Psycho-Socio Pedagogic Intervention Strategies for Autism

Psycho-Socio Pedagogic Intervention Strategies for Autism

Hema Nalini

AUTHORSPRESS

Worldwide Circulation through Authorspress Global Network
First Published 2010
by
Authorspress
E-35/103, Jawahar Park
Laxmi Nagar, Delhi-110 092
e-mail: authorspress@yahoo.com

Psycho-Socio Pedagogic Intervention Strategies for Autism
ISBN 978-81-7273-518-0

Printed by: Sri Krishna Offset Press,

"A scientific work... is never the work of a single person and each of those who collaborated in it have contributed many a sleepless nights."

—Louis Pasteur

Acknowledgement

I record my reverential gratitude to the great Architects of this Temple of Learning, Late Sri Avinashilingam Avargal, fondly remembered as "Ayya Avargal," for he was the source of inspiration for introducing Special Education as a field of study, and Former Chancellor Dr. Rajammal P. Devadas, fondly remembered as 'Amma Avargal' for raising the institution from its humble beginning in 1957 to its present status.

I wish to record my sincere thanks and appreciation to the Chancellor, Dr. K. Kulandaivel, for granting me permission to take up this research work.

I am appreciative of Dr. M. Chandramani, Vice Chancellor, Avinashilingam Deemed University for providing facilities to carry out the study.

I express my thanks to Dr. Saroja Prabhakaran, Registrar, Avinashilingam Deemed University for all the infrastructural help rendered in the conduct of this study.

My special thanks go to my dean, Dr. S. Meera, for the helpful suggestions and ideas and encouragement.

I thank profusely my guide Dr. Premavathy Vijayan, Ph.D, Professor and H.O.D, Department of Special Education, for her punctiliousness, valuable guidance, tireless striving and insightful suggestions that provided the right impetus for me.

Thanks are due to my mentors who sparked and kindled my interest in special education and prodded me to reach for the stars – my Professors at the University of Kentucky, U.S.A. Ms. Humble, Ms. Miller and her friends and colleagues at Good Samaritan Hospital, Lexington, Kentucky, U.S.A., Mrs. Gregory and Mrs. Sharp and the medical faculty that includes Drs. Farley, Maxson, Dawson, Shine and her numerous friends.

I would like to thank the special teachers, special children and their families without whose cooperation, this work would not have been possible. I thank profusely my colleagues and well-wishers in the university for all the help and encouragement.

I remain completely in the debt of my family. My parents provided a lifetime foundation of love and support and I continue to see the influence of my mother in every corner of my life and my father who serves as a beacon of light in my life. I will be failing in my duty if I do not mention my brothers, Raghuram, Raghavendra Prasad, Krishna Prasad and Srikanth, my sisters (in-law), Sujatha, Anuradha, Sri Vidya and Kasturi, my nieces—Subha and Shobana, and my nephew Abishek whose love and encouragement were instrumental in the fruition of the project. I offer my special thanks to my sister-in-law Sujatha and my brother Raghavendra Prasad who have helped me in innumerable ways. Thanks are due to my cousin, Dr. G. Srinivasan and his wife Dr. (Mrs). Meera Srinivasan who helped me in a variety of ways. Finally, I owe a great deal to my mother (in-law) and my father (in-law) who have been so supportive in all my endeavours and I remain grateful to them forever. Ultimately, I cannot too deeply express my sincere appreciation to my husband Sudaker and my child Rama for their understanding, support and love that make everything worthwhile.

Hema Nalini

List of Tables

List of Figures

List of Exhibits

List of Plates

Contents

List of Plates

Plate 1 : A girl with autism engaged in playing a game

Plate 2: A child with autism enjoying himself at the beach

Plate 3 : Multi-disciplinary specialists working as a team.

Plate 4 : Play as a therapy for children with autism

Plate 5 : A mother enjoying the company of her child with autism

Plate 6 : A grown up boy with autism, enjoying gardening

Plate 7 : A girl with autism engaged in making flower garlands.

Plate 8: A boy with autism with a fascination for water

Plate 9: Fixation for objects - a typical feature in autism

Plate 10: Fascination for bricks - a boy with autism obsessed with bricks

Plate 11: Developmentally-delayed children engaged in various activities

Plate 12: The author at a workshop on 'Multiple Intelligences'

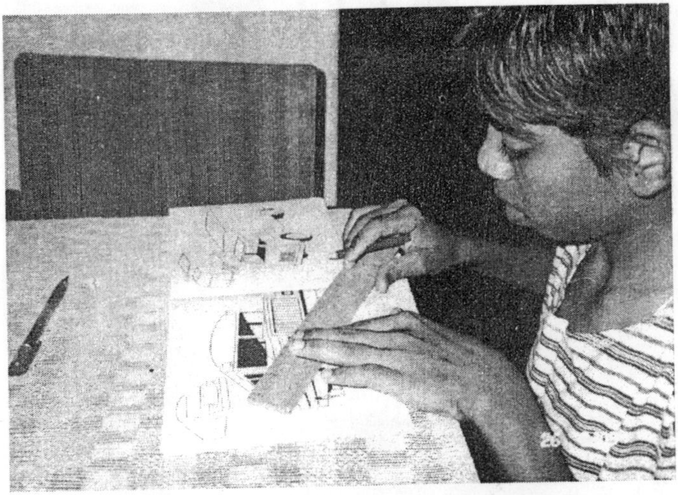

Plate 13: Development of splinter skill - typical feature in autism

Plate 14: The author playing with a child

Plate 15: A boy with autism working on the computer

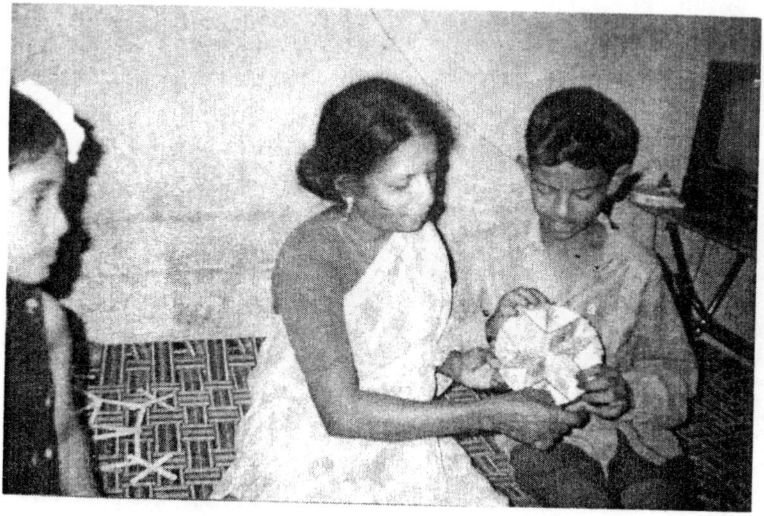

Plate 16: Mother teaching vocational skills to her child

(Contd...)

Plate 17: Sketches by children with autism

1

Introduction

Throughout centuries, education has been adapting itself to revolutionary changes and has metamorphosed from *gurukula parampara* to its current status. Education is one of the essential inputs to ensure the quality of life of an individual and is a potent instrument for change and the progress of a nation. It is a necessary investment in the present and the future for the development of human resources. That is why the right to education finds a paramount place in the Constitution; the 93rd Amendment of the Constitution of India makes education a fundamental right of every child. The goal of Universalisation of Primary Education (UPE) provides direction to planned developmental efforts and eradication of illiteracy has been the top of the agenda for all nations. 'Learning: The Treasure Within' is a historic report to the UNESCO of the International Commission on Education in the twenty-first century.

School education should aim at the all-round development of a child's personality by rebuilding it around the 'Four Pillars of Education' as suggested by Delores' Commission:

- Learning to Know
- Learning to Do
- Learning to Live
- Learning to Be

Education takes place throughout life in many forms, none of which ought to be exclusive. We must start to think about education in a more all-encompassing fashion. Likewise the four pillars cannot stand all alone. Without all the four pillars, education would not be the same.

National Initiatives in Special Education

Only in the past decade has the Indian government enacted legislation that has empowered children with disabilities and their families. This legislation has also provided for training of personnel working with children with disabilities.

Legislation

In 1992, India enacted its first piece of legislation related to special education: the Rehabilitation Council of India Act. The major purpose of this Act was to mandate minimum standards of education for professionals working with individuals with disabilities.

The Persons with Disabilities (Equal Opportunities, Protection of Rights and Full Participation) Act was initiated in 1995 and implemented in 1998. This comprehensive, breakthrough legislation provides for education and economic rehabilitation. This legislation stipulates that the government and local authorities ensure that every child under the age of 18 has a right to free education. In 1999, The National Trust for Welfare of Persons with Autism, Cerebral Palsy, Mental Retardation and Multiple Disabilities Act was passed. The focus of this act was to ensure the welfare of people with autism, cerebral palsy, mental retardation and multiple disabilities on a national level (Cardoza, 2000).

Personnel training

Lack of appropriately trained personnel has been one of the many constraints in providing services for children with disabilities in India. The Rehabilitation Council of India was developed under the Ministry of Social Justice and Empowerment to promote the training of personnel/professionals working with people with disabilities.

Education policy

After independence in 1947, India mandated its Universal Education for All policy, making education free and compulsory for all children ages 6-14 years (Saini, 2000). In India, despite the Persons with Disabilities Act (1995), most of the services seem to be provided to children with disabilities through private or non-government organisations. The Ministry of Welfare, with assistance from the Department of Health, Labour and Employment, is responsible for special education schools. Approximately 681 of them serve children with mental retardation. Non-government organisations serving children with disabilities exceed the number of government schools and receive 90 per cent of the funds earmarked for children with disabilities (Misra, 2000).

According to UNICEF as quoted by Kundu (2000), India has 300 million children between 0 and 14 years of age and 30 million children with different disabilities. This does not include children with learning disabilities, which constitute a substantial percentage.

Every disability gives rise to special educational needs and services. These must be met and appropriate services to be developed. Education For All has been the goal of UNESCO and education for all invariably includes children with special needs. Children with special needs is an encompassing term which covers a gamut of disabilities such as loco-motor disability, visual impairment, hearing and speech impairment, mental retardation, children with learning disabilities, autism, etc.

Autism—An Overview

Autism is a severe, neurobiological pervasive developmental disorder that was first termed "infantile autism" by an American physician, Leo Kanner (1943); Kanner described 11 children who shared the following symptoms - extreme autistic aloofness or self-absorption, anxiously obsessive and compulsive desire for the preservation of sameness, remarkable rote memory, limited or lack of language development, delayed echolalia, over/under sensitivity to stimuli and environmental demands, limitation in the variety of spontaneous activity and cognitive potentialities. A year later, an Austrian physician, Hans Asperger (1944), independently described a group of children with a similar pattern of symptoms. In a striking coincidence Asperger also chose the term 'autism' (the root is Greek 'autos' meaning self) thus emphasizing the social withdrawal evident in all cases. Kanner and Asperger both noted the children's poor eye contact, stereotypes of word and movement, and marked resistance to change. In fact, the triad of social impairment, reduced communication and decreased imagination characterises the whole spectrum of autistic disorders (Wing, 1986). Baron-Cohen, Leslie and Frith (1988) suggested that this association between these three areas of functioning could be explained by a single cognitive deficit, that is, an inability to cognitively represent mental states, otherwise called a theory of mind. Apart from the three impairments, there are several other impairments. Figure 1.1 provides a graphic representation of the impairments in autism.

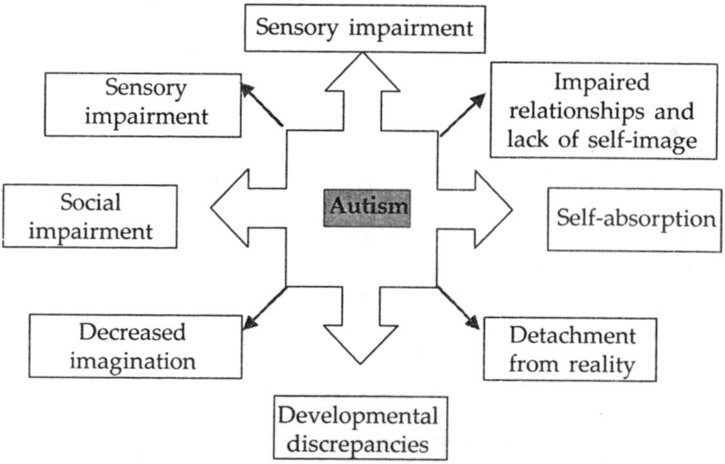

Figure 1.1 : Impairments in Autism

Autism is a combination of several developmental challenges. It is not an illness or a disease and is not contagious. Though many children with autism make great strides through early intervention, even today, most people with autism will find it difficult to lead a completely independent life, as lifelong support is required in most cases. Half of all autistic children will never learn to speak. It is not curable, but improvements can be made in all cases. However, individualised education programmes and structured support can maximise the child's progress, reduce pressure and stress upon the child and the family, and minimise the incidence of behavioural problems.

Diagnosis and Evaluation

The principal source for diagnosing autism is the *Diagnostic and Statistical Manual* of the American Psychiatric Association, Fourth Edition (DSM-IV, 1994). Developmental pediatricians, psychologists, child psychiatrists, or neurologists diagnose autism. At the time of (or prior to) diagnosis, a comprehensive evaluation is carried out. Such an evaluation usually includes a neuropsychological examination; tests for biochemical abnormalities, and other communicative patterns and adaptive functioning of the child and other assessments include physical and diagnostic conditions. It is absolutely crucial that intervention programmes derived from comprehensive evaluations are individualised to insure that they address the unique profile of needs and strengths exhibited by the given child. A battery of developmental and educational evaluations is also conducted to help develop an appropriate early intervention plan. Family involvement is integral to this entire process.

Studies over the past 20 years have demonstrated variations in the characteristics and severity of autism, now referred to as a spectrum of autistic disorders, including the classical form of the disorder as well as closely related disabilities that share many of the core characteristics. As per the DSM-IV criteria ASD (Autism Spectrum Disorder) includes the following diagnoses and classifications: (1) Pervasive Developmental Disorder-Not Otherwise Specified (PDD-NOS), which refers to a collection of features that resemble autism but may not be as severe or extensive; (2) Rett's syndrome, which affects girls and is a genetic disorder with hard neurological signs, including seizures, that become more apparent with age; (3) Asperger syndrome, which refers to individuals with autistic characteristics but relatively intact language abilities, and; (4) Childhood Disintegrative Disorder, which refers to children whose development appears normal for the first few years, but then regresses with the loss of speech and other skills until the characteristics of autism are conspicuous. Although the classical form of autism can be readily distinguished from other forms of ASD, the terms autism and ASD are often used interchangeably.

Prevalence

It is well established that autism occurs in four times as many boys as girls (NICHCY, 1999) and that there are no known racial, social, economic or cultural distinctions. At the Cure Autism Now Conference in California in October 2001, it was announced that there was an unprecedented rise in the prevalence of Autism in America. Reasons for this are varied and invalidated. While the earlier figure stood at 6 or 7 per 10,000 persons, today it has risen to one in every 500. Here in India, the trend is almost similar. Around two million in India are autistic.

Accompanying Disorders in Autism

Epilepsy, a brain disorder, often accompanies autism. Another frequent concomitant of autism is mental retardation; Sigman and Capps (1997) estimate that 75 per cent of autistic children are also classified as mentally retarded. Some individuals with autism may also have other disorders that affect the functioning of the brain, such as:

- Down syndrome
- Tuberous sclerosis
- Retinopathy of prematurity
- Neurofibromatosis
- Foetal alcohol syndrome
- Cerebral palsy

Genetic disorders such as:

- Fragile X Syndrome
- Landau-Kleffner Syndrome
- William's Syndrome
- Tourette's Syndrome.

There is no standard 'type' or typical features of autism. The terms that are often used to describe children who fall in the spectrum of autism are – autistic-like, autistic tendencies, autistic features, high functioning, low functioning, autism spectrum etc. Individuals with autism and ASD vary widely in ability and personality. While many individuals prefer isolation and tend to withdraw from social contact, others show high levels of affection and enjoyment in social situations. Some people with autism appear lethargic and are slow to respond, but others are very active and seem to interact constantly with preferred aspects of their environment. More important to understand is, whatever the diagnosis, children can learn and function productively and show gains from appropriate education and treatment.

Domains Affected by Autism

Autism is a spectrum disorder. In other words, the symptoms and characteristics of autism can present themselves in a wide variety of combinations, from mild to severe, from extremely gifted in their intellectual and academic accomplishments to developmentally and intellectually challenged.

Cognitive Competence includes thinking and information processing and intelligence (e.g., knowledge, understanding, application, analysis, synthesis, and evaluation).

Sensory Competence includes vision, hearing, speech mechanism, tactile, olfactory and motor/psychomotor (e.g., gross and fine motor, eye-hand coordination).

Language/Communication Competence includes expressive and receptive, nonverbal communication, language development (articulation, voice and fluency) and mode of communication.

Social Competence includes socio-psychological development, interpersonal skills, behaviour, personality, social skills and functional skills.

Educational Competence includes basic skills and achievement in content areas and school/study skills – functional numerical, academic skills.

Daily Living Skills include home, cultural and economic influences, and interactions in the home, school and community.

Vocational Competence includes general work behaviour, dexterity, following directions, working independently or with support, job preferences, career awareness, work skills etc.

Recreation and Leisure skills include use of free time, personal hobbies, use of community recreation resources, physical fitness, and degree of social involvement.

Figure 1.2 provides a graphic representation of some of the domains and possible ranges of functioning of students with autism. The figure gives a broad view of the continuum or spectrum nature of autism.

Cognitive Competence
Cognitively challenged ←============ → Savant/prodigy

Academic Competence
Low ←============ → High

Social Interaction/Reciprocity
Withdrawn ←============ → Extrovert

Language/Communication
Non-verbal ←============ → Verbal

Clumsy ←==========Gross-Motor==========→ Dexterous

Uncoordinated←=========Fine Motor========→ Coordinated

Hyposensitive ←===Sensory Competence====→ Hypersensitive

Figure 1.2: Spectrum Nature of Autism

Although autism is defined by a certain set of behaviours, children and adults can exhibit any combination of the behaviours in any degree of severity. Every person with autism is an individual, and like all individuals, they vary in their comprehension, skills and characteristics. There are great differences among people with autism. Some individuals mildly affected may exhibit only slight delays in language and greater challenges with social interactions and communication. Two children, both with the same diagnosis, can act very differently from one another; they have varying skills, personality traits, behavioural characteristics and learning strengths/deficits. The person may have difficulty initiating and/ or maintaining a conversation, or keeping a conversation going. Communication is often described as talking at others (for example, monologue on a favourite subject that continues despite attempts of others to interject comments). People with autism process and respond to information in unique ways. Figure 1.3 represents the pin men by National Autistic Society that have been selected to illustrate some of the different ways in which autism is displayed.

About Autism

These pin men have been selected to illustrate some of the different ways in which Autism is displayed.

It is a handicap which disrupts the development of communication at a very early age and leaves a child unable to form normal social relationships.

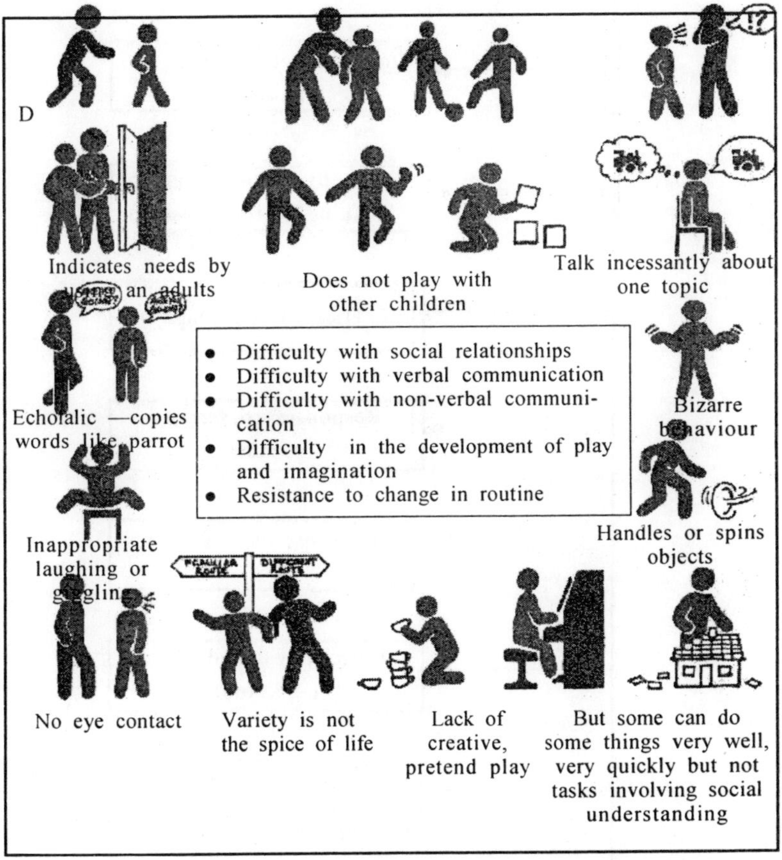

Figure 1.3 - Pin Men Depicting Unique Autistic Behaviours

(Courtesy-National Autistic Society, U.K)

Figure 1.4 illustrates the problems faced by children with autism in different dimensions of behaviour. The specific characteristics that are commonly found in autism are given under the following 10 broad categories.

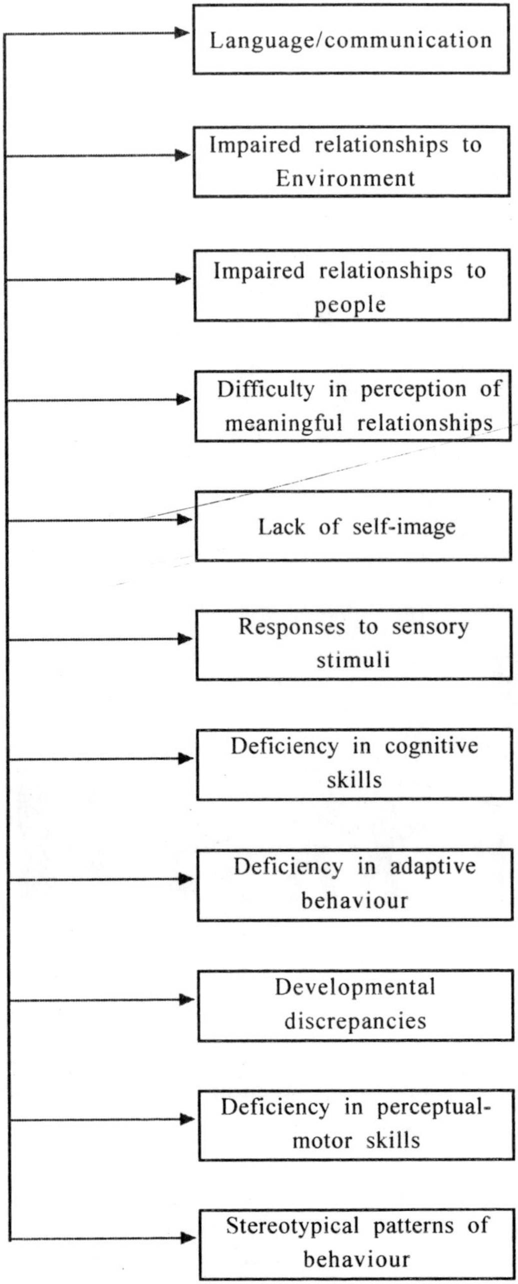

Figure 1.4: Behavioural Indicators of Autism

Autism impairs a person's ability to communicate, to understand language, to process information, to play, to form social relationships, and to interact with the world and it usually strikes some time in the first two years of life. Autism is a behavioural syndrome, which means that its definition is based on specific and distinct patterns of behaviours that a person exhibits.

Table 1.1 depicts various behavioural characteristics under each dimension of indicators of autism.

Table 1.1 - Behavioural Characteristics of Autism

Language/communication

- Delay in or total lack of development of spoken language
- Has limited or lack of facial expressions
- Failure to respond to the communication of others
- Failure to initiate or sustain conversation
- Lack of gestures
- Failure to imitate actions or sounds
- Repeats or echoes words and phrases (Echolalia)
- Stereotypical and repetitive use of language
- Use of 'you' when 'I' is meant
- May have little or no speech or may be verbal
- Idiosyncratic use of words
- Abnormalities in pitch, stress, rhyme and intonation
- Lack of creativity and spontaneity in social language
- Lack of varied/spontaneous 'make believe' play
- Seems not to understand meanings of words
- Takes literal meanings of words (Literalness of Language)
- Deficits in pragmatics (Social Usage of Language)

Impaired Relationships: To People

- Is unresponsive
- Lack of social smile
- Failure to use eye-to-eye gaze
- Impairment of the awareness of other people and their needs
- Inability to recognise human characteristics
- Does not play turn taking games
- Seeks social contact in unusual ways
- Limited/fleeting eye contact

- Uses adult's hands as tools
- Inability to express emotions

To the Environment

- Repetitive play
- Is upset by or resists changes
- Develops rigid routines
- Drifts aimlessly about
- Exhibits strong and inflexible interests

Difficulty in Perception of Meaningful Relationship

- Inability to see sequences of growth, time, action etc.,
- Inability to see similarities or differences
- Inability to relate to properties - Fire will burn
- Inability to generalise or transfer learning
- Lack of awareness of reality
- Inability to distinguish fantasy from reality and vice versa
- Impaired awareness of relationship of objects to each other, objects to persons, person to person
- Lack of judgement

Lack of Self-image

- Lack of personal identity and an impairment of self-image
- Remains isolated or engages in obsessional, ritualistic activities
- Lack of knowledge about his own personal territory or boundary
- Lack of body awareness, body control and perceptual control

Responses to Sensory-Stimuli

- Seems deaf
- Hypersensitive or hyposensitive to certain sounds, touch, smell and taste
- Plays with light and reflections
- Finger-flicking
- Pulls away when touched
- Hypersensitivity/hyposensitivity to certain textures, patterns, odours
- Is either hyperactive or hypoactive
- May whirl, spin, bang, bite wrist
- Hand-flapping
- Exhibits unusual or no response to pain
- Inappropriate reaction to sounds

— Inappropriate emotional response

Deficiency in Cognitive Skills

- Patchy development of splinter skills
- Difficulty in problem solving
- Poor imitation skills
- Difficulty in directing attention to meaningful features of the environment
- Lack of motivation and self-directed action
- Poor sequencing ability
- Difficulty in understanding the concept of time
- Difficulty in directing attention to meaningful aspects of the environment and events.
- Difficulty in the transfer and generalisation of knowledge
- Deficiency in adaptive behaviour
- Irrational phobias or fears
- Rigidity of thought and action
- Ritualistic, compulsive, obsessional behaviours
- Distorted reality

Developmental Discrepancies

- Good at puzzles but poor in following directions
- Lack of consistency - can do things sometimes, but not other times
- Reads but does not understand meanings
- Draws pictures in detail but does not understand the concept of 'finished' or 'over'
- Is verbal but cannot communicate properly his desires/thoughts/ needs

Deficiency in Perceptual Motor Skills

- Lack of body awareness
- Lack of body control and perceptual control
- Attachment to unusual objects
- Obsessive, compulsive rituals
- Preoccupation with certain objects and non-functional parts of toys or play materials
- Distress over changes in routines
- Rigidity of thought and action
- Poor organisation and planning

No single characteristic of behaviour indicates firmly the presence of autism. Children will not exhibit all the behavioural characteristics that are given in the table above. From the table it is quite palpable that autism is a complex disorder. A detailed look at the behavioural characteristics of autism is essential before embarking on any treatment programme.

Learning strengths and personality traits common in autism are discussed in the table given below.

Table 1.2: Learning Strengths in Autism

The ability to

- take in chunks of information.
- perceive and present information visually.
- retain information for a long time.
- learn and repeat long routines.
- organise information methodically and systematically.
- remember information by rote
- persevere.
- understand and use concrete, context-free information and rules.
- concentrate on narrow topics of interest.
- learn language without being taught.
- use advanced splinter skills (music, computers, puzzles) to learn
- new information.

Learning is an additive and growing process, and learning takes place only when an individual has an experience that influences behaviour and makes him or her a different person. The interventionist has to organise the programme, prepare the learning materials, present the materials to the child, guide and facilitate learning in a natural manner. It is imperative for teachers and interventionists to be eclectic and generate strategies built on the learning strengths of children with autism.

Learning deficits commonly found in children with autism are discussed in the table given below.

Table 1.3: Learning Deficits in Autism

Inability to

- process information and modulate or integrate sensory stimulation.
- focus on relevant and important information, elements or events.
- analyse, organise, interpret and integrate information to derive meaning.
- retrieve information in a logical sequential order.
- organise and understand events and language related to time.
- understand the complex, idiomatic nuances of the language.
- attach meaning to visual information.
- generate alternatives to solve problems.
- control motor and verbal responses.
- generalise or transfer information from one situation to the other.
- integrate auditory information efficiently.
- control thoughts, movements and responses.
- adjust to new situation and events.
- initiate communication to ask for help or assistance.
- perceive and observe socio-cultural rules.
- understand others' perspectives.

Etiology

Initially the condition was believed to be caused by inadequate parenting skills referred to as 'refrigerated mothers', but it is now recognised that this is definitely not the case. Autism is a pervasive developmental disorder involving a biological or organic defect in the functioning of brain. Infantile autism is a complex behavioural syndrome of unknown etiology. Recent research has shifted away from psychogenic hypotheses to a variety of possible genetic, neuroanatomical, neurophysiological, immunological, and neurotransmitter causes.

Anything that makes the central nervous system develop abnormally can cause autism—this abnormality may occur during foetal development, during birth or after birth. Although autism affects the functioning of the brain, the specific cause of autism is unknown. In fact, it is widely assumed that there are most likely multiple causes, each of which may be manifested in different forms, or subtypes, of autism. Future research will help us understand the etiologies of autism.

The supposition that only a single causative factor for autism exists—simple genetics—is proving increasingly flawed (even though a genetic basis is indicated by epidemiological studies). Study of simple genetic inheritance factors fails to explain the condition of children with regressive autism. The exact causes of autism spectrum disorders are not clearly understood but the following causes have been implicated.

- Genetic chromosomal factors as in Down syndrome, Fragile X syndrome etc.
- Metabolic imbalances such as phenylketonuria
- Diseases as diverse as tuberous sclerosis, or neurofibromatosis; cerebral lipoidosis, encephalopathy.
- Infections, for example, congenital/intrauterine rubella, cytomegalovirus, herpes simplex, HIV and so on
- Evidence of diffuse brain dysfunction (believed to be due to a physical or chemical fault affecting the developing brain); and brain abnormality like hydrocephalus; brain stem defect
- Postnatal conditions such as infantile spasms, herpes simplex, encephalitis and oxygen deprivation
- Heavy metal toxicity or exposure to environmental chemicals such as lead, mercury etc.
- Autoimmune disorders such as type-1 diabetes, adult rheumatoid arthritis, hypothyroidism, systemic lupus erythematosus and multiple sclerosis
- Anti-convulsant medications taken during pregnancy
- Food and inhalant allergies and digestive system deficiencies.

Objectives of the Study

- To enable individuals with autism to function as meaningfully and as independently as possible in the community;

- To discuss strategies that will provide the student a safe, positive atmosphere and environment for learning.
- To plan a curriculum that includes teaching basic living skills, social skills, functional skills, communicative skills, vocational skills etc.
- To devise and recommend appropriate intervention strategies based on the psycho-socio and educational characteristics of the children as well as the environment.
- To focus on the strength of the individuals and build strategies based on the propensities of the children.
- To determine the entry points to reach the core of the children based on the Multiple Intelligences of the children.
- To enable the children with autism to communicate with others.
- To keep communication open with parents and involve the parents and the family in the learning process.

Need and Importance of the Study

A variety of intervention strategies have been suggested ever since autism was first identified as a syndrome more than 50 years ago. These interventions and treatments are the results of a wide range of theories but most have not proven to be effective with large numbers of children, while some of the interventions have been successful with certain number of children with autism. This pattern continues today, with a large number of diverse treatment approaches being touted as uniquely effective in resolving patterns of autistic behaviour; it is rather imperative to evolve unique strategies that would help a large number of the affected group. It is this premise that provided the impetus for the investigator to evolve effective strategies.

It is also imperative for the teacher to enhance and develop all five domains of a child: the adaptive domain, the cognitive domain, the communication domain, the physical domain and the social or emotional domain. The teacher has to attend to, assess and enhance development in all five domains. By looking at the whole child, the teacher can help a child develop strengths and propensities/proclivities and enable a child to reach optimum development. Working at each child's 'zone of proximal development' challenge children's cognitive abilities and this develops the capacity for divergent thinking.

Deliberate and systematic endeavours are of seminal importance to enhance cognitive, communicative, social, functional and vocational skills through psychological, social and educational intervention programmes. Though the research work relating to causal factors of autism is still in an embryonic stage, the intervention programmes started earlier foster the development of skills in children with autism. Some very credible approaches have been demonstrated repeatedly to be effective in improving the behaviours and adaptability of people with autism. Interventions that are derived from an educational and behavioural orientation have been shown to help children and adults affected by autism, primarily by teaching new skills that enable the person to function more successfully in the daily world of home, school, work and community interactions.

Years of research and experience have produced some relevant guidelines for providing instruction and intervention for individuals with autism. For example, it is important that interventions be developed on an individualised basis. The label of autism by itself is not prescriptive. It does not indicate what intervention should be provided or how intervention should be provided.

As a set of general rules, it is widely agreed that people with autism respond better in a context where there is structure and clear guidelines regarding expectations for appropriate and inappropriate behaviour. It is also recommended that the environment include systems or materials, such as written or picture-schedules, that can help the person to comprehend and predict the flow and sequence of activities.

Another important guideline for intervention pertains to family involvement. To the greatest extent possible, family members should be encouraged to participate in all aspects of assessment, curriculum planning, instruction, and monitoring. Parents and other family members very often provide insight and useful information about an individual's history and learning characteristics; so effective intervention and instruction should take advantage of this vital resource. Furthermore, because families are so essential in the lives of people with autism, family support that helps strengthen the family system is regarded as a vital element in providing effective intervention for people with autism.

Scope of the Study

This study intends to provide help to individuals with autism to live as independently as they can and contribute meaningfully to the society. The study elaborately focuses on strategies that will provide the children a safe, positive atmosphere and environment for learning. The research work provides a curriculum that includes teaching basic living skills, social skill and communication skills etc.

This book devises and recommends appropriate intervention strategies based on the psycho-socio and educational characteristics of the children as well as the environment. Based on the strength of the students, the author builds strategies that would further enhance the propensities of the children. To reach out to the core of children with autism, it is imperative to determine the entry points. This study evolves strategies based on the Multiple Intelligences of the children—different learning styles of the students. The Strategic Intervention Package designed by the author suggests strategies based on psychological, sociological, cultural and familial dimensions of children, different learning styles of children as well as the entry points through which they can be reached. This book recommends multitude of strategies that help parents, care givers, therapists and special education teachers.

The focus of intervention and instructional efforts in this book is to develop functional, social, academic, cognitive, communicative and vocational skills that will be of immediate and ongoing value in the context of daily living. This typically includes strategies for enhancing a person's ability to communicate, to understand language, and to get along socially in complex home, school, work and community settings.

The key terms used in this book have the following connotations:

— *Psycho-social:* 'Psychological' dimension of the study includes the behavioural characteristics, personality traits, cognitive reactions, the implications of Multiple Intelligences and the intervention strategies that are based on sound psychological basis of 'behaviour modification'. Social skills and development refer to the way children interact and reciprocate with other children and adults in their lives.

- *Pedagogic:* Refers to educational and educable skills that involve emotional, cognitive, adaptive, communicative development of children that will eventually lead to sublimation of character.
- *Intervention:* Intervention refers to the treatment given to the children with autism that would create an environment which offers increased opportunities for intellectual, social, functional, emotional and personality development of the children.
- *Strategies:* Goal-directed and deliberately implemented mental operations used to facilitate task performance.

The sample drawn is restricted to 63 children with autism (only the children who met DSM-IV criteria for autism were chosen for the study). Chennai and Coimbatore were chosen for the study in special schools where the management was quite receptive to the author's ideas and suggestions. The investigation focused on children who fell under Autism Spectrum Disorder and not any other category.

The first chapter deals with introduction, objectives of the study, and the need and importance of the study.

Chapter two gives an account of the review of literature pertaining to the thesis.

Chapter three delineates the methodology that includes the method adopted in the study, focus, site description, data collection tools selected for the study, sample, setting, procedure, pilot study and final study.

Chapter four contains analysis and interpretations of the data collected through interview, observations and standardised tools.

Chapter five reports the findings, recommendations, suggestions and conclusion, and finally the appendices include references and copies of standardised tools used for the study.

2

Review of Literature

The survey of literature related to the problem under study is an eye opener for research work. Effective research is based upon past knowledge and this helps to eliminate duplication of what has been done and provides useful and helpful suggestions for significant investigation. Citing studies that show substantial agreement and those that seem to present conflicting conclusions help to sharpen and define understanding of existing knowledge in the problem area and a background for the research project. In general, relatively little has been written about autism in developing countries as India, compared to what has been published on autism in North America, Europe and Australia.

Diagnostic Point of View

DSM-IV specifies that "Autistic Disorder (defined as 'early infantile autism...or Kanner's autism') must be differentiated from other Pervasive Developmental Disorders... '. Autistic disorder differs from Childhood Disintegrative Disorder, which has a distinctive pattern of developmental regression following at least 2 years of normal development. In Autistic Disorder, developmental abnormalities are usually noted within the first year of life."

Wagner and Lockwood (1994) illustrate that the diagnosis of the pervasive developmental disorders relies on the detection of deficits in communication, social, and play skills relative to the child's mental age. Using a case example, their article illustrates the multidisciplinary process of making this diagnosis in very young children. Heubner (1992) says that autism is increasingly viewed as an expression of an unidentified neurological disorder. The research is categorised in four basic types: (a) neuropsychological testing of functional abilities, (b) treatment studies based on neuropsychological hypotheses, (c) autistic-related diseases and genetic disorders, and (d) neuro-anatomical and neuro-physiological studies.

Schopler et al. (1988) note, "Considering the very fact that the clinical picture of autism can arise from diseases as diverse as congenital rubella, tuberous sclerosis, encephalopathy...cerebral lipoidosis, and neurofibromatosis...it remains quite uncertain whether the...cases with a known pathologic cause represent phenocopies of some other unitary disorder with (an as yet undiscovered) single etiology...." Evidence for involvement in autism of the medical temporal lobe and related structures of the limbic system comes from a variety of sources, including behavioural/neuropsychological, animal lesion and autopsy studies. A neuropsychological study conducted by Barth, Fein and Waterhouse (1995) revealed that lower-functioning children with autism were impaired on a visual recognition memory task tapping medical temporal lobe functions. Furthermore, it is well established that individuals with autism have specific impairments in the processing of social and emotional stimuli, as evident on tasks such as face and emotion recognition, imitation of body movements, interpretations and use of body gestures, and formation of theory of mind (Baron-Cohen, Tager-Fluseberg & Cohen, 1993; Mundy, Bishop, Manstead & Tantam, 1994; Hobson, Ouston & Lee, 1988a, 1988b; Mundy Sigman, Ungerer & Sherman, 1986; Smith & Bryson, 1994; Teunisse & Degelder 1994). This pattern of behavioural impairments suggests that autism is related by dysfunction of a brain system involved in social cognition.

Prevalence of Autism

Presently the Centre for Disease Control admits to an estimated autism incidence of 1 in 500 (contrasted with an earlier estimate of 1 in 10,000). The actual incidence is suspected by the autism community to be at least this high, perhaps higher than 1 in 200, and to be increasing exponentially.

The California Department of Developmental Services in its report says that in 1987 there were 3,864 autistic children enrolled in the department's twenty-one regional programmes; in 1998, 11,995 autistic children were counted—a 210 per cent increase. Children with other disorders such as cerebral palsy and epilepsy increased at a rate consistent with the state's population growth (from 30-48%). The Illinois State Board of Education lists figures for the incidence of both autism and learning disabilities: autism cases on hand were 317 in 1991, and 2,305 in 1997. Another study was published in Copenhagen, Denmark (*Acta Psychiatrica Scandinavica,* 1999): "Autism: not an extremely rare disorder." Authors studied autism prevalence over time, "to determine whether there has been an increase in its prevalence in recent years. ...It is concluded that autism is considerably more common than was previously believed."

Genetic Component in Autism

Szatmari et al. (1999) observe that the genetics of autism in its various manifestations is likely to involve the complex interaction of multiple genes, but even in this event "it is too early to say what type of complex genetic disease autism/PDD represents." The authors venture so far as to say that "certain severe insults" during pregnancy and birth might "play a causative role in the development of PDD." Sigman and Capps (1997) state that "it is not clear, however, whether all forms of autism are genetically transmitted in the same way."

Immunological Point of View

Comi et al. (1999) say, "Autism is an age-dependent neurologic disorder that is often associated with autoimmune disorders in the patients' relatives... . The most common autoimmune disorders are type 1-diabetes, adult rheumatoid arthritis, hypothyroidism, and systemic lupus erythematosus... . An increased number of autoimmune disorders suggests that in some families with autism, immune dysfunction could interact with various environmental factors to play a role in autism pathogenesis."

Cohen (1998) is also of the opinion that "There is increasing evidence of immune system abnormalities in autism." Gillberg and Coleman (1992), note that "It is currently believed that a genetic disease underlies 10 to 20 percent of all autism cases...." There is another autism subgroup in which the autistic symptomatology is linked to disease processes currently thought to be, in many instances, of a non-genetic character. Ermann and Fathman (2001) discuss common themes from five articles regarding rheumatoid arthritis, systemic lupus erythematosus, insulin-dependent diabetes, autoimmune thyroid disease and multiple sclerosis.

Frith (1994) opines that the theory that psychotic illness can be due to immune dysfunction and/or viral infection has particular justification in the area of Autism. It has been shown that a virus infection in a young child preceded the onset of typical symptoms of autism, before which there was a period of apparently normal development. If the central nervous system becomes infected at a critical time, either before or after birth, autism may result. Trottier et al. (1999) opine, "The etiology of autism is complex, and in most cases the underlying pathologic mechanisms are unknown.... Recent research has investigated... immunological factors. On the basis of family and twin studies, there appears to be a genetic basis for a wide autistic syndrome."

Fudenberg (1998) notes, "The gene for classic autism has been localised to human chromosome-6, the site of human immune response genes and [is] linked to haplotypes containing the C4 null allele." Jyonouchi (2001) determines that a high frequency of excessive innate immune responses is seen in children with regressive autism, possibly explaining in part the apparent association between immunisation and the onset of regression and autistic behaviour.

Kawashima et al. (2000) characterise measles strains present in peripheral blood from eight patients with Crohn's Disease, three patients with ulcerative colitis, and nine with autistic enterocolitis. Hornig et al. (1999) are of the opinion that prenatal exposure to infectious agents and toxins is linked to the pathogenesis of neuropsychiatric disorders. Hornig et al. (2001) note that both genetic and environmental factors contribute to the pathogenesis of a variety of neurodevelopmental disorders, including autism, mental retardation and schizophrenia. Pletnikov, Moran and Carbone (2002) note, "One of the obstacles to understanding the pathogenesis of autism and its efficient treatment has been the paucity of animal models that could be used for hypotheses-driven mechanistic studies of abnormal brain and behaviour development and for the pre-clinical testing novel pharmacological treatments."

Montinari et al. (1996) observe that after 30 children were found to have signs of central nervous system and genetic damage following vaccination, the authors remark, "A study of the disease associated with genes of the HLA system has shown that this genetic complex can be responsible for a particular genetic susceptibility, predisposing to various diseases characterised predominantly by immune-system pathogenesis...." Schopler and Mesibov (1988) note that "the clinical picture of autism can arise from diseases as diverse as congenital rubella, tuberous sclerosis, encephalopathy treatments."

Singh (2001) is the first to report an association between virus serology and brain auto-antibody in autism; it supports the hypothesis that a virus-induced autoimmune response may play a causal role in autism. Singh (2002) concludes that autism involves a neuro-autoimmune response that occurs at the neuro-immune biology interface. Clinically, therefore, there is enormous potential for restoring brain function in autistic people through immunology. Binstock (1997) observes, (a) familial occurrences indicating an actual gene-mutation that is hereditary; (b) familial occurrences reflecting a genetically encoded susceptibility factor; (c) familial illness via environmental factors. (d) familial clustering of increased small intestinal permeability in families with Crohn's Disease.

The Center for Disease Control, (1998), says of autism, "Some prenatal factors included intrauterine rubella; tuberous sclerosis; chromosomal abnormalities, such as Down's Syndrome, as well as brain abnormalities, like hydrocephalus ....postnatal conditions associated with autism are untreated phenylketonuria, infantile spasms, and herpes simplex encephalitis. ...Evidence that genetics is an important, but not exclusive, cause of autism includes a three to eight percent risk of recurrence in families with one affected child. ..."

Gent et al. (1997) observe that "the immune response is regulated by genetic material located mainly on the sixth chromosome." Failure of components of this system can lead to disruption of normal cell-mediated cellular immune responses ... besides viral infections as a cause, it is possible that "a genetic predisposition to a relative deficiency of specific immune cells may be involved." Walsh and Usman (2001) provided a basis for possible mercury poisoning in autism. A total of 499 of 503 autism-spectrum patients exhibited evidence of a metal-metabolism disorder. Shaw (1998), reports finding in children with autism and PDD none of the signs characteristic of known, inborn (genetic) conditions causing metabolic disorders. "In several cases, electron microscopy has revealed live measles virus in the intestinal lining of children with the gastrointestinal abnormalities common in children with autism."

Psycho-physiological Perspective

The animal and brain damage literatures suggest that the limbic system, particularly the amygdala, is critical for social perception, such as recognition of faces and facial expressions (Aggleton, 1992; Jacobson, 1986; Nelson & DeHaan, 1996) the recognition of the affective significance of stimuli (LeDoux, 1984) and the perception of body movements and gaze direction (Brothers, Ring & King, 1990), and for certain cognitive disabilities that are likely to be important for social perceptions (Murray & Mishkin 1985) and recall of event sequences (McDonough, Mandlers, McKee & Squire, 1994).

Psychological Perspective

Baron-Cohen (1988) has given an extensive review of the theoretical assumptions and also the results of many studies relating to the social and pragmatic deficits among autistics. Whetherby (1986) asserts that autistic children are communicative, as they use language in an intentional way towards another person to achieve environmental or social ends.

Biological Bases of Autism

Cammisa and Hobbs (1993) in their paper examine recent research concerned with the major biogenic hypotheses. The principal conclusion of the review is that despite many promising hypotheses, the current literature is filled with conflicting findings and no one hypothesis has appeared to take centre stage. Cohen and Volkmar (1997) say that the claim has been made that a small but significant proportion of children develop autism as a result of pre-or post-natal infections—for example, with rubella, cytomegalovirus, herpes simplex, HIV, and so on.

Neurobiological Perspective

Bauman and Kemper (1994) examine the importance of genetic factors in the etiology of autism. It is known, for example, that autism can develop in association with etiologies as diverse as congenital rubella, tuberous sclerosis, and the fragile x anomaly, as well as in the absence of any identifiable, co-occurring, etiologically defined condition. Among autistic individuals without identifiable, associated etiologic conditions, several points suggest that there may also be genetic heterogeneity.

Behavioural Support for Young Children with Autism

Turnbull and Turnbull (1999) provide a description of behavioural support as applied in the context of a family-centred early intervention programme for young children with autism. Young children with autism sometimes display severe behaviour problems that can cause great disruptions in family life and interfere with attempts to provide needed services. Strategies are needed to resolve these behaviour problems in a manner that is effective, durable, and consistent with current approaches to positive, comprehensive, and inclusive practice in early childhood intervention.

Developmental Perspective

Sigman and Capps (1997) state, "Autism is not a unitary disease with a single etiology... . It is a heterogeneous behavioural syndrome found in association with many etiologies. Complications in any part of... development... could cause damage that leads to autism." Cohen says, "There is increasing evidence of immune system abnormalities in autism. A substantial number of reports of research on this subject have appeared in medical journals since the 1980s, and most of these articles present data that appear to support the theory of a connection between immune system dysfunction and some cases of autism...."

Watling et al. (1999) examine the current practice patterns of occupational therapists experienced with children with autism spectrum disorders. Practice patterns included frequent collaboration with other professionals during assessment and intervention.

Impairments in Autism

Sensory impairment

Autism is a developmental condition involving a triad of social impairments: in social relationships, communication, and imagination (Wing and Gould, 1979). Case-Smith and Miller (1999) in their survey elucidate very clearly that sensory integration and environmental modification approaches were used most frequently and effectively. Fisher and Murray (1991) describe sensory integration as both "a neurological process, and a theory of the relationship between the neurological process and behaviour."

Social impairment

Children with autism often have significant visual and auditory memory limitations children with autism need to use specific prompts and familiar cues learned in a high-support environment (optimal performance level) to develop long-term memory encoding enabling spontaneous regeneration of the new skill with reduced context support (functional performance level). The key symptom of autism is a strict adherence to specific routines and a need for sameness in the environment.

Children with autism become more socially responsive and attentive when information is provided in a highly predictable manner, and, conversely, that their behaviour is severely disrupted when the same stimuli are presented in an unpredictable manner children with autism have difficulty in the classroom with transition from one activity to another and with any unanticipated change from expectations children with autism have a need for predictability and routine, which may be due to:

1) difficulties in arousal modulation
2) impairments in memory
3) impairments in processing of temporal information

Programmes must facilitate successful transition from preschool to kindergarten or first grade due to the challenge children with autism have making changes and generalising previously acquired skills to new environments. Children with autism are most often not capable of gaining skills in more complex environments that typically involve small or large groups of impairments that they have difficulty attending to and encoding critical information such as gestures, language and facial expressions.

Language/Communication Impairment

Rapin and Allen (1987) commented that one subtype of developmental language disorder—'semantic-pragmatic syndrome' — was frequently seen, in a severe form, in verbal children with autism. As researchers are becoming increasingly interested in the communication, sensory and social impairments in autism, much focus is given to language impairment as it is the primary cause for social and communication impairments. First, there is a debate as to whether children with this type of impairment exist as a valid separate clinical group (Brook and Bowler, 1992;Gagnon et al., 1997). From a clinical perspective, children with primary pragmatic language impairments have been described as having superficially normal language development, unusual language constructions, difficulty using pragmatic cues in conversation, difficulty in turn-taking and complex difficulties with comprehension (Bishop and Rosenbloom, 1987; Rapin and Allen, 1987; McTear and Conti-

Ramsden, 1992; Attwood, 1998). Thus, there is controversy as to whether in fact they should be diagnosed instead as having high-functioning autism or Asperger syndrome (Gagnon et al., 1997). The characteristics of children classified by DSM-IV (American Psychiatric Association, 1994) as having pervasive developmental disorders not otherwise specified (PDD-NOS) are also similar to those associated with pragmatic language impairment (Mahoney et al., 1997; Buitelaar and van der Gaag, 1998; Prior et al., 1998).

Currently the term 'semantic-pragmatic disorder' is used (in Britain at least) to refer to children who do not meet a diagnosis for autism. However, Rapin and Allen originally used the term as a descriptive one, which applies to children with specific language impairment, but mainly to those with autism. This is highlighted recently in Rapin's (1996) 'update' paper. The term 'pragmatic language impairment' (PLI) is very recent and represents an attempt to specify more precisely the relevant features of this clinical group. It is used in this article and in Bishop's (1987) work to replace the term 'semantic-pragmatic disorder' for children without autism.

Theory of Mind

The ability to mentalise, or ability to attribute mental states to others, has been argued to be at the basis of autism and in most cases of Asperger's Syndrome patients. This "Theory of Mind" hypothesis was proposed and tested by Baron-Cohen, Leslie and Frith in a first-order Theory of Mind Task (1985) and in a second-order Theory of Mind task (1989). The first-order test required the subject to recognise a character's false belief in a story about two dolls (Sally and Ann).

Baron-Cohen, et al. (1997) designed a new "adult test of theory of mind ability", where information about a person's mental state can be acquired only from photographs of a person's eyes. Other literatures have argued that there may be other deficits, more primary to the Theory of Mind deficit, such as inability to disengage from an object (Hughes and Russel, 1993), since recent studies have shown a lack of universality in autistics failing the Theory of Mind tests (Yirmiya, et al., (1996). There have been other studies attempting to attribute an anatomical region of the brain to the "theory of mind" (Baron-Cohen et al., 1994; Happe, et al., 1996, 1999; Karmiloff et al., 1995).

Executive Function and Theory of Mind

As defined by Duncan (1986), "Executive Function" refers to the various processes which underlie purposeful behaviour, such as planning, focusing of attention and memory. Executive Function (EF) would be perceived, therefore, as a complex cognitive construct typically associated with the operations of the (pre) frontal cortex.

However, evidence exists from neuroanatomy and developmental psychology (as reviewed by Hughes 1998) that basic prefrontal and executive functions emerge during early infancy. While it might appear initially that these two areas are quite separate aspects of cognitive development, there are both theoretical and empirical reasons for their linkage. For example, Frith (1992) has argued that the meta-cognitive skills necessary for understanding mental states are a necessary prerequisite for executive control. McEvoy et al (1993) have demonstrated that, among high functioning autistic children, a capacity to engage in joint attention (which is a plausible precursor of theory of mind) is strongly correlated with performance on EF tasks. In sum, the study suggests that several precursors may be involved in the development of theory of mind; and that both executive function and theory of mind are complex constructs with specific rather than general relationships between the two areas.

Eye Gaze and Mind Reading

Continuing with the theme of developing a theory of mind, one may refer to the work of Lee et al., (1998) who introduce their work by describing how increasing significance has been attached to the role of (the direction of) the eye gaze in social interaction. In animals, eye gaze may establish dominance, initiate or terminate aggressive behaviours, indicate the source of food, and signal approaching danger. The role of eye gaze has been extended in human interactions, and it has been suggested (Baron-Cohen 1994) that a uniquely human function of eye gaze and eye gaze monitoring is the revealing of mental state — mind reading, or provision of clues about the focus of another person's attention, desire, or belief.

Communication Breakdowns in (Verbal) Autistic Children

On a different aspect of Autism, Geller (1998) describes how the analysis of pragmatic skills has contributed to the understanding of the particular language capacities and deficits that are typically observed among children with autism. It is normally assumed that the (child) speaker genuinely wishes to communicate, is monitoring the listener's comprehension and trying to ease understanding. Among children with autism, communication breakdowns and non-repair are significant areas of difficulty in that, when an exchange falters, such children appear to lack strategies to bring the conversation back on track, and one notes the common situation where the autistic child will seek to initiate a conversation by reference to some topic or event, and will assume (given an inadequate theory of mind) that the listener will immediately be able to "tune in" without any confusion.

Paul and Cohen (1984) raise the question, whether the child is unwilling or unable to work towards repairing the exchange. These authors observed adults with autism in conversation with a confederate who made frequent requests for clarification. Geller reviews existing studies that appeared to confirm that children with autism are rarely able to modify messages to fit the needs of the listener, even when they were able to work out what the listener's understanding might be.

Developmental Patterns among Children with Autism

The general theme of the paper by Sigman (1998) is that each developmental phase has both its own particular characteristics and requirements, which will guide interventions, and consequences for subsequent development. Reference is made to three basic approaches to the study of developmental trends:

- The behaviour of children who share a particular diagnostic label is compared with that of ordinary children matched for mental age in order to explore ways in which the disorder has caused deviation from the normal progression.

– Stability in the observable characteristics is examined by comparing the diagnostic groups at different ages, or by examining an individual's performance in a given area over time.

– Precursors of characteristics or disabilities are investigated by examining how the ranking of a child within the group on some element is correlated with the child's ranking on a different element measured at a later time.

In her review, Sigman chose to focus upon social competence because of its significance in shaping the children's day-to-day experiences; and her general theme tends to echo that of the implication in the preceding section, viz., that early interventions should be directed towards improving basic communication skills given their significance in influencing later verbal and social skills.

Autism and the Use of "Circles of Friends"

In respect of classroom practice, Whitaker et al (1998) describe the outcome of the use of the Circle of Friends' technique with autistic children in mainstream schools as the focus. This technique seeks to promote inclusion of pupils with disabilities, and provides one means of including (socially) vulnerable children within a peer group, which is seen as having considerable potential influence upon the behaviour of individuals.

In autism, the core issue is that of impaired social interactions compounded by problems in communication and imagination. Lord and Magill-Evans (1995) held that individuals with autism had particular difficulty in seeking to coordinate eye contact with smiling or other communicative behaviours, and that other children tended to make little response to the attempts to initiate interactions that were made, or did not even recognise them as attempts to communicate. Therefore, they conclude that, while one cannot be certain how much of the changes in behaviour are directly the result of the Circles of Friends, it is legitimate to regard this approach as a means of mobilising practical support for the children with autism, while gaining benefits for peers, all with minimal costs, and minimal drawbacks for any participants.

Therapeutic Perspectives

Because of the spectrum nature of autism and the many behaviour combinations that can occur, no one approach is effective in alleviating symptoms of autism in all cases. Various types of therapies are available, including behaviour modification, speech/ language therapy, sensory integration, vision therapy, music therapy, auditory training, medications and dietary interventions, among others.

Music Therapy

Akogiounoglou (1990) explores the ability of school-age autistic children to respond overtly to familiar and novel auditory stimuli: environmental, vocal, and musical sounds. He also outlines detailed behavioural profile of an autistic child. He reports a strong preference of autistic children to respond with movement and indicates weak preference toward musical excerpts rather than toward environmental and vocal sounds.

Clauss (1995) investigates the effects of music on attention and self-stimulation. He hypothesizes that background music would improve attention and reduce auditory self-stimulation and reports findings that indicate music may help improve attention and communication. Edgerton (1993) attempts to determine the effectiveness of improvisational music therapy on autistic children's communicative behaviours.

Hairston (1984) suggests that use of art and music therapy can improve four areas of development: behaviour, communication, socialisation and pre-academics. Leopold (1997) hypothesizes that language deficits in savants, in addition to a particular developmental profile, allow for the flourishing of musical skill. Simpson (1997) examines the effect of musical tempo, which either matched or did not match a child's preferred tempo, on the quality of interaction with the researcher. He hypothesizes that there would be more positive behaviours of emotional connection (e.g., smiling, mutual eye contact) and more reciprocal behaviours (action imitation, turn-taking) during the attunement condition than in the non-attunement condition.

Sensory Integration Therapy

Ayres (1979) describes sensory integration therapy as sensory stimulation and subsequent adaptive responses evolve according to the child's neurological needs. Therapy techniques include vestibular stimulation such as swinging in a hammock, and tactile stimulation achieved by brushing parts of the child's body (Smith, 1996). SI therapy is viewed as a direct intervention that can improve nervous system function. This is done by providing the child with enhanced levels of sensory information gleaned during physical activities that are meaningful to the child, and that elicit adaptive behaviours (Koomar & Bundy, 1991).

SI therapy does not seek to teach higher order skills, but rather to rearrange brain functioning (sensory processing capability) as a precursor to learning (Arendt, Maclean, & Baumeister, 1988). Ray, King and Grandin (1998) examined the effect of vestibular stimulation (swinging) on speech sounds in children with autism. The researchers found a 15 per cent increase in vocalisations while the child was on a swing than in the absence of this vestibular stimulation.

Cook (1991) presents anecdotal case studies of on-task behavior and attending skills in three children with autism who received sensory motor interventions. Cook reported both teachers and parents noted significant improvements in both domains, and in all three children. According to Murray and Anzalone (1991), "care is required not to overstep the boundaries of sensory integration theory when applying these procedures to children and adults with autism. " In a study designed to test the effectiveness of SI on self-injurious behaviours (SIB), Mason and Iwata (1990) found that SI was less effective than behavioural treatment in reducing SIB; in one case, the rate of SIB actually increased with SI treatment. A review of the literature did not yield any study concluding SI is an effective treatment for SIB or self-stimulation.

Arendt (1988) examined the effectiveness of SI therapy as it applied to individuals with mental retardation. He found that the database of studies was small, and that the methodology in most of the studies under his consideration had serious flaws that included examiner bias and uncontrolled variables. Zissermann

(1992) describes the effects of deep-pressure tactile stimulation in reducing self-stimulating behaviours in a child with multiple disabilities including autism. These behaviours include hitting the hands together, one hand on top of the other, so that the palm of one hand hits the dorsum of the other, or hitting a surface with one or both hands.

Aroma Therapy

The brain relies on information gathered by various sensory receptors such as touch, smell, taste, hearing and sight in order to make sense of our environment. The disruption caused by a sensory disorder as to how the information is organised in the brain can have a devastating effect on how a situation is perceived and understood (Siegel 1996, p79). Many people with autism will experience hypersensitivity to certain stimuli resulting in actual physical pain of sensory over load (Waterhouse 1995, p.19.

Occupational Therapy

Calhoun et al (1991) in their article summarise the occupational therapy assessment and intervention with a high functioning autistic child over a four-year period. It documents her initial presentation with communication, imaginative activity, social and emotional delays. Case-Smith and Bryan (1999) examined the effects of an occupational therapy intervention emphasizing sensory integration with five preschool children with autism. The results support descriptions in the literature regarding the behavioural changes that children with autism can make when participating in intervention using a sensory integration approach.

Ermer and Dunn (1998) determine which factors on the Sensory Profile, a measure of children's responses to commonly occurring sensory experiences, best discriminate among children with autism or pervasive developmental disorder (PDD), children with attention deficit hyperactivity disorder (ADHD), and children without disabilities. The researchers conclude that Sensory Profile is useful in discriminating certain groups of children with disabilities.

Watling et al. (1999) examine the current practice practices of occupational therapists experienced with children with autism spectrum disorders. Practice patterns included frequent collaboration with other professionals during assessment and intervention. Intervention services were typically provided in a one-to-one format with the most common techniques being sensory integration (99%) and positive reinforcement (93%). Theoretical approaches included sensory integration (99%), developmental (88%) and behavioural (73%). Evaluations relied heavily on nonstandardised tools and clinical observations. Educational methods identified as most helpful were weekend workshops (56%) and on-the-job training (52%).

Play Therapy

Restall and Magill-Evans (1994) focused on two questions. First, how does the play of children with autism differ from that of normally developing children? Second, what are the relationships between play performance and adaptive abilities? The researchers conclude that the results suggest that deficits in social development are a primary feature of autism. Stancliff (1998) opines developmental toys as the ideal method of sensory integration treatment for children with autism.

Approaches to Autism

Approaches have been developed in three main areas: (1) Communication Approaches (2) Interactive Approaches (3) Behaviour Approaches.

Proximal communication

There are a range of non-verbal techniques that adults can use to engage children with autism in social interactions. The Proximal Communication has theoretical foundations in work on social interactions between adults and children in infancy

Burst/Pause Approach to the Development of Intentional Communication: This approach is more effective with older non-verbal children with severe or profound learning disabilities as well as with other children with autism who do not speak. The main aim of the approach is to get the child to look at an adult for a tickle, in order to show acknowledgment.

The Picture Exchange Communication System (PECS): It was based on observations that 80 per cent of the preschool children admitted they had no functional communication skills. The aim is for children to acquire key communication skills, especially initiating communication in a social exchange.

Interactive Approaches: Interactive approaches are based on an understanding of autism as rooted in difficulties with intersubjectivity and emphasises the importance of building relationships with teachers and careers which can then be used as the basis for further educational development.

Music Interaction Therapy: An autistic spectrum approach. Music is a useful way of developing communication skills, it allows emotions to be expressed. It can include directive and in-directive strategies.

Interactive Curriculum: The actions of the child or adult are imitated and incorporated into turn taking routines. This can help to build relationships.

Option Approach: The philosophy of the approach is that feelings are governed by attitudes and to empower personal growth. If attitudes can be changed feelings can be changed.

Behaviour Approaches: It focuses on specific behaviours rather than on the diagnostic entity of autism and it emphasises the immediate environment rather than etiology or early history. Skills are built up in small steps, often through a process of backward chaining. "Because autistic children have so many difficulties that need to be addressed separately, they need to be taught virtually everything, and the teaching needs to proceed piece by piece instead of in major steps."

The TEACCH Approach: There are many different opinions regarding this approach. TEACCH stands for Treatment and Education of Autistic and Related Communication Handicapped Children. Their main aims are to develop communication skills and to help individuals work and play independently of adults. The types of intervention enforced are structured teaching, communication, leisure and social development and stress reduction. TEACCH programme also combines treatment with diagnostic and assessment methods.

Daily Life Approach (The Higashi School): Children are put through intensive physical activities under a regimented schedule. The emphasis is on teaching and learning within a group. It appears to be founded in Eastern philosophy which accepts a relationship between an individual's mind, body and spirit, and Japanese pedagogy, which focuses on group education and group performance.

Assessment in Autism

Daly et al. (1997) sum up in their paper that conventional tests of infant-toddler development confound the measures used to infer mental ability with the child's disability. A new approach involving assessment of central information processing ability is described as a complement to conventional tests that permits the identification of intact mental ability in the face of pervasive developmental delays and autism.

Stress in Families

Peck (1998) says that Families of children with autism experience increased amounts of family stress, as compared to families without a child with autism. Many family support initiatives have addressed the lack of resources in these families to cope with the increased stress they face from day to day.

Aarons & Gittens (1994) review psychiatric problems in children and adults with autism and related disorders and their first-degree relatives, with a focus on: (1) why they present with psychiatric problems; (2) rates of psychiatric disorders; (3) clinical features important in diagnosis and differential diagnosis; (4) treatment. The data suggest that depression, anxiety, impairing compulsive behaviours, attentional problems, hyperactivity, and sleep problems occur commonly in individuals with autism.

Services for Autism

Attwood (1998) suggests the importance of using a functional assessment of the problem, the benefits of utilising the school psychologist as a behavioural consultant in developing, implementing and evaluating treatment and that treatment integrity can be monitored and improved through the use of videotape review for feedback to treatment staff. Sperry et al. (1999) explore the perspectives of services providers and parents of children diagnosed with autism spectrum disorder regarding service systems. A comparison of parent and provider focus group transcripts yielded points of convergence in the areas of collaboration, family support, financial issues, equity, early identification, advocacy, training and inclusion.

3

Methodology

Crawford (1928) writes, "Research is simply a systematic and refined technique of thinking, employing special tools, instruments and procedure in order to obtain a more adequate solution of a problem that would not be possible under ordinary means".

The present chapter deals with methodology of the study under discussion and delineates in detail the method undertaken in carrying out the study.

A single subject experimental design is used in this study. The key element of this design is the introduction and manipulation of an independent variable under controlled conditions (Cook and Campbell, 1979). Single subject experimentation is indicated when the research question addresses the behaviour of individuals rather than group behaviour, characteristics of individual subjects vary greatly, and representative sampling of individual behaviours is difficult to achieve (Herson and Barlow, 1987; Sidman 1960; Tawney and Gast, 1984, Elder, 1997b). This type of experimental design is being used for several reasons. First, it allows for careful inspection of the individual interacting with the environment. Second, investigators are able to incorporate new knowledge into the intervention when appropriate without compromising the scientific integrity of the experiment. Finally, this research design allows investigators to take multiple "behavioural snapshots" over time, providing quantitative descriptions of behaviour that are sensitive to the dynamic property of behaviour (Johnston and Pennypacker, 1986 a/b).

The issue studied is the development of psycho-socio-pedagogic intervention strategies for children with autism. This study was accomplished by exploring the people and the environment that a child with autism came into contact with. The author conducted extensive interviews with key informants and reviewed the records maintained by the school and family.

The subjects involved in the study were from the two important metropolitan cities in Tamil Nadu: Chennai and Coimbatore. Chennai is the capital of Tamil Nadu and various government and non-government organisations have been making great strides in special education. The city of Coimbatore is landlocked and its economy is based on textile industries and agriculture. The city has a number of children with autism, studying in special and integrated school settings. 'Autism' as a study is relatively new in this country, as many people have had little or no experience with it. However, teachers working in special schools have undergone basic training and are well equipped to handle this group of children.

Both participant and non-participant observations were conducted in several settings – at school and at home. These observations were recorded immediately in field notes. On the note-taking form was a place for the date, place of observation and beginning and ending times of observation. Observations in several settings allowed the evaluator to see how the individual functions and the impact of environmental conditions and factors on the ability to function. Multiple observations in different settings enabled the author to set reasonable expectations, to understand conditions and factors necessary for optimal performance and to determine the conditions that disrupt effective functioning. (Photocopy of the Note-taking form is given in the Appendices).

Extensive interviews were conducted before developing the intervention strategies. Initial interviews were open-structured to collect information from various sources, although at times probes were used to clarify or expound points (ATEC checklist is given in Appendix-II). The interviewees were asked to share freely and then were asked questions based on information received from previous interviews. The later interviews were semi-structured and structured, and these interviews were intended to gain more information about the intervention strategies or questioning to clarify or extend meaning, based on platforms of information already obtained.

Written sources included doctor certificates, reports from clinical pathologists and speech pathologists, official agency reports and school records. Copies of the records were examined individually and notations were made or paragraphs and points were highlighted in a search for developmental or social information (A copy of a child's record is enclosed in the appendices).

Informants included persons who had known the children since birth or preschool years, including long-time friends, maternal/paternal grandparents, mother's/father's sisters/ brothers, para-professionals, past teachers, present school staff, a close neighbour, other close relatives who had known the children intensely for one period of the life of the children with autism etc. The extensive interviews combined with observations and document review provided a rich database for exploration of the subjects. Informants described events and provided interpretations grounded in years of close contact with the child with autism.

Assessment Tools

Forms I-IV given in the Appendices were prepared to gather information about the sample selected to be adopted for the study. The following procedures had to be adopted to elicit and develop the instructional, behavioural support plan and the intervention strategies:

- Identify priority goals
- Assess social skills
- Assess daily life activities
- Identify preferences and interests

The procedures and forms developed by Falco and associates (1990) were used for Project QUEST (Quality Educational Services Training Project), Portland State University, Portland, Oregon as models. The forms and procedures served only as guidelines. The author developed her own tools that are given in the Appendices (Forms I- V). These forms were especially helpful in eliciting the kinds of detailed information needed to develop effective intervention strategies and programmes for children with autism. Opinionaires were also prepared to find out about the effectiveness of intervention strategies (Photocopies of the forms used are given in the Appendices).

Pilot Study

A pilot study was conducted to have an idea about the feasibility and practical difficulties. This also enabled the author to have a thorough knowledge and understanding about the key problems. A matrix was prepared before determining the intervention strategies (Matrix of Priority Problems for Effective Intervention is given in the Appendices).

Setting

There are two settings for this study. The first is the classroom in special school where the children regularly got together. The second setting is the subject's home where the child lives with his/her parents and siblings. In many cases, siblings played a key role in providing the strategic intervention suggested by the author.

Psychometric Properties

Any good instrument should have sound psychometric properties: reliability and validity. In general, an instrument is reliable when it measures what it is supposed to measure; it is valid when it accurately predicts performance.

Reliability may be defined as the level of internal consistency or stability of the measuring device over time. All observations were recorded and in order to provide indications of reliability of the observation procedure employed, the behaviour of the subject during the particular session and all observers kept separate and independent records were also recorded. Reliability was calculated using the formula:

$$\text{Percentage of agreement} = \frac{\text{No. of agreements}}{\text{No. of agreements \& disagreements}} \times 100$$

Inter-observer agreement data for the observation sessions ranged from 89 per cent to 100 per cent with a mean of 96 per cent.

Garrett (1973) defines validity of a tool as "accuracy with which a tool measures whatever it is supposed to measure. The efficiency with which a test measures, what it attempts to measure." A careful analysis of the intervention strategies and treatments by experts in special education and clinical psychologists was carried out and found to be valid.

Variables and Sampling Used in the Study

Selection of proper variables is an important ingredient of a good research. There are two types of variables in behavioural research and application: dependent and independent variables. The value of the dependent variable is said to depend upon the value of the independent variable. In this research, the dependent variables were the positive behaviour changes in the children. The independent variables that brought forth the changes were: the dominant intelligence of the child, the obsession or fixation or the splinter skill of the child and the intervention strategies that were used as channels to reach him or her out.

Sampling

Purposive sampling that falls under non-probability sampling method was used in the study. 'Purposive sampling' means sample with a purpose in mind. One of the first things, one has to do is verify that the respondent does in fact meet the criteria for being in the sample. Purposive sampling can be very useful for situations where sampling for proportionality is not the primary concern.

The sample selected for the final study included 63 children with autism. (For single-subject experimental design, the sample size was large.) Subjects were chosen from specific special schools that had a large number of children with autism-like features and only the children who met the DSM-IV criteria for Autistic Spectrum Disorder (Diagnostic and Statistical Manual, 1994) were chosen for the final study. (Photocopy of the DSM-IV is given in the Appendices.) Distribution of the sample is diagrammatically represented in Figure 3.1.

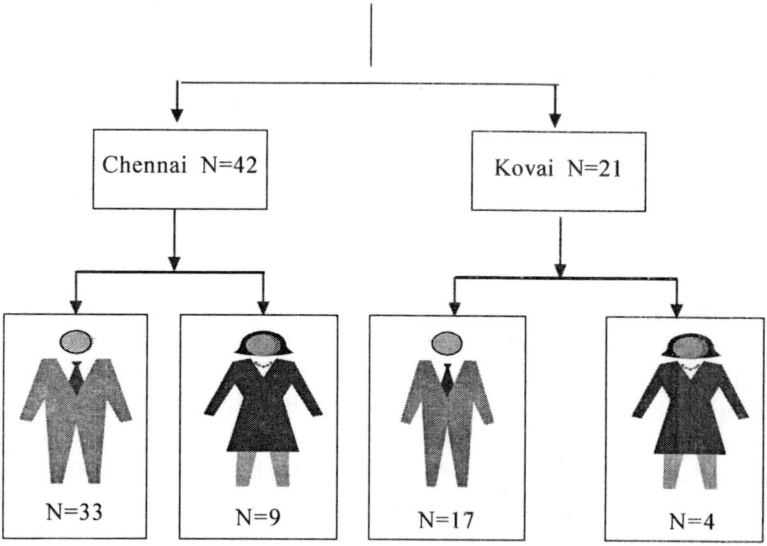

Figure 3.1: Distribution of the Sample N=63

Curricular Framework

An eight-sided curriculum was developed, which presents academic areas structured in a developmental approach with an evaluation that coordinates the curriculum. This provided the framework for the strategic management. The eight areas involved are:

1. Communication skills
2. Social-interaction skills
3. Academics
4. Functional skills
5. Motor skills
6. Prevocational and vocational skills
7. Behavioural skills
8. Recreational skills

Figure 3.2 illustrates all the areas that are covered by the curriculum.

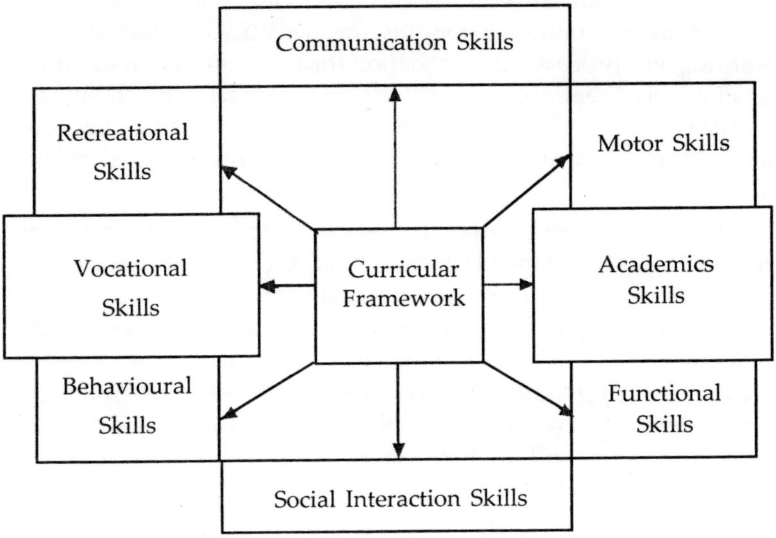

Figure 3.2: Curricular Framework

Learning Styles

According to Drs. Rita and Kenneth Dunn, there are a number of specific elements that comprise a person's learning style, including:

Environmental elements (sound, light, temperature, and design)

Sociological elements (pair-oriented, peer-oriented, team-oriented, self-oriented, self-oriented, and authority-oriented)

Emotional elements (motivation, persistence, responsibility, and structure)

Physical elements (perceptual/modality strengths, time of day, need for intake – eating, drinking and need for mobility)

The intervention strategies were designed, based on the theory of Multiple Intelligences and Piagetian and Vygotskian principles of linguistic, communicative and play development of children.

Rationale

'Learning styles' influence our way of thinking, our ways of learning and our ways of teaching. In educational psychology, the term 'individual differences' is given due weightage. Every individual has unique strengths, propensities, preferences for learning and processing information through different modalities or channels (hearing, seeing, touching and feeling - there are auditory learners, visual learners, tactile-kinesthetic learners, analytic and global learners, innovative learners and dynamic learners).

It is rather imperative for teachers to bear in mind the individual differences, which has significant pedagogic implications. Individuals learn, represent and relate information, knowledge, insight and inspiration in multitudinal ways. Teachers have to understand the propensities, strengths, weaknesses, preferences and aversions of the learners. First of all a teacher has to take a closer look at her/his own functioning as a learner. This will in turn pave the way for new teaching strategies and techniques.

Multiple Intelligences

Professor Howard Gardner, Professor of Education at Harvard University, developed the theory of Multiple Intelligences (MI). In his book *Frames of Mind* (1983), he says, "People use at least seven relatively autonomous intellectual capacities – each with its own distinctive mode of thinking – to approach problems and create products. Every normal individual possesses varying degrees of each of these intelligences, but the ways in which intelligences combine and blend are as varied as the faces and the personalities of individuals."

It was rather imperative for the investigator to find out the entry points or learning styles of the children so that appropriate interventions could be devised. The intervention strategies were based on the theory of Multiple Intelligences. The general characteristics associated with each of these intelligences are described in Figure 3.3.

Verbal-Linguistic Intelligence: Word Smart refers to an individual's capacity to use language communication and is good at playing games such as scrabble, cross word puzzles etc. (examples: poets, journalists, broadcasters, lawyers, teachers, novelists and writers). These individuals are adept in verbal and language skills (reading, writing, speaking).

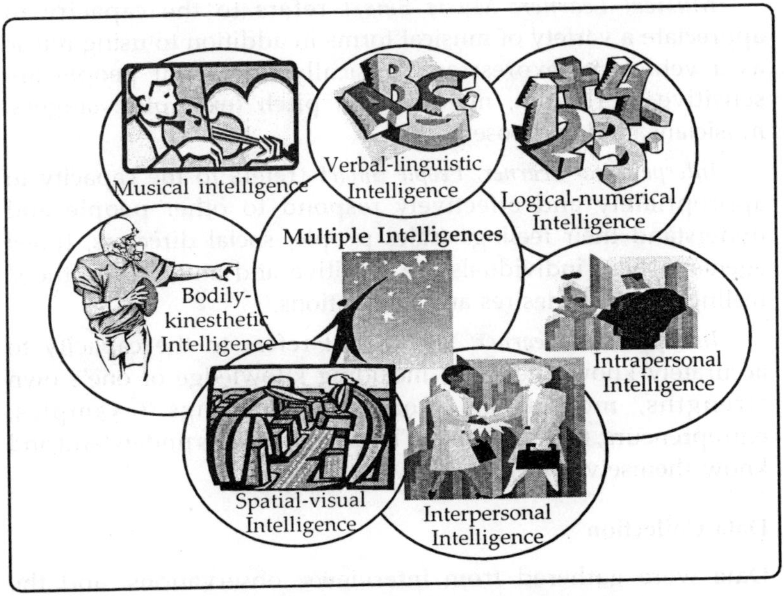

Figure 3.3: Types of Multiple Intelligences

Logical Mathematical Learner: Number Smart refers to an individual's capacity to think and analyse logically, use numbers effectively, solve problems scientifically, and discern relationships and patterns between concepts and things (example: mathematicians, engineers, architects and scientists). These individuals learn best through the opportunity to experiment, search for patterns and make their own discoveries. They typically enjoy games of strategy such as chess, bridge and various card games.

Spatial Learner: Art Smart refers to the capacity to think visually and orient oneself spatially. In addition, spatially intelligent people are able to graphically represent their visual and spatial ideas (examples: artists, decorators, architects, surveyors, inventors, and guides).

Bodily-Kinesthetic Learner: Body Smart refers to the capacity of using one's own body skilfully as a means of expression or to work skilfully to create or manipulate objects (examples: dancers, actors, athletes, sculptors, surgeons, mechanics, and craftspeople). They learn best by doing through active learning, movement, and hands on activities.

Musical Learner: Music Smart refers to the capacity to appreciate a variety of musical forms in addition to using music as a vehicle of expression. Musically intelligent people are sensitive to rhythm, melody, and pitch (examples: singers, musicians, and composers).

Interpersonal Learner: People Smart refers to the capacity to appropriately and effectively respond to other people and understand their feelings (sales people, social directors, travel agents). These individuals are sensitive and attuned to others' feelings, moods, desires and motivations.

Intrapersonal Learner: Self Smart refers to the capacity to accurately know one's self, including knowledge of one's own strengths, motivations, goals, and feelings (examples: entrepreneurs, therapists, etc.). These individuals understand and know themselves well.

Data Collection

Data were gathered from interviews, observations, and the artefacts of the lives of all the children involved in the research. Triangulation was accomplished within and across multiple data sources that included several interviews of different individuals across two different settings such as home and school, and two methods of recording – field notes and participant and non-participant observations; and extensive document review, including artefacts from the lives of children deemed important enough by the family to save, along with school records, etc.

Both quantitative and qualitative strategies were employed in the study, exploring different questions with different methods of data collection, and triangulation using different methods or sources to answer the same question to obtain information from more than one viewpoint.

Triangulation is the application and combination of several research methodologies in the study of the same phenomenon.

By combining multiple observers, theories, methods, and empirical materials, researchers can hope to overcome the weakness or intrinsic biases and the problems that come from single method, single-observer, single-theory studies. There are five basic type of triangulation:

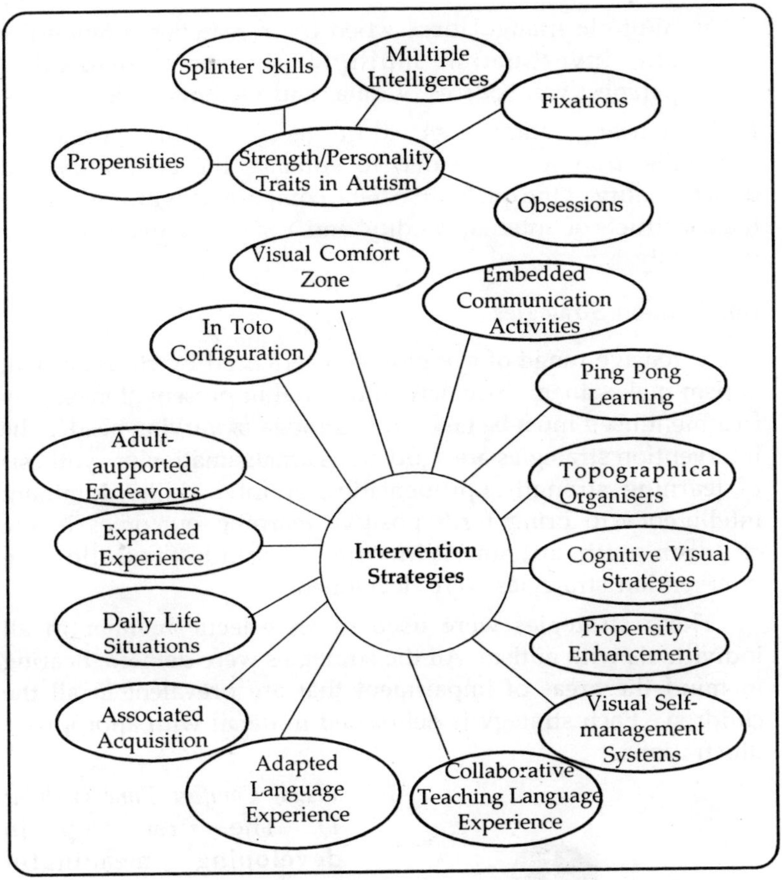

Figure 3.4: Intervention Strategies

a) data triangulation, involving time, space and persons.

b) investigator triangulation, which consist of the use of multiple, rather than single observers.

c) theory triangulation, which consists of using more than one theoretical scheme in the interpretation of the phenomenon.

d) methodological triangulation, which involves using more than one method and may consist of within-method or between-method strategies.

e) multiple triangulation, when the researcher combines in one investigation multiple observers, theoretical perspectives, sources of data, and methodologies.

Multiple triangulations are used in this study. This approach to data collection was intended to enhance the credibility and dependability of the qualitative data, comparable with addressing the constructs of 'internal validity' and 'reliability' in quantitative data analysis.

Intervention Strategies

The extensive range of symptoms experienced by children with autism makes them extremely individual in presentation, so any treatment used must be tailored to a range of varying needs. The intervention strategies are a judicious amalgamation or synthesis of learning strengths, propensities, splinter skills, dominant intelligence to bring forth positive learning outcomes in the children with autism. With this in mind, the following intervention strategies were developed.

These strategies were used in an eclectic manner in all individuals with autism. All the strategies were devised, bearing in mind the areas of impairment that are prevalent in all the children. Each strategy is delineated in detail with appropriate illustrations.

Visual Comfort Zone (Exhibit 1): The first step in developing meaningful communication is to maintain and improve eye contact with children with autism. The adult caregiver has to make sure that the developmentally delayed children are kept at the eye level of the caregiver. Eye contact helps to develop increased body awareness, attention to surroundings and perceptual motor coordination.

Embedded Communication Activities (Exhibit 2): Functional routines such as getting dressed, school interval or recess, lunch, play time, going to the doctor and leisure activity have a lot of potential for communi-cation and these can be capitalised on to communi-cate with the child with autism. Life is full of series of such activities or events; these events can be utilised to teach functional, social and communication skills. Any opportunity that arises during the day should be made use of as a teachable moment.

In Toto Configuration (Exhibit 3) : The child with autism has to be accepted in totality with his/her propensities, fixations/ obsessions, interests, dominant intelligence, learning strengths and deficits. While developing an effective Individualised Education Programme (IEP), it is important to consider the big picture or complete picture, the gestalt. The IEP is much like a travel plan or an itinerary. The plan for those with autism has to be drawn with great and elaborate details. Just like a travel plan, it should be developed with understanding the starting place (current level of functioning), places of stay (teaching strategies, inter-ventions, modifi-cations and adapt-ations) and final destination (the ultimate goal). The ultimate goal is to enable the child to lead an independ-ent and meaningful life and to contri-bute to the society.

Ping Pong Learning (Exhibit 4): As the urge to interact and communicate is almost absent in autism, young children need many opportunities to interact and to communicate. The adult care giver/ sibling/ teacher/ therapist/ friend or anyone who interacts with a child with autism has to start an activity or imitating, matching the child's actions provide a chance for the child to reciprocate. Enhancing and improving social, functional and communication skills is the most challenging task for people who support individuals with autism. In order to expand and improve communication skills, it is imperative to provide opportunities for interaction, turn-taking, giving and receiving. The activity or a game should be selected in such a way that it requires both players to interact with each other as in a ping-pong game. These types of structured play-based strategies provide a context for spontaneous communication and social interaction.

Topographical Organisers (Exhibit 5): Children with autism have problems in understanding the locations and boundaries. Sometimes temporary markers have to be used to define a particular area, location or boundary. The environment, the events, the space and the time should be organised and structured in such a way that optimal level of stimulation is maintained for effective learning to take place. Children with autism have difficulty in processing sensory information and they have to depend upon others to provide external structure. It is

important to highlight on critical and seminal information, to provide clarity, meaning and purpose, provide scaffolding and to reduce anxiety from distractions.

Cognitive Visual Strategies (Exhibit 6) : As children with autism are visual learners, pairing signs with speech are useful in teaching basic language concepts because some of the attributes of an object such as shape, colour, size and movement are graphic. Words have to be taught as a whole supported by pictures. Planning and preparing visual references to augment and support communication are of paramount importance. This strategy is based on the previous knowledge of the learner.

Propensity Enhancement (Exhibit 7): Activities, people and objects that are liked by the children with autism have to be enhanced and expanded further to provide meaningful learning situations. Obsessions, fixations and intense interests act as natural reinforcers and tremendous motivators. Teaching new skills through special interests serve as entry points through which the children can be reached. A narrow, fixated interest needs to be broadened into constructive activities.

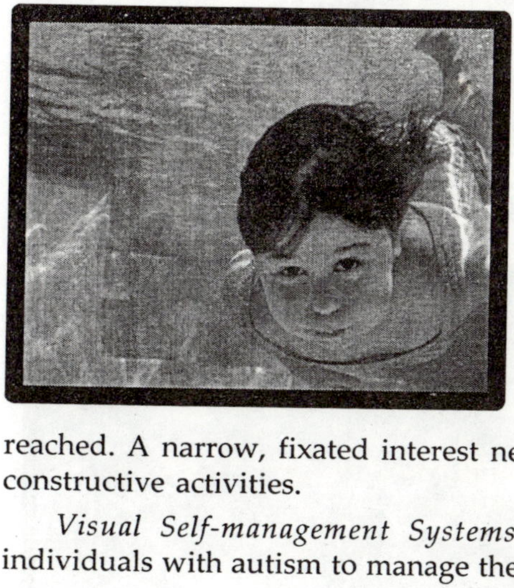

Visual Self-management Systems (Exhibit 8): To enable individuals with autism to manage themselves independently in

the society, in order to organise information, to prepare for changes and transitions and to clarify time, concepts and ideas the learner needs information in a concrete and visual format. Visual references and organisers include calendars, mini calendars, cue cards, semantic maps, thematic webs, stories, etc., Visual instructional strategies provide new teaching skills and also enable to solve behaviour problems in children with autism.

Collaborative Teaching (Exhibit 9): Parents, special education teacher, therapists, siblings and friends should work together as a team to integrate all therapies and services to teach useful and meaningful skills in a holistic manner and to avoid con-fusion and to prevent the learning of unrelated splinter skills. Every member of the team has to collaborate, share information and expertise.

Adapted Language Experience (Exhibit 10): Those with autism live in a verbal world; they have to understand other people's words in order to learn and function effectively and efficiently. Hearing the language in natural contexts is a prerequisite for understanding and using the language for communication. Adaptations and positive language experiences such as 'parallel talking', 'exaggerated facial expressions', 'animated facial expressions', 'visual cues' and 'reflective listening' will result in better and more meaningful use.

Adult Supported Endeavours (Exhibit 11): Quite often children with autism are controlled by adults and care givers and they do not get to exercise their rights, wants and desires. Activities related to the subject of their interest ought to be explored in as much detail as time and enthusiasm allow. This sort of spontaneous learning does much to encourage a curious and questioning attitude in children. They are much more likely to continue to explore objects and ideas if they are supported in their endeavours by a thoughtful and responsible adult. The adults must be alert to provide assistance at the most optimal point for the child to communicate his needs.

Expanded Experience (Exhibit 12): While playing with a child with autism, every activity is to be treated as a form of interpersonal communication. Talking with children about their activities can clarify or confirm their understanding. An important part of this is asking questions and keeping the communication channel open. While talking about a particular concept or while engaging the child with autism in a particular activity, it is important to include all related concepts, themes, interests and activities. Novel actions added to the natural interaction and new dimensions of the actions increase flexibility and tolerance for new and complex information and prevent rigid routines in children with autism.

Daily Life Situations (Exhibit 13): Many types of activities and situations of home life provide opportunities for children to learn various concepts and to interact with people in real life. Focused and structured experiences that enable the children to develop communication and social skills, independence, positive self-concept and autonomy to make choices must be provided. These will ultimately help the child to make transitions smoothly from one situation to another, from home to community at large.

Associated acquisition (Exhibit 14): A child acquires language through cognition, generalisation, discrimination and classification of concepts. The child perceives an object through his senses and adds meaning to his/her perception and these two processes occur together. Two brain functions of joint attention and the ability to focus along with another person enable a child to acquire language. It is of vital importance to provide a language-rich environment where the child can match or associate objects or activities with their names. While helping the child to acquire language, it is important to present real objects, models, pictures juxtaposingly. Creating appropriate communication enabling environments and providing communication-enabling activities will enable children with autism to acquire language and lead to spontaneous communication.

Procedure

The children were observed, extensive interviews were held with key informants, the artifacts were reviewed and the problems were held, the strengths and weaknesses, preferences and interests, priority goals and routines and learning styles were identified, and assessment was made through standardised tools or forms and devised appropriate strategies.

Parents, guardians and intervention team members were consulted and permission sought before implementation the of intervention. For each child with autism, a supporting team was constituted. The special teacher, the parents and the siblings/peers (in case the child with autism was the only child, the peer or a friend or a neighbour who cared for the child) constituted the support team. The profile of each child with details such as propensities, proclivities, learning style, dominant intelligence, splinter skill, obsession, fixation, learning strengths and learning defects was discussed extensively with all team members. There are certain characteristics that are syndrome-specific and there are certain characteristics that are specific to a particular individual. For instance, lack of eye contact, echolalia, using adult's hands as tools, hyperactivity or hypoactivity etc., are syndrome-specific, and a child biting, hitting and spitting on other children are specific to a particular child. Distinction was made between what is applicable to all children and what characterises a particular individual.

The intervention strategies were synthesised taking into account the unique information processing styles, the propensities/proclivities, splinter skills, dominant intelligence, fixations / obsessions, learning strengths and learning deficits. The Theory of Multiple Intelligences and Piaget's principles of play development of children and Vygotskian views of language and communication development in children provided the theoretical framework for the study. All 14 intervention strategies devised by the investigator, their salient features and the purpose of each strategy and the implementation and the expected learning outcomes of each strategy were also discussed in detail with all members of the support team. The judicious and eclectic use of all the fourteen strategies was stressed upon.

The special teacher, parents, siblings and other members of the family and peers, whoever constituted the support team were oriented by the investigator. After the initial training was completed, follow-up was carried out at scheduled intervals. Strategies developed by the author both at school and at home. All observations were immediately recorded in a notebook.

One palpable limitation in this kind of study is the examiner's bias. To eliminate this bias and to ensure reliability of the study, all observations were recorded and ahered to.

Each experiment was conducted by manipulating the independent variables such as the splinter skill/obsession/fixation of the child and dominant intelligence of the child. The experiment was constructed with the focus on the unique learning styles of the children. This was useful in manipulating the independent variable and in generating the desired learning outcomes in each subject and that is the function of single-subject experimental design. Each experiment comprised 20 sessions of treatment or implementation strategy stretched over a period of two months. For observation purposes of the investigation the timeframe was specified but the interventions are still carried out in all the schools.

Occurring concurrently with the recorded sessions was the ongoing process of coding the previously recorded sessions. The outcome of each session of treatment was discussed with the support team and modifications were made immediately. The on-going process of the research stands testimony to the success of the investigation. The author has developed 'Strategic Intervention Paradigm' (a manual for special teachers, parents, siblings, family members, caregivers and therapists and others who are involved in helping children with autism) and 'Picture Enhanced Communication Competency Model for Children with Autism' in a compact disc format. The compact disc is prepared to develop communication skills in children with autism. Creating communication-enabling environments and providing communication-embedded activities to facilitate language acquisition and spontaneous communication are of paramount importance.

Several workshops were conducted on 'Multiple Intelligences' for special teachers, teachers in general, B.Ed students and Special Education students. Practical 'Demonstrations on the Sensory Impairment of children with Autism' and lectures were given by the author for parents, students, special teachers, doctors, anganwadi supervisors, social workers. The author actively served as resource person for projects sponsored by World Bank. (The e-mail sent by Dr.Lenaghan stands testimony to the success of the workshop on 'Multiple Intelligences' and a copy of his e-mail is enclosed in the Apppendices). These activities helped in gaining more insight into autism and in creating awareness about 'autism' among the general public. Articles published copies of in leading newspapers are enclosed in the Appendices. After the publication of the articles, several parents came forward to share their experiences and to get their queries clarified.

Data Analyses

The collected data were consolidated, tabulated, classified, analysed and interpreted. The single subject experimental design discussed in this study does not by itself determine the effectiveness of treatment procedures. Instead it provides an argument for ruling out contributions from other sources and it allows one to determine the effectiveness of a procedure either by observing graphs or by making a few calculations, opines A. Repp (1983). Calculations are of two types: (1) statistical (2) arithmetical. The statistical analyses are plentiful but their use in behavioral work is debatable. Several reasons are given for not using statistical analyses in behavioral science research.

Sulzer-Azaroff and Mayer (1977) have written that when behaviour has changed as a result of an intervention an important question to ask is the following: "Of what significance is this demonstrated relation?" One traditional approach has been to base interpretation significance upon probability theory asking, "What is the likelihood that these results could have been obtained by chance alone?" If it is concluded that chance was unlikely to be accepted as "statistically significant". In applied behaviour analysis, however, the emphasis is more on social, personal or clinical significance than on statistical significance (emphasis added). The applied behaviour analyst asks the question "What importance does the demonstration of this functional relation have for particular individuals and their society?"

Arithmetical determinations of the effectiveness of behaviour change procedures are much less controversial among behaviourists. In this study, the Multiple-Baseline Design was chosen. Multiple-baseline across behaviours of the same individual examines several behaviours of a single individual with each being brought sequentially into contact with the independent variable.

4

Results and Interpretations

This study aims to recommend psycho-socio, pedagogic paradigm of intervention strategies for autism. The results of the analyses of data are discussed and interpreted here in detail. The research methodology adopted was single study experimental design and hence each subject of the sample is given the appropriate intervention strategy, and the results of each and every experiment is delineated in detail. "Graphical analysis of data is often neglected because of the large sizes of data sets and the emphasis on randomization theory and this neglect can lead to flawed data analysis," says Lohr (1999). Care has been taken to avoid this flaw and hence every single subject is analysed in detail and the positive changes in behaviour observed are graphically represented.

Data Analyses

The collected data were analysed both qualitatively and quantitatively.

The below table provides background information about the sample. From the table it is quite palpable that the prevalence of autism is four times more in boys than in girls. In the current study it was found that the percentage of boys affected by the disorder was 79 per cent and girls 21 per cent. Autism can occur in people of all ethnic, social, education and income groups. Autism is found in families of all racial and social backgrounds. In rural area, the percentage of children affected by autism was 34 per cent and even in rural areas, there were special schools catering to the children with special needs.

Table 4.1: Socio-demographic Details of the Sample

S.No	Particulars	Further details	%
1	Gender	Boys	79
		Girls	21
2	Locality	Rural	34
		Urban	66
3.	Age Group	5 - 9	40
		10 - 14	47
		15 - 19	13
4	Causal Factors	Genetic	40
		Non-genetic	60
5	Educational Qualification.of fathers	Illiterate	-
		Primary	2
		High school	12
		Collegiate	86
6	Educational Qualification of mothers	Illiterate	-
		Primary	7
		High school	16
		Collegiate	77
7	Occupation of Fathers	Labourers	8
		Agriculturists/Businessmen	11
		Government servants	17
		Teachers/professors etc.	28
		Professionals: doctors/ lawyers/engineers	36
8	Occupation of Mothers	Housewives	10
		Agriculturists/Businesswomen	5
		Government servants	29
		Teachers/Professors	35
		Professionals: doctors/ lawyers/engineers	21
9	Family Income*	Low income: less than Rs. 2,500-4,500	7
		Middle income Rs. 4,501-7,500	38
		High income above Rs.7,500	55
	Age of Diagnosis of Autism	Before 3 years of age	25
		After 3 years of age	75

*Based on HUDCO (2002) income classification

The educational qualifications of parents of the sample studied reveals that there were no illiterates. Even in rural areas, where the the study was conducted it was found that even the mothers were functionally literates. They understood the complexity of autism perfectly, and provided insight and different perspectives about their children.

Another important point that is worth mentioning in the present study was that the highest percentage of autistic children (36%) were born to professionals such as doctors, engineers and lawyers. In some cases, it was difficult for parents, especially the educated fathers, to accept their children. As the parents of the children with autism in the selected sample were highly educated (64%), they fell under high-income group. Among the mothers of children with autism, 56 per cent were professionals. In 40 per cent of the sample the cause of autism is attributed to genetic factors and 60 per cent to non-genetic factors. Another important feature that was observed in the study is that only 25 per cent of the children were diagnosed before they started their preschool. Majority of the children (75%) were diagnosed only after the age of three years. This emphasizes the necessity for early diagnosis and early intervention.

Early diagnosis and early intervention brings in dramatic changes in the children. There are several factors that mould and shape the child. It is imperative to identify, classify, analyse and evaluate the factors operating on the behaviour of the child. These factors include heredity, physical, physiological, emotional, cognitive and interpersonal factors such as familial, social and cultural factors. The background information provides a detailed glimpse at the factors that shape the child. Figure 4.1 presents the demographic details about the children.

Gender-wise distribution of the sample (%)

Locality-wise distribution of the sample (%)

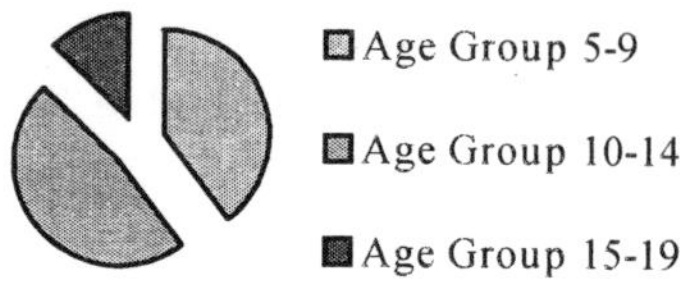

Age Group of the Sample (%)

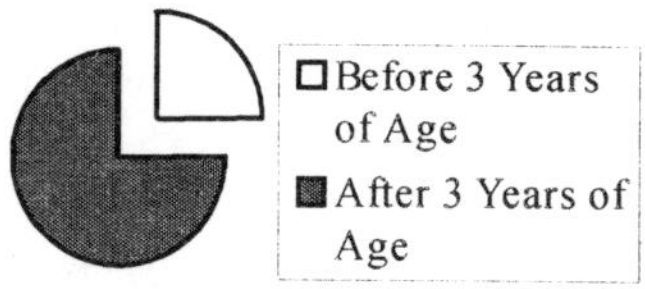

Age of Diagnosis of Autism (%)

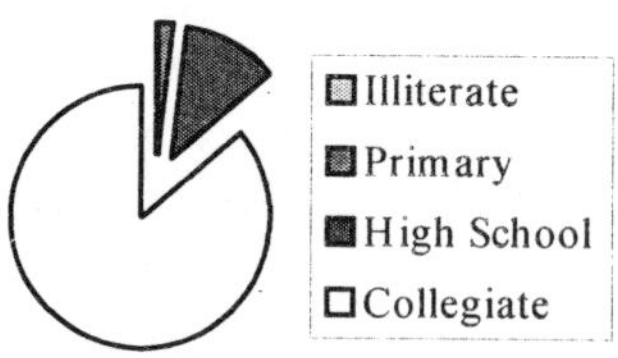

Educational Qualification of Fathers (%)

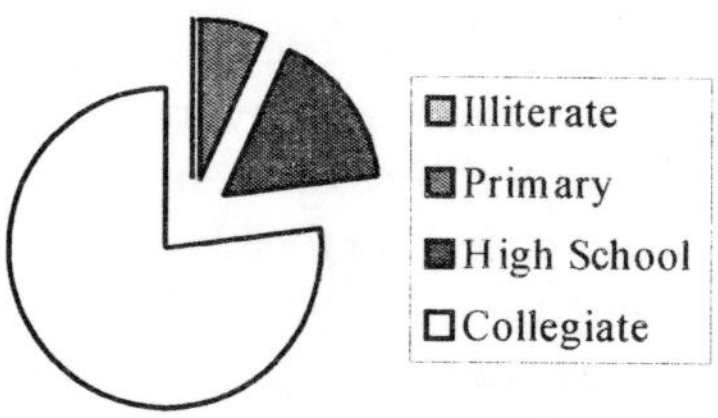

Educational Qualification of Mothers (%)

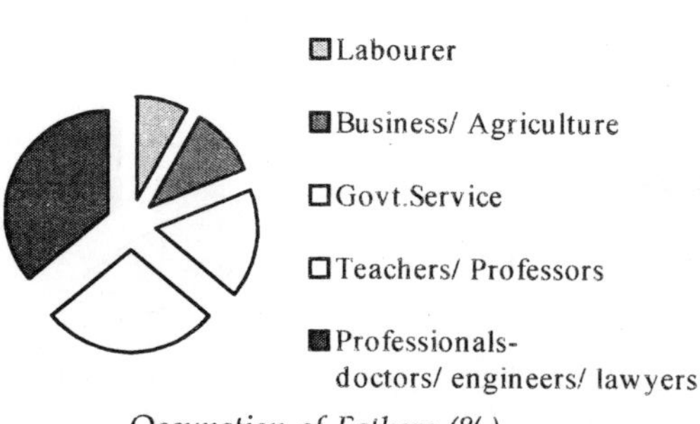

Occupation of Fathers (%)

(Fig. 4.1: Contd...)

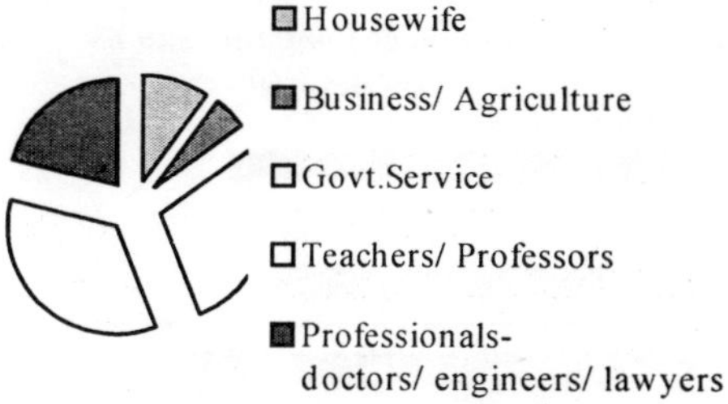

Occupation of Fathers (%)

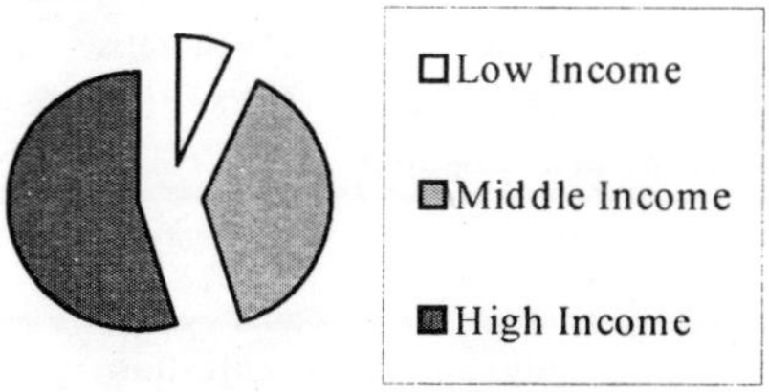

Family Income (%)

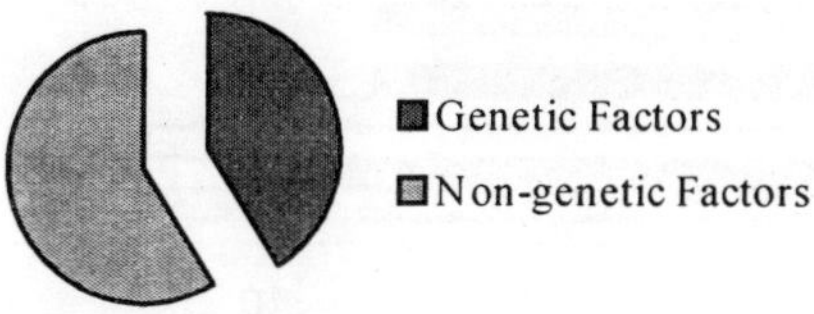

Causal Factors of Autism (%)

Figure 4.1: Demographic Details of the Sample (%)

Language /Communication

Language and communication, an important dimension of human beings is impaired in children with autism that many of them are totally non-verbal or have minimal speech characterised by inappropriate social reciprocity.

The various components that enhance language/ communication but those that are impaired in children with autism are given below and the number of children who have difficulties with each component are given with the help of a graph.

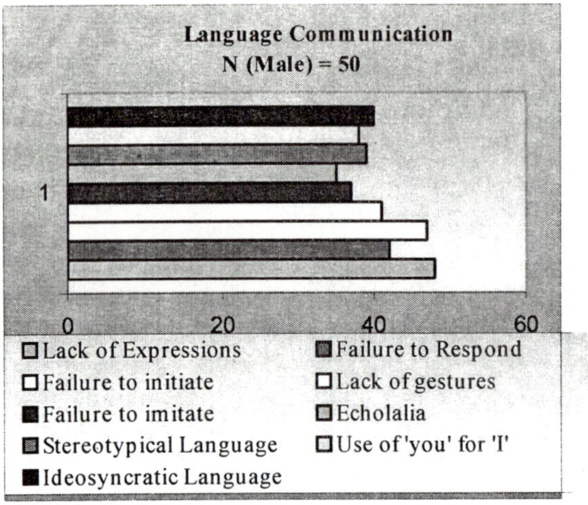

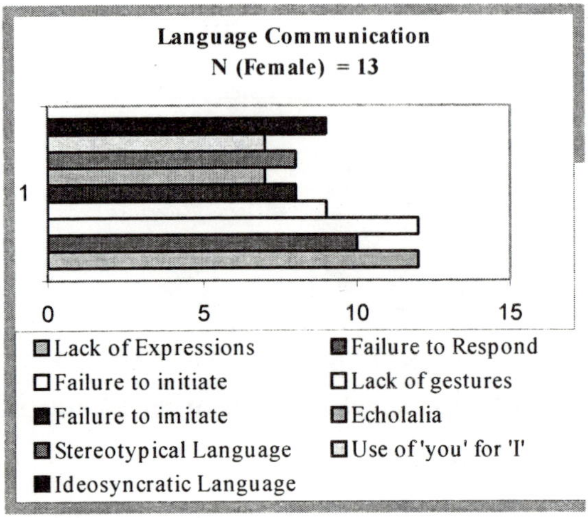

Figure 4.2 Language/Communication

1. Has limited or lack of facial expressions
2. Failure to respond to the communication of others
3. Failure to initiate or sustain conversation
4. Lack of gestures

5. Failure to imitate actions or sounds
6. Repeats or echoes words and phrases (echolalia)
7. Stereotyped and repetitive use of language
8. Use of 'you' for 'I'.
9. Idiosyncratic use of words.

Among all the behavioural characteristics listed under the category of 'Language/communication', the one that majority of children had problems with happened to be 'lack of facial expressions' and 'failure to initiate or sustain conversation'. Figure 4.2 is a graphic representation of the behavioural characteristics that fall under the category of 'Language/ Communication'.

Impaired Relationships: To People

The predisposition and preference for social stimuli that is critical in social interaction is totally lacking or weak in children with autism. "What makes autistic children 'autistic' is the quality of their engagement with others"(Hobson, 1992). Hobson adds that even the awareness of others is missing in some of these children. The components of the characteristic of 'Impaired Relationships: To People' and the number of children who fall under each component of the sample selected for the study are described below. They:

1. is unresponsive.
2. lack of social smile.
3. failure to use eye-to-eye gaze.
4. impairment of the awareness of other people and their needs.
5. are unable to recognise human characteristics.
6. do not play turn taking games.
7. use adult's hands as tools.
8. are unable to express emotions.

The graph (Figure 4.3) gives a clear vignette of children with impaired relationships with particular reference to people.

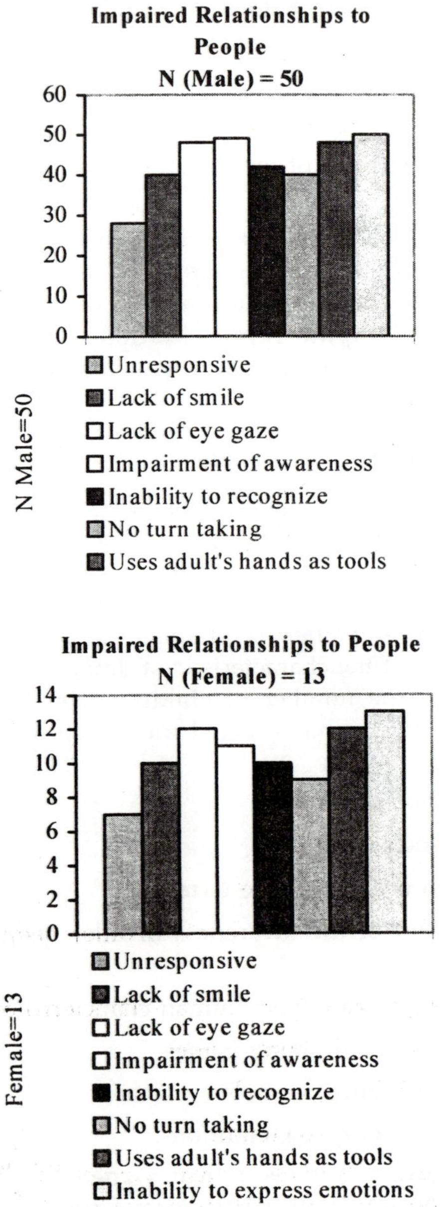

Figure 4.3: Impaired Relationships to People

Impaired Relationship: To the Environment

The inability to modulate and adapt to the stimulation provided by people and the environment or social situations is stifling and suffocating for most of the children. The inability to respond properly to the environment of the children with autism is listed below.

1. Repetitive play
2. Are upset by or resist changes
3. Develop rigid routines
4. Drift aimlessly about
5. Exhibit strong and inflexible interests

Figure 4.4 gives a clear picture of impaired relationships with reference to the environment and the number of children who fall under each dimension listed under the characteristic.

Difficulty in Perception of Meaningful Relationships

Children with autism have difficulty in understanding the sequences of growth, time, action, similarities and differences among things and to transfer learning to different novel situations. Different components of the characteristic or specific difficulties faced by children with autism are listed below:

1. Inability to see sequences of growth, time, action etc.
2. Inability to see similarities or differences
3. Inability to relate to properties, e.g., fire will burn
4. Inability to generalise or transfer learning.
5. Inability to distinguish fantasy from reality and vice versa
6. Impaired awareness of relationship of objects to each other, objects to persons, person to person
7. Lack of judgement

The graph (Figure 4.5) illustrates clearly the difficulties encountered by children with autism in perception of meaningful relationships and the number of children who come under different dimensions.

Lack of Self-image

Children with autism remain isolated as they engage in obsessional and ritualistic activities. Lack of body awareness, body control, lack of personal identity and lack of knowledge about one's own personal territory and boundary lead to lack of self-image, a devastating impairment in autism.

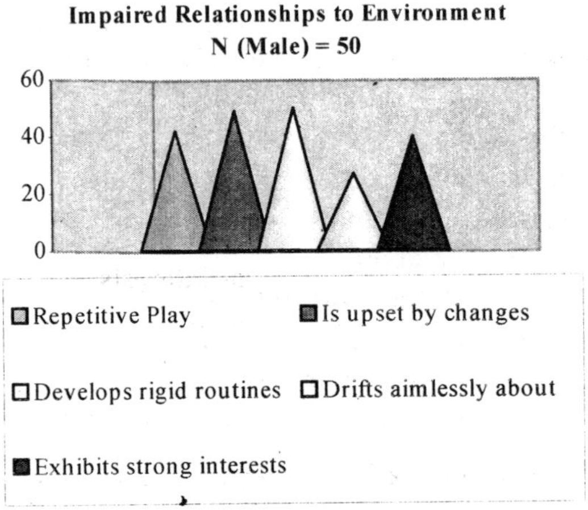

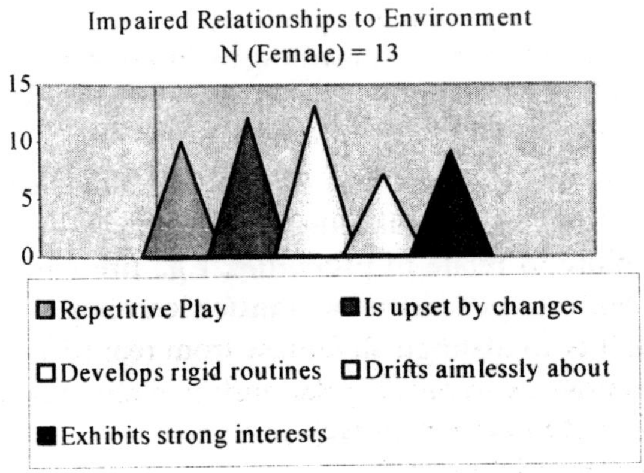

Fig.4.4: Impaired Relationships to Environment

1. Lack of personal identity and an impairment of self-image.
2. Remain isolated or engage in obsessional, ritualistic activities
3. Lack of knowledge about their own personal territory or boundary.
4. Lack of body awareness, body control and perceptual control.

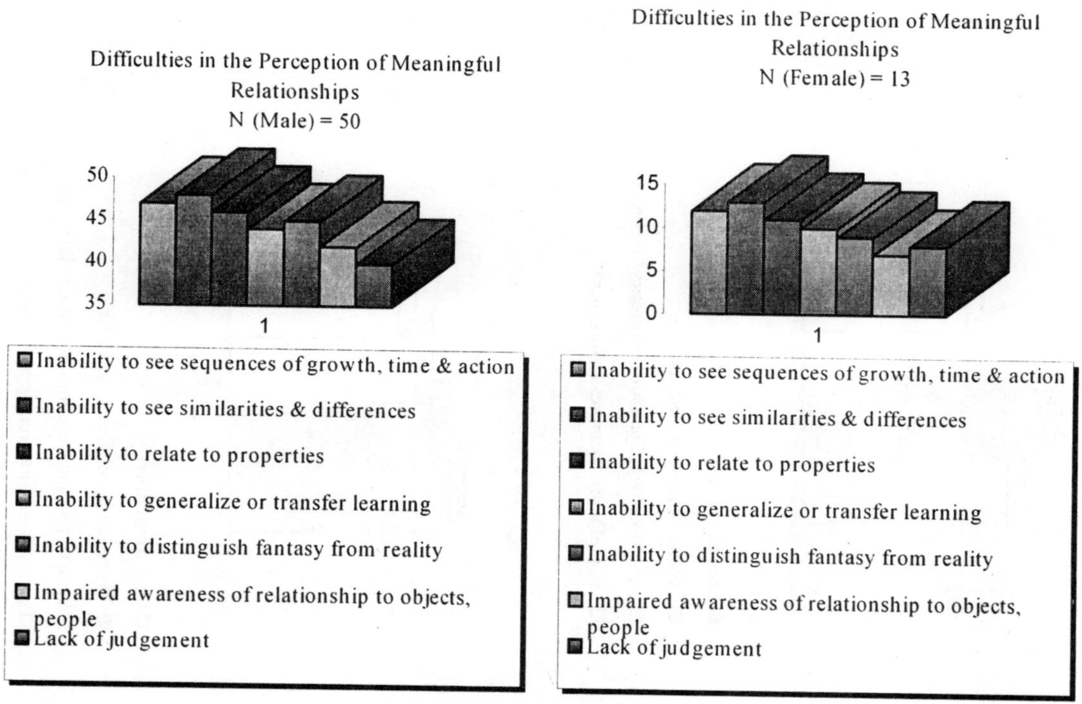

Figure 4.5: Difficulties in the Perception of Meaningful Relationships

The graph (Figure 4.6) portrays the number of children who lack self-image due to impairment in different components of the behavioural characteristic of lack of self-image.

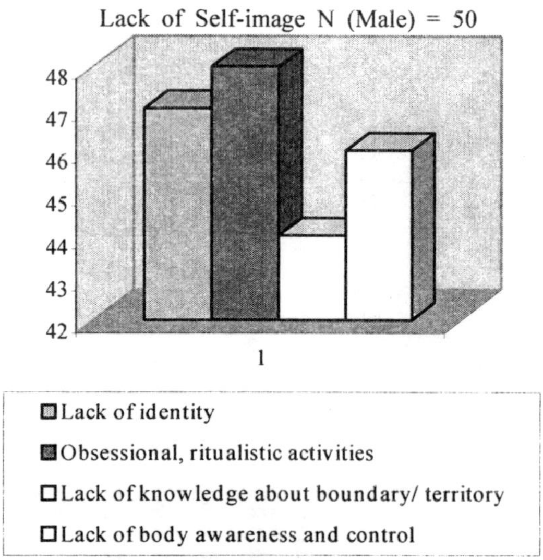

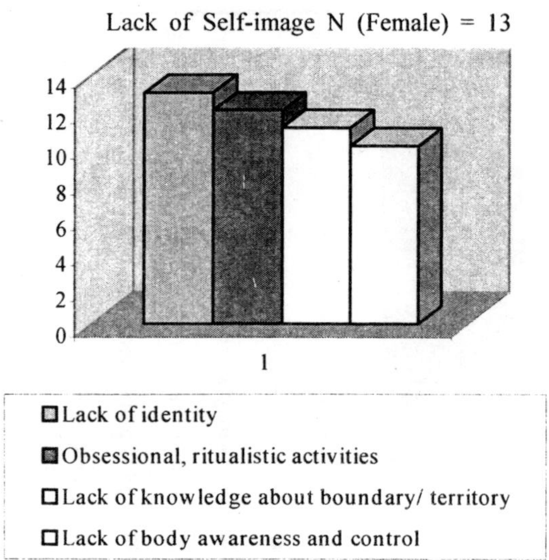

Figure 4.6: Lack of Self-image

Responses to Sensory Stimuli

Repetitive and stereotypic behaviours occur due to problems, stress and excitement. The root causes of the behaviour have to be understood and the interventions have to be devised as to eliminate the problem behaviour and enhance productive and acceptable behaviour among the children. The components of responses to sensory stimuli that are commonly found among autistic children are given below. They:

1. seem deaf.
2. hypersensitive or hyposensitive to certain sounds.
3. play with light and reflections.
4. are constantly finger-flicking.
5. pulls away when touched.
6. are hypersensitive/hyposensitive to certain textures, patterns, odours.
7. are either hyperactive or inactive.
8. may whirl, spin, bang, bite wrist.
9. are constantly hand-flapping.
10. exhibit unusual or no response to pain.

Figure 4.7 indicates the responses of children with autism to sensory stimuli.

Deficiency in Cognitive Skills

The inability to focus on the relevant information when engaged in any activity coupled with development of splinter skills and lack of self-directed action in children with autism leads to deficiency in cognitive skills. Cognitive skills enable an individual to learn with understanding and apply what they have learnt in different and novel situations. It fosters creativity and problem-solving skills in individuals.

1. Patchy development of splinter skills
2. Difficulty in problem solving
3. Poor imitation skills

4. Difficulty in directing attention to meaningful features of the environment
5. Lack of motivation and self-directed action
6. Poor sequencing ability

Figure 4.8 delineates deficiencies faced by children with autism with reference to cognitive skills.

Developmental Discrepancies

The hallmark feature of autism is the 'Developmental Discrepancies'. Quite often, children with autism display behaviour that is quite paradoxical and contrary to their skills. Their social interactions and reciprocities to sensory/social stimuli are often out-of-step and inappropriate. Some of the components of developmental discrepancies experienced by the children are given below:

1. Rigidity of thought and action
2. Good at puzzles but poor in following directions.
3. Lack of consistency—can do things sometimes, but not at other times
4. Attachments to objects rather than human beings
5. Poor organisation and planning
6. Sleep, eating/elimination problems

The graph (Figure 4.9) portrays the developmental discrepancies faced by the sample.

Decades of research have proved that those with autism could learn and did respond to instructions based on the principles of psychology that is quintessentially the study of human behaviour. The focus of treatment for autism in the current decade is behaviour modification. Behaviour could be moulded and modified; appropriate behaviour could be taught and inappropriate and problem behaviour in a child could be completely eliminated. Behavioural characteristics as profiled in this section provide a broad perspective for understanding the behaviour of children with autism.

All 63 children with autism who constituted the sample of the study were given interventions based on the strategies evolved by the author. Each subject and the treatment given are discussed elaborately.

Experiment 1: Subject 1

The Experiment 1 was aimed at helping the subject make eye contact and improve his communication skills and living skills through his obsession with toys and dolls.

Subject 1 had the extraordinary skill to perceive the visual world accurately, and he was able to recreate aspects of his experience even in the absence of visual stimuli. He was so good in visual, spatial intelligence that it was not necessary for him to draw the elements in a sequential order — he could start drawing the headlights first and complete the picture of a car. However he had difficulty in drawing a tree, a tall building or any object that was beyond his eye level. All the intervention strategies were synthesized and attempts were made to reach out to him through his extraordinary visual spatial intelligence and non-verbal means of communication.

The author, along with the special teacher and the parents decided to communicate to the child through puppets and dolls. Soon it was known that the child opened out more when he was contacted indirectly through puppets and dolls, as he hated any kind of direct contact and communication. Instructions and directions given to him through puppets/dolls were more meaningful than direct communication.

He was also given opportunities to draw, colour and paint various objects that he enjoyed. He soon learnt to name the objects, the sizes and shapes such as big tree/small tree, green/blue ball etc.

His verbal communications skills and eye contact are still low. The special teacher, the parents, the subject's sister took turns in implementing the strategies in order to prevent the child developing a rigid pattern with reference to the setting and people. The child was rather inactive and withdrawn because of the seizure medications that were given to him every day in the mornings. The physician was consulted and the medications were changed. The child was more attentive after this change was made.

Table 4.2 Behavioural Characteristics, Strengths and Deficits in Subjects

Age	*Sex*	*Behavioural Characteristics*	*Splinter skill/ Obsession*	*Learning Strength/ Dom.Intelligence*	*Learning Deficit*
11	M	Non-verbal; Withdrawn; has seizure disorders; lack of eye contact; abhors social contact.	Drawing and playing with puppets and dolls.	The ability to transfer visual world into motor patterns. Visual-spatial, Bodily-kinesthetic & Interpersonal intelligence	Inability to perceive & organise events in time and understand language
6	M	Non-verbal; demonstrates needs by leading adult by the hand; no symbolic play.	Water long time.	The ability to remember information for a Visual-spatial and bodily-kinesthetic intelligence	Inability to analyse. Organise and integrate information.
9	M	Short attention span; no language; poor social skills.	Cell phone/ telephone	Musical intelligence & Bodily-kinesthetic Intelligences	Appears deaf but talks to himself. Treats toys as functional objects.

(Contd...)

(Contd...)

6	M	Non-verbal; hypersensitive to sounds; poor social skills; echolalic.	Dancing.	Phenomenal memory; exceptional motor skills. Bodily kinesthetic intelligence & Interpersonal	Poor pretend & symbolic play; resists change; needs adults to sustain interest in activity.
9	M	Verbal; physically aggressive; lack of eye contact; self-hurting.	Watching Television	Good rote memory; the ability to take in chunks of information. Verbal-linguistic intelligence & Intrapersonal	Exhibits strong and inflexible interests.
7	F	Verbal; poor social skills' throws temper tantrums; finger flicking and rocking.	Fond of animals.	Musical intelligence, Inter-personal & Intra-personal Intelligence	Inability to work independently on the given task.
10	M	Non-verbal; engages in repeated play; withdrawn; lack of eye contact.	Bricks.	The ability to transfer visual world into motor patterns. Spatial visual and logical-mathematical intelligence.	Inability to understand the presence and the perspectives of others.

(Contd...)

(Contd...)

9	M	Non-verbal; Withdrawn; has sleep and elimination problems; anxious; physically aggressive; poor social skills.	Bubbles.	Visual-spatial and bodily-kinesthetic intelligences.	High levels of physical activity. Inability to perceive and organise events and language related to time.
16	F	Non-verbal;. withdrawn; anxious; throws temper tantrums; poor social skills; echolalic.	Jewellery.	The ability to transfer visual world into motor patterns; phenomenal memory. Visual-spatial intelligence & Inter-personal Intelligence	Lack of understanding of symbols. Poor motor planning and motor skills.
5	F	Verbal; hyperactive; aggressive; short attention span.	Garlands/ garland making.	The ability to use language effectively. Verbal-linguistic intelligence	Poor eye-hand coordination.
10	M	Non-verbal; hypersensitive to sounds; abhors social contact.	Kites.	The ability to concentrate on narrow topics of interest, Visual-spatial intelligence and inter-personal intelligence	Motor clumsiness.

(Contd...)

(Contd...)

10	M	Non-verbal; engaged in solitary play; poor social skills.	Blocks.	Bodily-kinesthetic and visual-spatial intelligences.	His frustration and anxiety transformed into temper tantrums.
11	M	Verbal; impatient; violent; keeps to himself.	Paper shredding.	The ability to remember visual information and imagery. Visual-spatial intelligence	Ataxia and general motor clumsiness.
14	M	Non-verbal; hyperactive; abhors social contact.	Bats and balls	The ability to remember information for along time; reels out calendar dates and events. Logical-mathematical & Inter-personal intelligences	Inability to write.
8	F	Verbal; talks incoherently; agitated; poor social skills; withdrawn.	Dolls.	The ability to concentrate on narrow topics of interest. Visual-spatial and intra-personal intelligences	Inability to understand language and use semantics appropriately.

(Contd...)

(Contd...)

13	M	Non-verbal; anxious; has seizure disorders; lack of eye contact; abhors social contact.	Fans.	The ability to understand concrete, context-free information and rules. Visual-spatial and bodily-kinesthetic intelligence	Communicates by pointing; difficulty in focusing.
7	M	Non-verbal; hypersensitive to sounds; poor social skills; echolalic.	Puzzles.	The ability to take in chunks of information. Verbal-linguistic and visual-spatial intelligences.	Inability to follow directions and understand language.
13	M	Non-verbal; anxious; lack of eye contact; abhors social contact.	Boxes.	The ability to learn language without being taught. Verbal-linguistic & Bodily-kinesthetic intelligences.	Engages in repetitive play and drifts aimlessly about.
8	M	Non-verbal; hyperactive; hypersensitive to visual stimuli; echolalic.	Microphone	The ability to sing songs both forward and backward. Musical and bodily-kinesthetic intelligences.	Seeks social contact in unusual ways.

(Contd...)

(Contd...)

5	F	Non-verbal; Withdrawn; self-hurting; lack of eye contact; abhors social contact.	Balloons	The ability to persevere. Visual-spatial and bodily-kinesthetic intelligences.	Inability to perceive and people around.
19	M	Non-verbal; hypersensitive to sounds; socially withdrawn; lack of eye contact.	Stained glass	The ability to perceive and present information visually. Visual-spatial & Bodily-kinesthetic intelligences	Inability to understand others perspectives.
11	M	Non-verbal; non-compliant; impatient; has panic attacks.	Kitchen utensils.	Inter-personal intelligence.	Has poor gross motor skills; grasps things with his palm; has problems with motor imitation.
13	F	Non-verbal; Withdrawn; abhors social contact.	Rangoli:	The ability to learn and repeat long routines, the ability to transfer visual world into motor patterns. Visual-spatial and bodily-kinesthetic intelligences.	Inability to use and understand language; communicated with others by pointing.

(Contd...)

(Contd...)

12	M	Verbal; talks constantly and incoherently; echolalic.	Ships and sailboats.	The ability to take in chunks of information. Verbal-linguistic and visual-spatial intelligences.	Inability to understand complex and idiomatic uses of language.
15	M	Non-verbal; hyperactive; hypersensitive to sounds; abhors social contact.	Stars; observing the night sky.	The ability to read and write volumes of materials. Verbal-linguistic and Visual-spatial intelligences.	Inability to understand the perspectives of others.
12	M	Non-verbal; self-hurting; has seizure disorders; lack of eye contact.	Block printing and vegetable dyeing.	The ability to transfer visual world into motor patterns. Visual-spatial intelligence	Inability to do things consistently; can do sometimes and cannot do other times.
13	F	Verbal; poor social skills and lack of eye-hand coordination.	Candles.	The ability to focus. Verbal-linguistic & Visual-spatial intelligences	Inability to understand language and semantics of language.
8	M	Non-verbal; Withdrawn; has seizure disorders; lack of eye contact; abhors social contact.	Paper craft.	The ability to transfer visual world into motor patterns. Visual-spatial intelligence	Lack of body awareness, body control and perceptual control.

(Contd...)

(Contd...)

7	M	Non-verbal; wringing hands; self-hurting.	Camera.	The ability to concentrate on narrow topics of interest. Visual-spatial intelligence	Inability to imitate and understand language.
11	M	Non-verbal; hypersensitive to sounds; self-hurting.	Sand-play.	The ability to transfer visual world into motor patterns. Bodily-kinesthetic and Visual-spatial intelligences.	Inability to perceive and organise events in time and understand language; uses adult's hands as tools.
17	F	Non-verbal; Withdrawn; anxious; self-hurting.	Hairdressing.	The ability to transfer visual world into motor patterns. Bodily-kinesthetic and visual-spatial Intelligences.	Pulls away when touched. Inability to perceive and organise events in time and understand language.
18	M	Non-verbal; Withdrawn; has seizure disorders; lack of eye contact; abhors social contact.	Dolphins.	The ability to transfer visual world into motor patterns. Visual-spatial intelligence	Inability to attach meaning to visual information.
17	M	Non-verbal;Self-hurting; lack of eye contact; abhors social contact.	Coconuts.	The ability to use advanced splinter skill to learn new information. Visual-spatial intelligence	Inability to recognise human emotions and characteristics.

(Contd...)

(Contd...)

14	M	Non-verbal; hyperactive and poor social skills.	Yarn.	The ability to transfer visual world into motor patterns. Visual-spatial intelligence	Inability to work within boundary.
16	M	Non-verbal; had outbursts of anger and defiance; poor gross and fine motor skills.	Computers.	The ability to focus on narrow topics of interest. Visual-spatial intelligence	Inability to generalise or transfer information from one situation to the other.
11	M	Verbal; lack of social smile; limited language skills.	Buttons.	The ability to transfer visual world into motor patterns. Visual-spatial intelligence	Deficiency in understanding everyday situations. Is overly when asked to complete even simple tasks.
14	M	Verbal; has seizure disorders; lack of eye contact; abhors social contact.	Mythological figures.	The ability to organise information methodically and systematically. Verbal-linguistic skills. Visual-spatial intelligence	Inability to focus on relevant information.

(Contd...)

(Contd...)

(Contd...)

10	M	Non-verbal; gets upset by change; Impulsive and unresponsive.	Cars.	The ability to transfer visual world into motor patterns. Visual-spatial and bodily-kinesthetic intelligences.	Inability to understand everyday life situations.
8	M	Non-verbal; anxious; physically aggressive; lack of eye contact; abhors social contact; echolalic.	Robots.	The ability to transfer visual world into motor patterns. Musical and visual-spatial intelligences.	Inability to control motor and verbal responses.
7	M	Verbal; hyperactive; physically aggressive; abhors social contact; motor clumsiness.	Airplanes/ Helicopters	The ability to organise information methodically and systematically. Verbal-linguistic & Visual-spatial intelligences.	Has motor planning difficulties; bumps into things.
13	M	Non-verbal; hypersensitive to touch; echolalic; abhors social contact.	Pottery.	Attachment to objects rather than people. Musical and Visual-spatial intelligences.	Resists change and gets upset by change.

(Contd...)

18	M	Non-verbal; aggressive; has seizure disorders; lack of eye contact; abhors social contact.	Shoes, sandals, footwear.	The ability to rely on visual cues and visual organisers. Visual-spatial intelligence	Inability to retrieve information in a logical and sequential order.
9	M	Verbal; hypersensitive to sounds; echolalic; abhors social contact.	Trees and plants information.	The ability to control and scan important and relevant Visual-spatial intelligence	Inability to generalise or transfer information from one situation to other.
13	M	Non-verbal; hyperactive; lack of eye contact; abhors social contact.	Furniture designing; carpentry.	The ability to use visual information meaningfully. Visual-spatial intelligence	Inability to initiate communication.
8	F	Verbal; talks incoherently; poor social skills.	Hand wringing.	The ability to concentrate on narrow topics of interest. Verbal-linguistic & Visual-spatial intelligences	Inability to process information and modulate or integrate sensory information.

(Contd...)

(Contd...)

10	M	Non-verbal; anxious; has seizure disorders; lack of eye contact; abhors social contact.	Telephone directory	The ability to rely on concrete, visual cues; phenomenal memory. Visual-spatial intelligence	Inability to perceive and organise events in time and understand language.
7	M	Non-verbal; hypersensitive to sounds; lack of eye contact; stressful; lacked direction and focus.	Marbles.	The ability to learn and repeat long routines. Visual-spatial intelligence	Is upset by any change in routine; Responds unpredictably to noise.
8	M	Verbal; anxious; lack of eye contact; abhors social contact.	Newspaper.	The ability to transfer visual world into motor patterns; exceptional reading skills in English. Verbal-linguistic & Visual-spatial intelligences	Inability to speak and write in English.
12	M	Non-verbal; hyperactive; hypersensitive to sounds; screaming and shouting; self-destructive.	Calligraphy.	The ability to rely on visual cues and visual information. Visual-spatial intelligence.	Inability to perceive and organise events in time and understand language.

(Contd...)

(Contd...)

7	F	Non-verbal; withdrawn; self-hurting; lack of eye contact; abhors social contact.	Coins.	The ability to take in chunks of information. Verbal-linguistic and visual-spatial intelligences.	Inability to follow even simple commands.
9	M	Non-verbal; hypersensitive to sounds; socially withdrawn.	Crayons.	The ability to remember information for a long time. Visual-spatial intelligence	Inability to control thoughts, movements and responses.
12	M	Non-verbal; anxious; physically aggressive.	Match boxes.	The ability to understand concrete, context-based information. Visual-spatial intelligence	Inability to indulge in parallel play.
11	F	Non-verbal; has down syndrome; withdrawn; lack of eye contact; abhors social contact.	Toothpicks.	The ability to remember information for a long time; rote memory. Visual-spatial intelligence	Inability to generalise information.

(Contd...)

(Contd...)

13	M	Verbal; talks constantly but incoherently; neologisms; indulges in meaningless and incoherent talk.	Lights and driving.	The ability to process and integrate sensory stimulation. Visual-spatial and Bodily-kinesthetic intelligences	Inability to perceive and organise events in time and understand language.
10	M	Non-verbal; hyper-active and hyper-sensitive to sounds.	Caterpillars/ Worms.	The ability to transfer visual world into motor patterns. isual-spatial & Inter-personal intelligences	Inability to perceive and organise events in time and understand language.
V					
8	M	Non-verbal; Withdrawn; has seizure disorders; lack of eye contact; abhors social contact.	Clock.	The ability to transfer visual world into motor patterns. Visual-spatial intelligence	Inability to perceive and organise events in time and understand language.
10	F	Verbal; Withdrawn; lack of eye contact; abhors social contact.	Straws.	The ability to use visual information meaningfully. Visual-spatial intelligence.	Inability to modulate and process sensory stimulation and information.

(Contd...)

8	M	Non-verbal; Withdrawn; has seizure disorders; lack of eye contact; abhors social contact.	Cards/ playing cards.	The ability to concentrate on narrow topics of interest. Visual-spatial intelligence	Inability to focus on relevant information.
7	M	Non-verbal; anxious; self-hurting.	Umbrella.	The ability to transfer visual world into motor patterns. Visual-spatial intelligence	Inability to organise and integrate information.
10	M	Non-verbal; hyper-sensitive to sounds; self-hurting.	Locks and keys.	The ability to take in chunks of information. Visual-spatial and bodily-kinesthetic intelligences.	Inability to engage in pretend play or imaginary play.
12	M	Non-verbal; hyperactive; anxious; aloof and withdrawn.	Puppets.	Visual-spatial, bodily-kinesthetic and musical intelligences.	Inability to engage in social interaction and communication.
14	M	Non-verbal; hyperactive; anxious; self-hurting; has seizure disorders.	Sponge.	The ability to take in chunks of information; Visual-spatial, bodily-kinesthetic, interpersonal and musical intelligence.	Inability to work within boundary.

(Contd...)

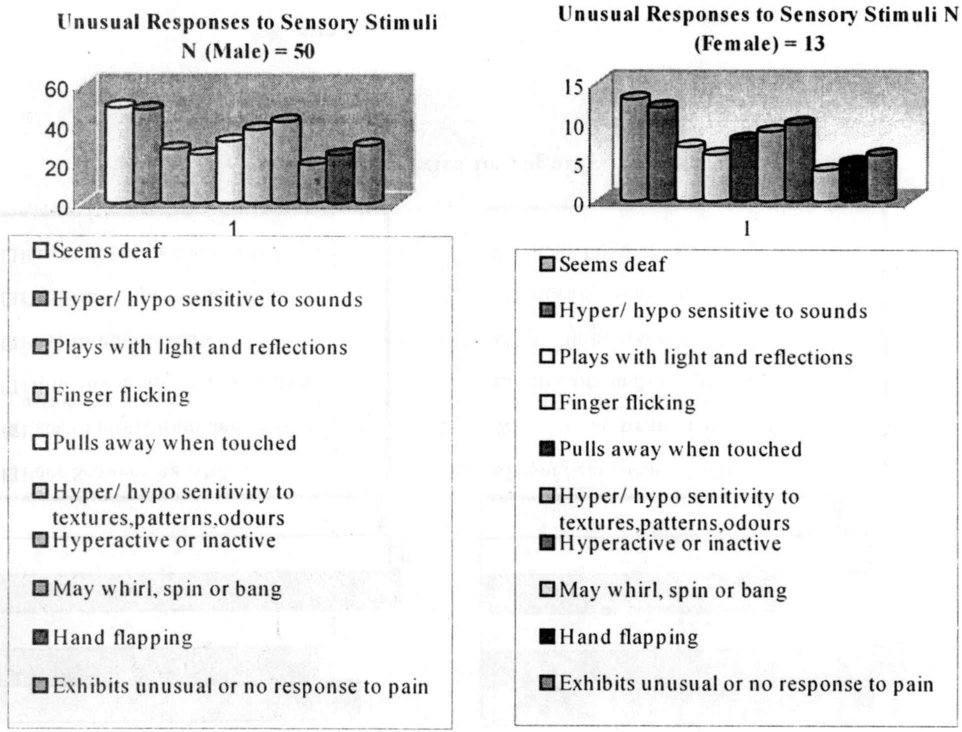

Figure 4.7 Unusual Responses to Sensory Stimuli

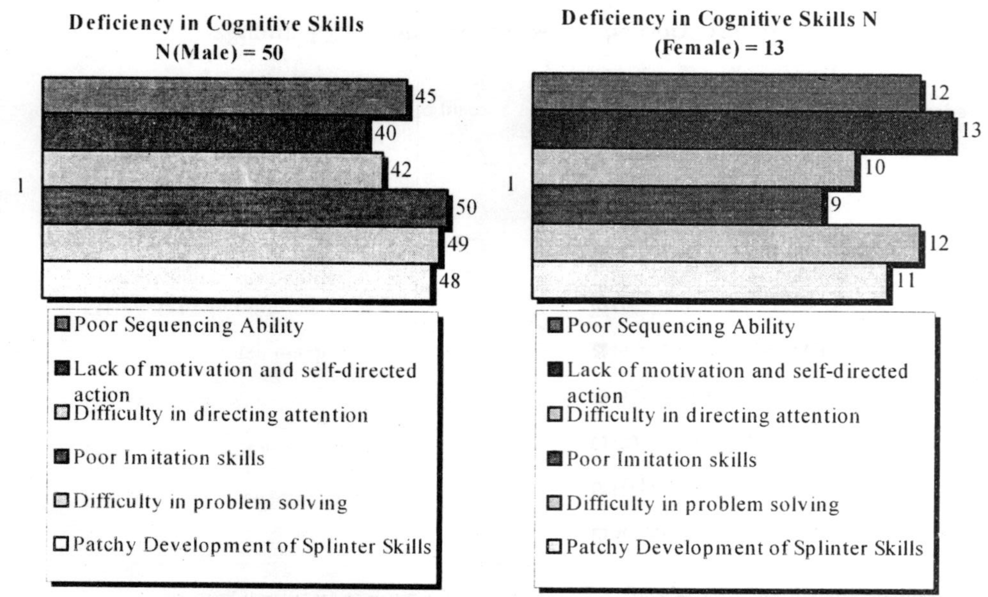

Fig 4.8 Deficiencies in Cognitive Skills

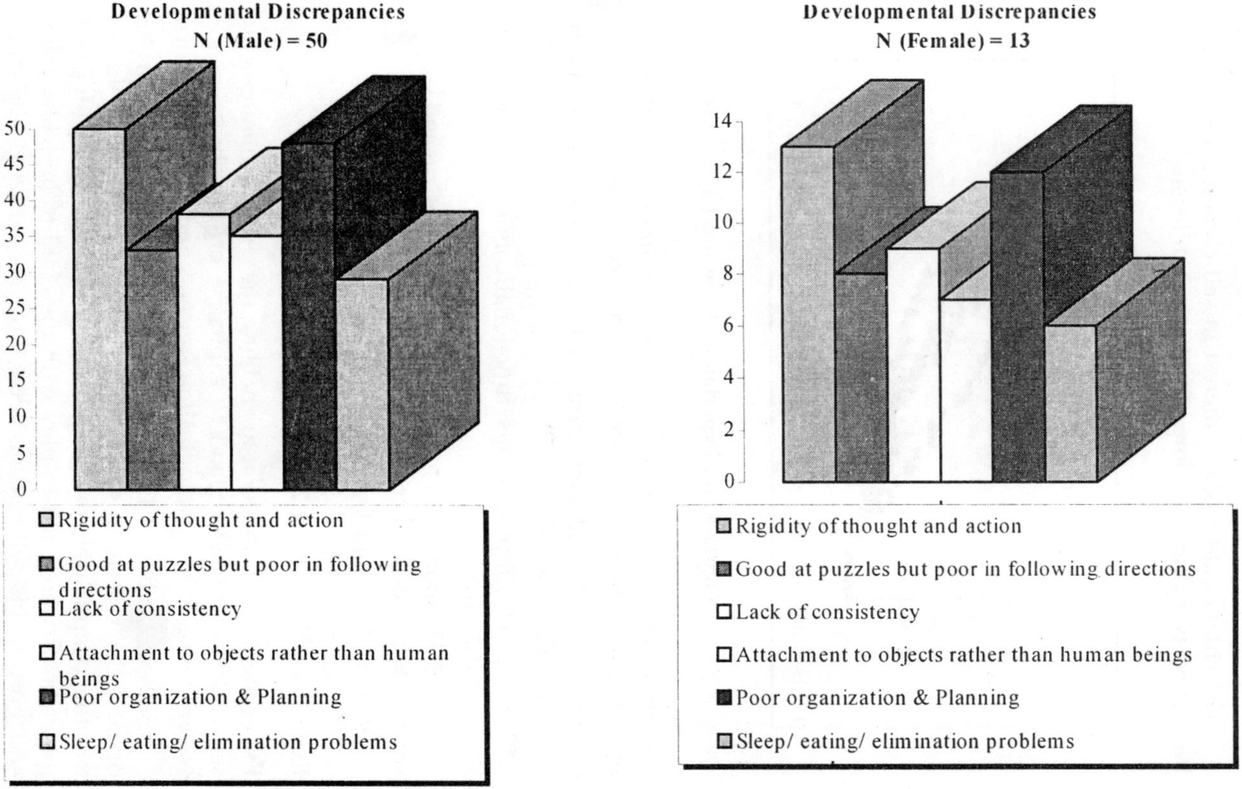

Figure 4.9 Developmental Discrepancies

The child could sustain interest in self-chosen activities and he started enjoying the company of other children.

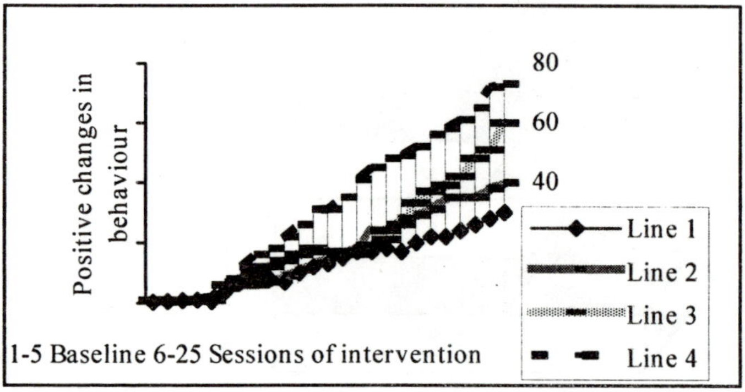

Figure 4.10 : Experiment 1—Subject 1

The above graph gives a clear picture of the improvements made by the child. The positive behaviour changes were :

Line 1. The child communicated with friends and family through puppets/dolls.

Line 2. He improved his functional/communication skills through drawing/painting.

Line 3. He soon learnt to name the objects, the sizes and shapes such as big tree/small tree, green/blue ball etc.

Line 4. The child learnt to relax and enjoy.

Experiment 2 : Subject 2

Experiment 2 was aimed at to enabling the child to eliminate his self-injurious behaviour and to capitalise on his obsession for water to teach him communication concepts and functional skills.

Subject 2, a boy of 12 years, had an obsession for water as he opened the faucets in the bathroom and watched it for hours together. Capitalising on this passion of the child water toys and paper boats were used to play with the child to help him relax and prevent his self-hurting behaviour. As expected, the child responded positively to the water games, and as he was always actively engaged in some kind of activity, his self-injurious behaviour reduced drastically. The author planned every step in the implementation of the strategy with other members/ facilitators of the support team that included the special educator, the parents and sibling/s so that opportunities could be provided for the child to communicate, such as stopping the activity in the middle/ hiding the toy/ not providing him water immediately, the child started communicating his needs non-verbally. The child was orally explained the activity (by indulging in parallel talking), the name of the toy/object, for instance, 'water turtle', 'green turtle' etc. Slowly the child started saying the names of the objects and could express his desires such as 'want water', 'like paper boat', etc.

Table 4.3: Behavioural Characteristics, Strengths and Drawbacks in Subject 2

Age	*Sex*	*Beh. Characteristics*	*Splinter skill/ Obsession*	*Learning Strength/ Dom. Intelligence*	*Learning Deficit*
6	M	Non-verbal; demonstrates needs by leading adult by the hand; no symbolic play.	Water	The ability to remember information for a long time; visual-spatial and bodily-kinesthetic intelligence.	Inability to analyse; organise and integrate information.

Since all these games were played, maintaining the same eye level with the child, his eye-to-eye gaze improved dramatically. He wanted to learn swimming. He enjoyed anything to do with water—boat rides, gardening, watering and tending plants in the garden. The child's ability to analyse, organise and integrate information is still low, and he is still echolalic but the other changes in his behaviour will enable him slowly to conquer the deficits in other areas.

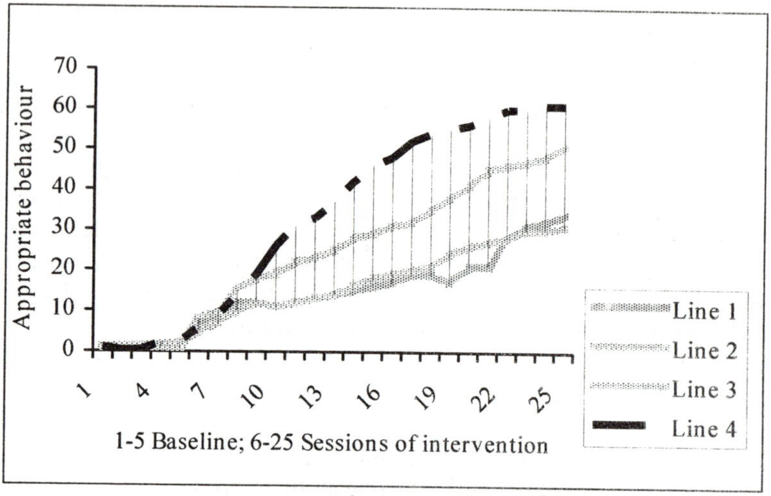

Figure 4.11: Experiment 2 — Subject 2

The graph given above illustrates very clearly the impact of the intervention strategies and the positive changes in the behaviour of the child. The positive behaviour changes were:

Line 1. The child's eye gaze improved.

Line 2. Capitalising on his passion for water, the child could be taught to frame sentences with one or two words.

Line 3. His communication and social skills were enhanced through the activities that he enjoyed.

Line 4. Engaging him in his favourite activities reduced his self-injurious behaviour.

Experiment 3 — Subject 3

Experiment 3 was aimed at enabling the child to communicate with family and friends, to reduce hyperactivity and enable the child to be more focused.

Subject 3, a boy of 9 years, was engrossed for hours together in self-directed, solitary play — playing with cell phone/ telephone. What was quite paradoxical about this child was that he did not respond when someone called him or to any verbal stimulus but could identify the sound of his father's car way ahead. He liked one particular song very much that he wanted played over and over again. This desire of the child to the optimum make the child do various activities on the condition that the song would be played once he accomplished a particular task. The child also responded better when verbal instructions were given to him through a toy cell phone/toy phone. He soon started saying a few words to people over the phone. He started communicating freely with his teachers, friends and family members. His favourite song was used as a trump card to motivate him to do an activity that he would not do otherwise. The graph below delineates the positive changes that occurred in the child's behaviour after the implementation of interventions.

Table 4.4: Behavioural Characteristics, Strengths and Drawbacks in Subject 3

Age	*Sex*	*Beh.Char*	*Splinter Skill/ Obsession*	*Learning Strength/ Dom.Intelligence*	*Learning Deficit*
9	M	Short attention span; no language; poor social skills.	Cell phone/ telephone	Musical intelligence	Appears deaf but talks to himself; treats toys as functional objects.

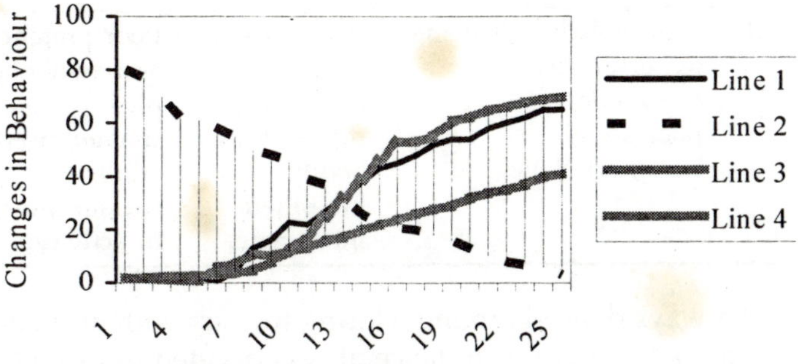

1-5 Baseline; 6-25 Sessions of Intervention

Figure 4.12: Experiment 3 — Subject 3

The positive behaviour changes were:

Line 1. Using his fixation for the phone the child could be taught to communicate with people around him.

Line 2. Hyperactivity reduced by engaging him in more productive work.

Line 3. Musical intelligence was used as a channel to reach out to him.

Line 4. He used words meaningfully to communicate with people.

His verbal and social skills were not quite refined. He could communicate his desires and thoughts in one or two words with his friends and family members. Whenever the child had free time, he knew how to relax and enjoy.

Experiment 4 : Subject 4

Experiment 4 was aimed at enabling the child improve his social skills and help him communicate his desires through his exceptional bodily kinesthetic intelligence.

Table 4.5: Behavioural Characteristics, Strengths and Drawbacks in Subject 4

Age	*Sex*	*Beh.Char*	*Splinter Skill/ Obsession*	*Learning Strength/ Dom. Intelligence*	*Learning Deficit*
6	M	Non-verbal; hypersensitive to sounds; poor social skills; echolalic.	Dancing.	Phenomenal memory; exceptional motor skills; bodily kinesthetic intelligence	Poor pretence and symbolic play; resists change; needs adults to sustain interest in activity.

Subject 4 always danced around, closing his ears with his hands. As he had a keen interest in dance, it was decided to reach him out through his exceptional bodily-kinesthetic intelligence. Movement stories and movement songs were designed to teach him various concepts and skills. Opportunities to move to music were provided — marching, walking, bending, hopping, galloping, swaying arms are examples of large muscle activities that accompany music. Hand and finger activities to musical accompaniment provided opportunities for small muscle development. Moving like a rabbit, elephant or giant provided a dramatic play opportunity with music. He was hypersensitive to sounds and closed his ears when there was too much noise in the classroom. Whenever there was a heavy wind, the sound made by the leaves rustling in the gust and the calendars, window screens, charts, pictures scrapping on the wall were so overpowering for him that he screamed. It was decided to explain to him the source of the noise/sound and move him to a quieter place with little or no distractions, and if possible the things that produced the annoying the sounds were removed. He began to concentrate more when he was occupied in a task in a quieter place. He started communicating with the teachers, friends and members of the family through body gestures, actions and movements, and he enjoyed doing those.

Movement education provided opportunities for the child to gain body awareness, spatial directions, locomotion, to work with others, to repeat his favourite actions, to point out his preferred activities/objects/toys, etc. Slowly, music was introduced and the child was engaged in rhythmic activities. This enabled the child to gain body balance, self-concept and to express his feelings.

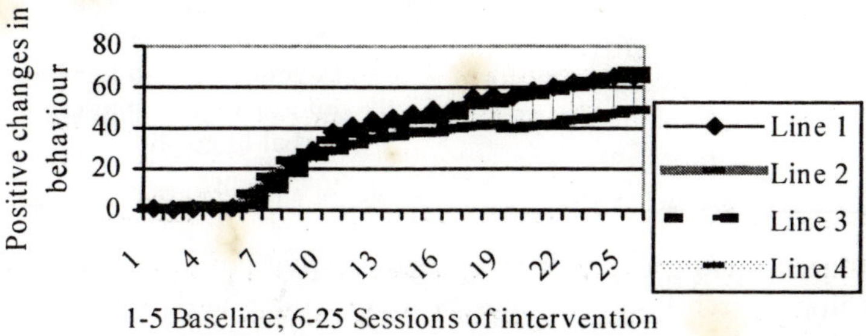

Figure 4.13: Experiment 4 — Subject 4

The above graph clearly portrays the changes in positive behaviour.

The positive changes in behaviour were:

Line 1: Movement education provided opportunities for the child to gain body awareness, spatial directions, locomotion.

Line 2: The child learnt to work with others, to repeat his favourite actions, to point out his preferred activities/objects/toys etc.

Line 3: The child could engage in social activities, and understood turn taking and reciprocity in social interactions

Line 4: The child gained body balance, self-concept and was able to express his feelings.

He was still non-verbal but gained more control over his body and there was terrific improvement in his motor skills and motor planning.

Experiment 5 : Subject 5

Experiment 5 was aimed at helping the subject reduce his physical aggression and self-hurting behaviour.

Table 4.6 : Behavioural Characteristics, Strengths and Drawbacks in Subject 5

Age	*Sex*	*Beh. Characteristics*	*Splinter Skill/ Obsession*	*Learning Strength/ Dom.Intelligence*	*Learning Deficit*
9	M	Verbal; physically aggressive; lack of eye contact; self-hurting.	Watching television	Good rote memory; the ability to take in chunks of information; verbal-linguistic intelligence.	Exhibits strong and inflexible interests.

Subject 5 had exceptional rote memory that he could deliver the dialogues rendered by famous Tamil comedians, Kaundamani and Senthil, in various Tamil movies. He was reluctant to write, even though he had good linguistic skills. He was obsessed with watching television. It was decided to teach him computer skills and, as expected, the subject could use word processor effectively to communicate with outside world. He improved his verbal, linguistic skills by expressing his ideas, thoughts, wishes, requests and desires by typing them on the computer. He began to write small poems. He slowly began to understand that he had problems.

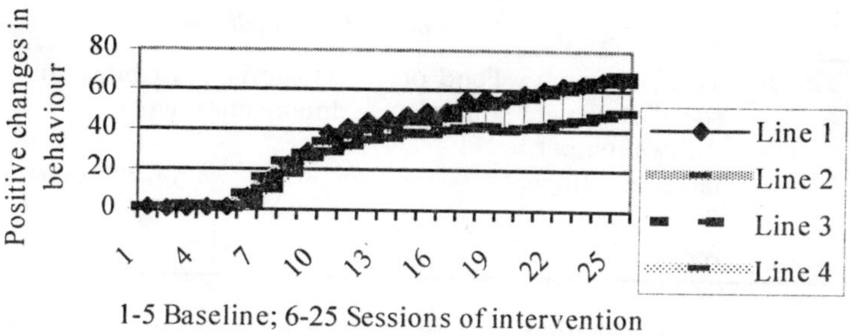

Figure 4.14: Experiment 5 — Subject 5

The child could express the underlying reason for any of his physical aggression and he was taught breath control and how to control his anger. Once he identified the reason or the source of irritation, he could eliminate the object or the activity and thus he gained control over objects, activities and environment.

Figure 4.14 clearly portrays the positive changes in the behaviour of the subject brought out by the intervention strategies based on the subject's exceptional verbal-linguistic intelligence.

The positive behaviour changes were:

Line 1. His verbal/ linguistic skills improved dramatically.

Line 2. He could express ideas and thoughts by typing them on the computer.

Line 3. He could express underlying reason for discomfort and aggression.

Line 4. He gained control over objects, activities and environment.

Experiment 6 — Subject 6

Experiment 6 was aimed at capitalising on the child's passion for animals and music, and help the child eliminate temper tantrums and stereotypical activities such as finger flicking and rocking.

Table 4.7: Behavioural Characteristics, Strengths and drawbacks of Subject 6

Age	*Sex*	*Beh. Characteristics*	*Splinter Skill/ Obsession*	*Learning Strength/ Dom.Intelligence*	*Learning Deficit*
7	F	Verbal; poor social skills; throws temper tantrums; finger flicking and rocking.	Fond of animals.	Musical intelligence	Inability to work independently on the given task.

Subject 6 was a girl who was very fond of dogs and cats (and animals in general). Her favourite toy was a stuffed Pomeranian puppy that she wanted to hug and cuddle all the time. Whenever she threw tantrums, she was shown the puppy with tears in its eyes and told that the puppy was crying and turning away from her. It was explained to her that the puppy did not like her tantrums and did not want to be friends with her. Immediately she stopped her tantrums.

She had exceptional musical skills and always carried a toy keyboard. Her parents were advised to put the subject in music classes (especially keyboard music). As expected, she learnt to play the keyboard exceptionally well so that she could play both Indian classical music as well as film songs. Whenever she refused to cooperate, it was explained to her that her favourite dog was disappointed with her. This strategy paid off well and the child could be put back on the track again. As an extension of her mastery of keyboard, it was decided to teach her computer skills and she picked up that with ease as well.

Through her love for animals, various concepts and skills were taught, such as:

— 'What is Dolly the dog, doing now?'

— 'Dolly is sleeping'.

— 'When will Mala go to bed?'

— 'At 9 o'clock in the night'.

— 'What do you see in the night sky?'

The graph given below portrays the positive changes in her behaviour.

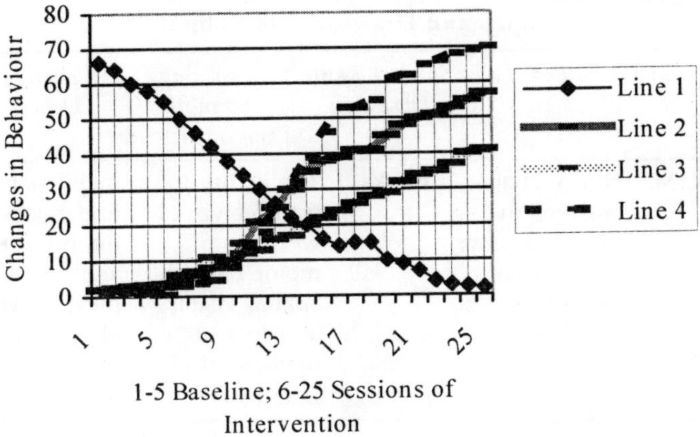

Figure 4.15: Experiment 6 — Subject 6

The positive behaviour changes were:

Line 1. Her adamancy and temper tantrums dwindled down considerably.

Line 2. She could work independently on her music lessons for longer periods.

Line 3. She acquired mastery in music as well as computer skills.

Line 4. Her stereotypical activities, such as hand flicking, wringing and rocking diminished significantly.

Experiment 7 — Subject 7

Experiment 7 was aimed at enabling the child to improve his functional and social skills through his exceptional visual-spatial skills and logical-mathematical skills.

Subject 7, a 10-year-old boy had a special obsession for bricks. This was known when the subject was seen holding the bricks and playing with them, at the time of construction of their house. He lined up the bricks in perfect rows and columns as if he was constructing rooms, buildings, towers, etc.

Table 4.8: Behavioural Characteristics, Strengths and Drawbacks in Subject 7

Age	*Sex*	*Beh. Characteristics*	*Splinter Kkill/ Obsession*	*Learning Strength/ Dom.Intelligence*	*Learning Deficit*
10	M	Non-verbal; engages in repeated play; withdrawn; lack of eye contact.	Bricks.	The ability to transfer visual world into motor patterns; spatial visual and logical-mathematical intelligence.	Inability to understand the presence and the perspectives of others.

The investigator it was realised that he had the vast potential of learning various skills and concepts through his passion for bricks. Blending this passion with his spatial-visual skills, he was taught fundamental mathematical concepts such as length, width, depth etc. The child learnt to use the same bricks for various purposes, such as sofa, dining table, television, kitchen counter, etc., using half brick or a small piece depending upon the requirement.

As an expanded experience, the child was taken to various construction sites such as hospital, school, house, office, etc. This exposure widened his horizon of learning. He could get the whole picture or the picture in totality — various rooms in a house, what purpose they serve, what kind of furniture is used in each room. The activity was deliberately stopped in the middle when it was really exciting for the child and waited for the child to respond.

The child began to talk in sentences that other people could understand. Before doing the mock construction, a plan was drawn and adequate visual cues were provided. These visual organisers enabled the child to grasp the whole picture. The graph given below portrays the changes that were observed in the child due to the intervention.

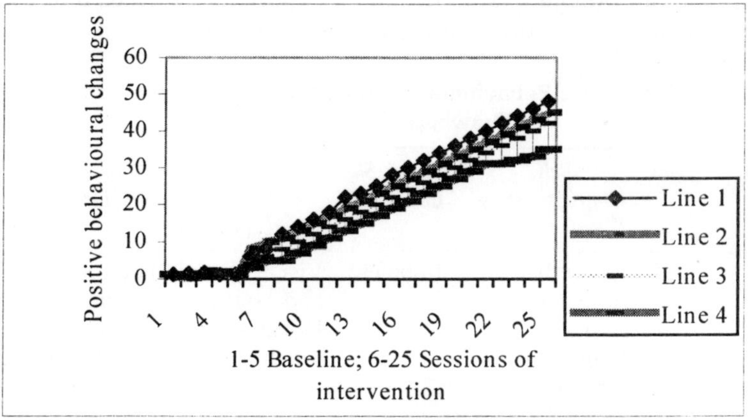

Figure 4.16: Experiment 7 — Subject 7

The positive behaviour changes were:

Line 1. Improvement in social interactions.

Line 2. Improvement in eye contact.

Line 3. Responded to people around him.

Line 4. Expressed his desires and needs verbally.

Experiment 8 : Subject 8

Experiment 8 was aimed at capitalising on the subject's interest in making bubbles to reduce anxiety and aggression and to improve his communication skills.

Subject 8 had a fascination for bubbles and he kept watching other children making bubbles for hours together. But he would never make bubbles and he did not know how to make it. This was an opportunity for the child to utilize this as a learning/ teaching. Bubbles were deliberately made in front of the child so that he would ask for a chance. Initially for a few days, he just observed this drew and whenever he wanted the activity to be continued, he closer to the author touched her. She set up the activity in such a way that she involved the sibling, peers and children in the neighbourhood to join in. The child slowly started uttering a few words, such as 'want bubs'. She took advantage of the situation and taught him a lot of new words such as 'bubble bottle', 'big bubble', 'rainbow bubble', 'pop', 'gone', etc., and the child started repeating the words after a few times.

Table 4.9 : Behavioural Characteristics, Strengths and Drawbacks of Subject 8

Age	*Sex*	*Beh. Characteristics*	*Splinter Skill/ Obsession*	*Learning Strength/ Dom. Intelligence*	*Learning Deficit*
9	M	Non-verbal; withdrawn; has sleep and elimination problems; anxious; physically aggressive; poor social skills.	Bubbles.	Visual-spatial and bodily-kinesthetic intelligences.	High levels of physical activity; inability to perceive and organise events and language related to time.

The child was taken to an aquarium, and the fish making bubbles in the water fascinated the child. He soon learnt a lot about fish. Several games and activities were devised using fish as the centrepiece of all his activities; fish cutouts were made and words were written in the back of the cutouts; they were put in a tub and word matching games were played by fishing the right word from the tub which stood for the pond. He also learnt to play pretend or imaginary plays and games. Introducing interesting objects or activities expanded the child's horizon. It was decided that the child's keen interest in fish could lead him to a career in marine biology or fish cultivation. He could also spend his free time fishing in the pond/lake. He kept a fish tank at home and he took care of the fish. He learnt the concept of time management by feeding the fish at appropriate intervals.

He could also build and design fish tanks and water fountains. He drew several designs for fish tanks and water fountains, and what was amazing was that he asked his parents as to the feasibility of designing musical water fountains.

The graph given below gives a vignette of the positive changes in the behaviour of the child.

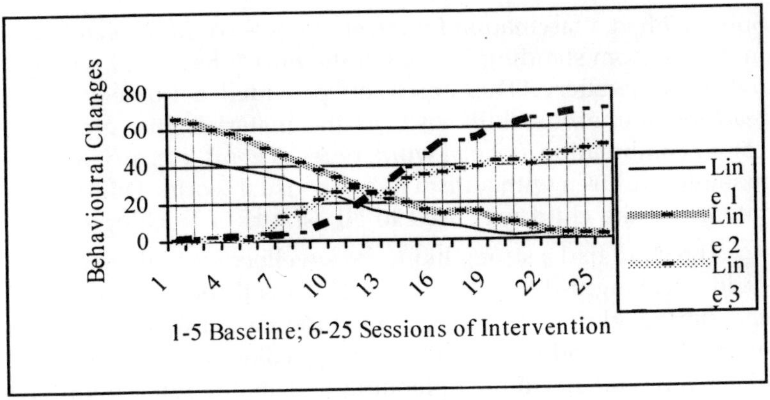

Figure 4.17: Experiment 8 — Subject 8

The positive changes in behaviour were:

Line 1. Physical aggression decreased considerably.

Line 2. His anxiety dwindled down to a considerable extent.

Line 3. He started communicating with his friends and family members.

Line 4. He could utter a few sentences.

Experiment 9: Subject 9

The investigator's aim in Experiment 9 was aimed at reaching out to the child through her visual-spatial intelligence.

Table 4.10: Behavioural Characteristics, Strengths and Drawbacks of Subject 9

Age	*Sex*	*Beh.Char*	*Splinter Skill/ Obsession*	*Learning Strength/ Dom. Intelligence*	*Learning Deficit*
16	F	Non-verbal;. withdrawn; anxious; throws temper tantrums; poor social skills; echolalic.	Jewellery	The ability to transfer visual world into motor patterns; phenomenal memory; visual-spatial intelligence.	Lack of understanding of symbols; poor motor planning and motor skills.

Subject 9 had a fascination for jewellery. She could be seen in her mother's room standing in front of the mirror bedecked with her mother's jewellery. This obsession provided a framework for teaching numerous skills such as the materials that are used, colour combination, enamel work, types of gems, etc., in jewellery making. Children with autism live in a visual world. This distinct interest of the child was used to all aspects of teaching.

The child had a strong liking for jewellery set with gems. The child was taught different colours of gems through confetti and she started gluing the confetti in different configuration. This enabled her to understand how different colours can be combined effectively and her motor planning and motor skills improved tremendously. Slowly she was given opportunities to work with fake gems. Finally, she was taught the names and properties of different gems, and to differentiate real gems from synthetic gems and precious metals from base metals. She also learnt to design and set gems.

Jewellery designing and jewellery making demanded total concentration and involvement, and hence her tantrums and anxiety dwindled down. Her good visual skills and phenomenal memory helped her to devote herself completely to learn the subtle nuances of the profession. Her social skills were still poor and she was echolalic even though there were slight improvements. A local jewellery shopowner suggested a short-term course in gemmology and promised to provide employment opportunities to her. The positive changes that occurred in the behaviour of the child are portrayed in the graph below.

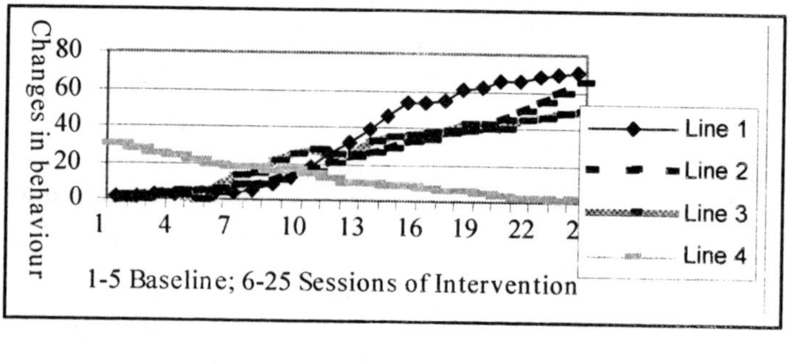

Figure 4.18 : Experiment 9 — Subject 9

The positive changes in bahviour were:

Line 1. Learnt the concepts of colour, shape, size, precious metals, gems and synthetic gems, etc.,

*Line 2.*Improvement in small motor skills.

*Line 3.*Developed language skills and social skills.

*Line 4.*Temper-tantrums reduced to a considerable extent.

Experiment 10 : Subject 10

Experiment 10 was aimed at improving the eye-hand coordination, eye contact and to enable the child to channellise her hyperactive nature and also to reduce her aggressiveness.

Table 4.11: Behavioural Characteristics, Strengths and Drawbacks of Subject 10

Age	*Sex*	*Beh.Char*	*Splinter Skill/ Obsession*	*Learning Strength/ Dom. Intelligence*	*Learning Deficit*
5	F	Verbal; hyperactive; aggressive; short attention span.	Garlands/ garland making.	The ability to use language effectively, verbal-linguistic intelligence	Poor eye-hand coordination.

Subject 10 is a five-year-old girl who likes garlands and garland making. Taking advantage of this spontaneous interest of the child, it was decided to teach her functional skills. The child was shown different flowers in the garden, how each flower was different from the other and how they had to be strung together. Soon she learnt to identify the flowers and which flower and which colour and size could be put together. She enjoyed this activity so much that her physical aggressiveness reduced considerably.

The activities were further extended by giving word games such as visual matching tasks. The subject learnt a few words such as 'flower', 'petal', 'leaf', 'dewdrops', etc. As the child was verbal, she could put words together in a meaningful manner and construct relevant sentences of her own. She also learnt to make organdie roses, ribbon roses, lace roses, paper roses and other flowers. Apart from flowers, she also learnt to make garlands with other materials for birthday celebrations/parties. Her aesthetic sense developed tremendously and her hyperactivity dwindled down considerably. She was also more focused and she could concentrate more on her work at hand.

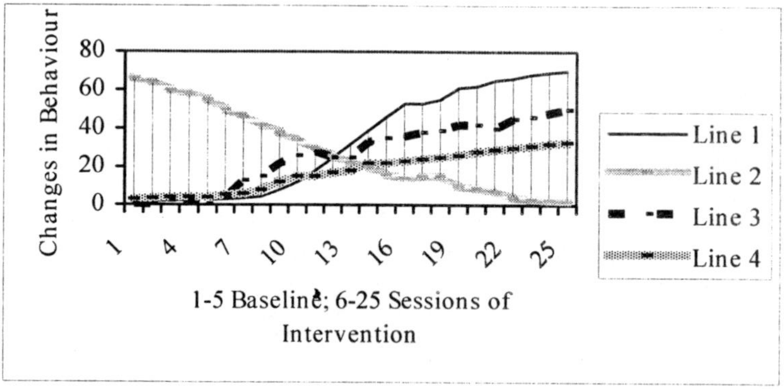

Figure 4.19 : Experiment 10 — Subject 10

Behavioural changes are given in the graph below.

Line 1. Developed concepts about colour, shape and size.

Line 2. Reduction in physical aggressiveness and hyperactivity.

Line 3. Improvement in eye contact and self-expression and language skills.

Line 4. Developed aesthetic sense - appreciation for beauty.

Experiment 11 : Subject 11

Experiment 11 was aimed at improving the child's social skills and communication skills, and to reduce his motor clumsiness through his passion for kites.

Subject 11 was passionate about flying kites. This obsession of the child was used to develop balance, coordination and body awareness. Kites of different shapes were made — animals, birds, mythological figures, letters of the alphabet, etc., Knowing the alphabet is a key to successful reading in later years. While flying kites, the alphabet song was also sung drawing the child's attention to the letters of the alphabet.

Table 4.12: Behavioural Characteristics, Strengths and Drawbacks of Subject 11

Age	*Sex*	*Beh.Char*	*Splinter Skill/ Obsession*	*Learning Strength/ Dom. Intelligence*	*Learning Deficit*
10	M	Non-verbal; hypersensitive to sounds; abhors social contact.	Kites.	The ability to concentrate on narrow topics of interest, visual-spatial intelligence	Motor clumsiness.

Initially the child was taught to make kites of different shapes. To teach the concept of 'symmetry' to the child, several cut outs were made in the shapes of fish, boats, birds, folded in half. The child was also given opportunities to cut on perforated lines. This activity helped the child to develop drawing skills, cutting things to shape, symmetrical patterns, mathematical concepts.

The childwas told the story of Benjamin Franklin who found out that lightning is electrically charged by flying a kite. The child also learnt various other science concepts. To everyone's surprise, he asked whether lightning generates the electricity that is provided to our homes. He wanted to know more about generation of electricity by different means such as hydroelectric, atomic, nuclear, etc.

The subject evinced keen interest in physics and he wanted to be a physicist when he grew up. He was also taken to various hydroelectric and atomic power generation sites. Apart from electricity, airplanes and aeronautics fascinated him and he could tell everyone in detail the history of aviation. The changes that took place in the behaviour of the child are given in the graph.

The changes in the target behaviour were:

*Line 1.*The child's motor clumsiness reduced significantly.

Line 2.He evinced keen interest in science especially physics.

Line 3.His visual spatial and bodily kinesthetic intelligence improved considerably.

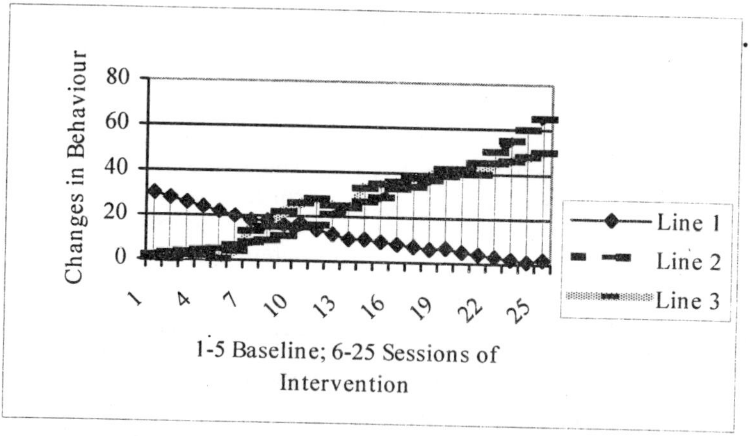

Figure 4.20: Experiment 11 — Subject 11

Experiment 12 : Subject 12

Experiment 12 was aimed at teaching the child social interaction and to enable to ehim xpress himself.

Table 4.13 : Behavioural Characteristics, Strengths and Drawbacks of Subject 12

Age	*Sex*	*Beh. Char*	*Splinter Skill/ Obsession*	*Learning Strength/ Dom. Intelligence*	*Learning Deficit*
10	M	Non-verbal; engaged in solitary play; poor social skills.	Blocks.	Bodily-kinesthetic and visual-spatial intelligences.	His frustration and anxiety transformed into temper tantrums.

Subject 12 had an obsession for blocks and he could arrange them in amazing order that defied even gravity. His interest in blocks was capitalised on, to teach him various communications skills especially in the context of turn-taking interaction activities. The child was always engaged in solitary play and he threw tantrums if his personal space was invaded. A few blocks were put in front of the child and herself in suthe author ch a way that the child could observe all the movements made by her and child imitated the actions of the child. The child did not establish eye contact with her but was observing through his strong peripheral vision. After some time, she stopped imitating him and observed his actions. He (through signs) instigated her to imitate or repeat his actions.

After playiñg with him for a few more days, his peers observed that he started taking the initiative he seeking partners and carrying on conversations with them. Slowly started asking for the required items and started verbalising his desires and needs. When his request was fulfilled immediately, his communication effort was reinforced. Block-building games enabled him to work within boundaries. Pairing the signs with speech while interacting with the child provided a language-rich environment.

The positive changes in the behaviour of the child are given in the graph below.

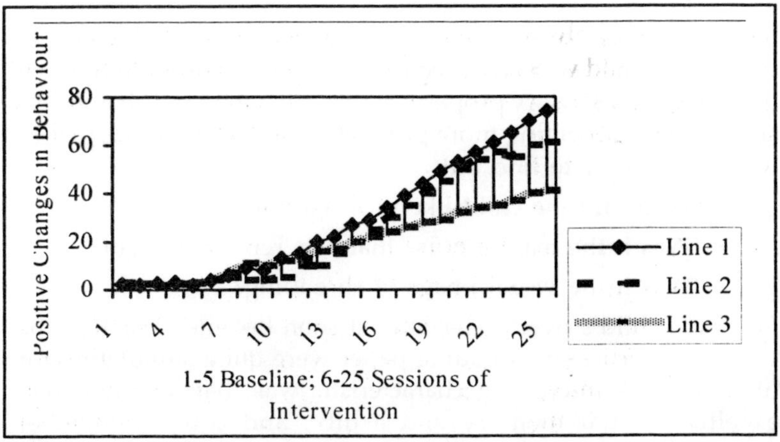

Figure 4.21: Experiment 12 — Subject 12

The positive behaviour changes were:

Line 1. Improvement in communication skills and turn-taking interactions.

Line 2. Worked within boundaries.

Line 3. Initiated conversation and engaged in cooperative learning.

Experiment 13 : Subject 13

Experiment 13 was aimed at helping the child gain manual dexterity and to improve his language skills.

Table 4.14: Behavioural Characteristics, Strengths and Drawbacks of Subject 13

Age	*Sex*	*Beh. Char*	*Splinter Skill/ Obsession*	*Learning Strength/ Dom. Intelligence*	*Learning Deficit*
11	M	Verbal; impatient; violent; keeps to himself.	Paper shredding.	The ability to remember visual information and imageryl visual-spatial intelligence.	Ataxia and general motor clumsiness.

Subject 13 was always seen tearing papers and vinyl sheets to pieces. The child was onserved for a few days in order to find out the reinforcing sensory property of this behaviour and change this activity into something more productive and socially acceptable. It was necessary to find out:

— 'What did the child like in shredding?'

— 'Was it the tearing noise that was reinforcing?' or

— 'Was it the visual image of shredding?'

From the child's overt behaviour, it soon became clear that the visual properties of shredding paper were quite stimulating for him. Another interesting characteristic was that the child had excellent visual memory and acuity, and could remember contours, shapes and sizes of various objects, and transfer them into appropriate motor patterns. He was given opportunities to progress from tearing paper with his fingers to snipping with scissors, cutting on lines, cutting curves and finally cutting out shapes and objects. He was given training to make papier-mâché objects, which he enjoyed very much.

The changes in the behaviour of the child are graphically represented in Figure 4.22.

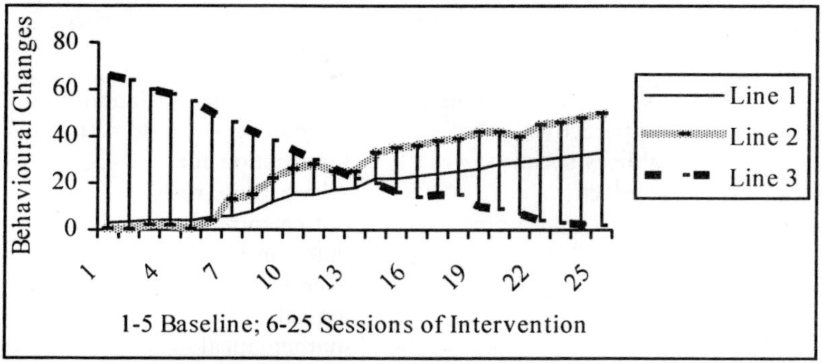

Figure 4.22: Experiment 13 — Subject 13

The positive behaviour changes were:

Line 1. His oral language skills improved.

Line 2. He could change his negative activity into positive activity.

Line 3. His motor clumsiness reduced and he gained manual dexterity.

Experiment 14 : Subject 14

Experiment 14 was aimed at improving the communication skills and to reduce hyperactivity in the child through his fondness for bats and balls.

Subject 14 had a fascination for bats and balls, and he would never pretend to play any game. He would hold the cricket bat in his hands and keep examining it. It decided to teach him the game. When the author came closer to him to ask for the bat, he hit her with his bat as she invaded his personal space. He rubbed his head (an example of echo praxis) and started crying without realising that it was he who had hit a person. He was cajoled to play the game but he never wanted to play the game. The strategy was changed a little by asking him to be the scorekeeper that he enjoyed very much.

Table 4.15: Behavioural Characteristics, Strengths and Drawbacks of Subject 14

Age	*Sex*	*Beh.Char*	*Splinter Skill/ Obsession*	*Learning Strength/ Dom. Intelligence*	*Learning Deficit*
14	M	Non-verbal; hyperactive; abhors social contact.	Bats and balls.	The ability to remember information for a long time; reels out calendar dates and events; logical-mathematical intelligence.	Inability to write.

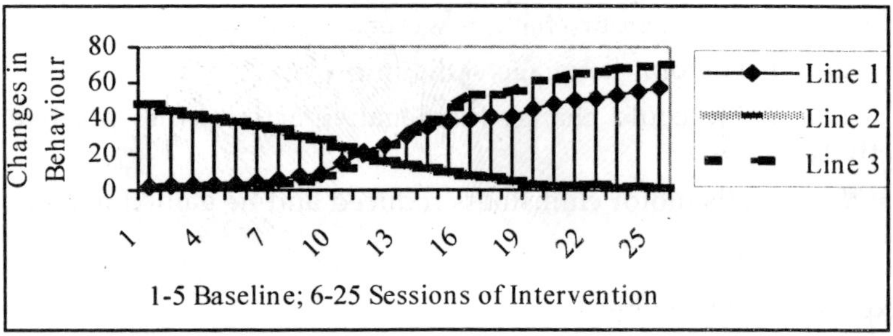

Figure 4.23 : Experiment 14 — Subject 14

He could remember the runs scored by each and every player in all the games with great accuracy. Even though he never played the game, he could tell the players why they failed to score a hundred or why a particular player was run out. This helped the players to improve their style of batting or spinning or running. Other children in the neighbourhood considered him a valuable member of their cricket team. He slowly started writing everything, and improved his writing skills and social skills. He was still non-verbal but he was communicative.

The changes that took place in the observable behaviour of the child are above below in the graph.

The positive behaviour changes were:

Line : Improved his communication skills.

Line 2: Hyperactivity reduced.

Line 3: Improved his writing skills.

Experiment 15 : Subject 15

Experiment 15 was aimed at fostering independence and social interaction skills in the subject through her love for dolls.

Table 4.16 : Behavioural Characteristics, Strengths and Ðrawbacks of Subject 15

Age	*Sex*	*Beh. Char*	*Splinter Skill/ Obsession*	*Learning Strength/ Dom. Intelligence*	*Learning Deficit*
8	F	Verbal; talks incoherently; agitated; poor social skills; withdrawn.	Dolls.	The ability to concentrate on narrow topics of interest; visual-spatial intelligence.	Inability to understand language and use semantics appropriately.

Subject 15 had a huge collection of dolls. It was decided to teach her functional and social skills through her obsession for dolls. The child was helped to identify her dolls by giving them different names, and she was also taught numerical skills by counting her dolls. She soon learnt that people also have different names. Because of her collection of dolls, the girls in the neighbourhood flocked into her house. As she was the only child, the it was decided to include her friends in the support team. Her peers deliberately dismantled some of the dolls, and she started complaining to her parents that the girls broke the limbs of her dolls.

Everyone joined her in mending the dolls. She learnt human anatomy through this activity. She started playing with the other girls. She was taught to make stuffed toys, such as teddy bears, dogs, bunny rabbits and rag dolls. She made a lot of toys and she started enjoying this activity. She was also taught to count money, and to maintain an account that would enable her in future to run a shop. She also enjoyed making lovely dresses for her dolls. She could also give suggestions to her friends as to how to make clothes for their dolls. The changes that occurred in the observable behaviour of the child can be portrayed through a graph given below:

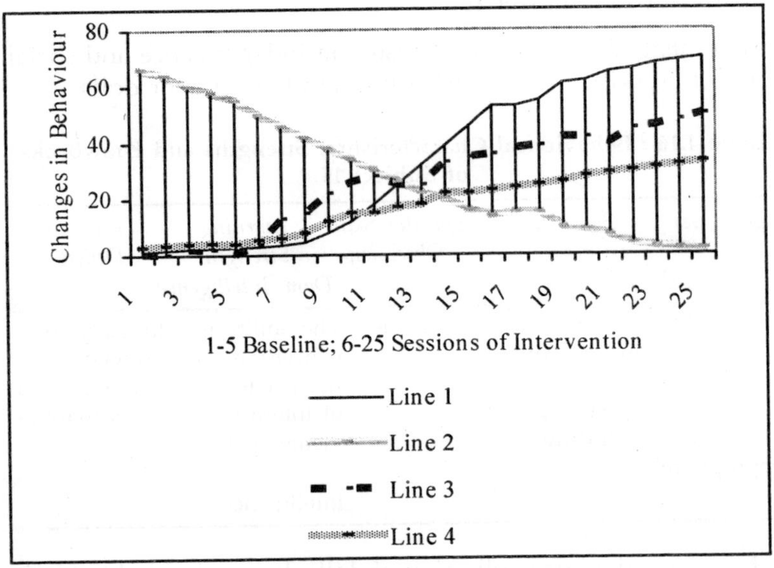

Figure 4.24 : Experiment 15 — Subject 15

The positive behaviour changes were:

Line 1. She started talking meaningfully and coherently.

Line 2. As she was engaged in some useful activity all the time, her agitation and restlessness reduced.

Line 3. Small motor activities that she engaged in fostered independence and social interaction skills.

Line 4. She developed persistence in her task, and manipulative skills and perceptual motor skills.

Experiment 16 - Subject 16

Experiment 16 was aimed at eliminating the self-destructive behaviour and help the child to focus on a given task more through his obsession for spinning objects.

Subject 16 was always engrossed in watching a fan. His entire world spun around fans. He would not see any other object or person in the room. He was quite violent and would not allow anyone to come close to him except his mother. It was decided to approach the child only through his mother. The mother bought a few toys, such as toy fan, pinwheel, spinning wheel, tops, toy windmill, etc., Initially, the child did not even bother to look at the toys. But slowly he started observing them. The windmill and the spinning wheel fascinated him in particular. He was given an activity book that described a lot of easy-to-assemble paper models. The book had the paper model of a windmill which he enjoyed making all by himself.

Table 4.17 : Behavioural Characteristics, Strengths and Drawbacks of Subject 16

Age	*Sex*	*Beh. Char*	*Splinter Skill/ Obsession*	*Learning Strength/ Dom. Intelligence*	*Learning Deficit*
13	M	Non-verbal; anxious; has seizure disorders; lack of eye contact; abhors social contact.	Fans.	The ability to understand concrete, context-free information and rules; visual-spatial and bodily-kinesthetic intelligence.	Communicates by pointing; difficulty in focusing.

The child was taken to a windmill energy generation site. He was so thrilled and overwhelmed that he started expressing his happiness in small sentences. He was taught to spin cotton with a spinning wheel that he enjoyed very much. With the cotton spun by him, he got a shirt made and he was proud of wearing it. He was still non-verbal and developed reading skills. He started reading *My experiments with Truth* by Mahatma Gandhi and he enjoyed reading it. He collected pictures of Mahatma Gandhi with his famous spinning wheel.

He was also given books about Amsterdam, and he wanted to know the technical details about windmill power generation. The parents were advised to buy a few books about 'windmill'. It was decided that he could pursue a course in this line and he could find employment in this line. The changes that took place in the child are given in Figure 4.25.

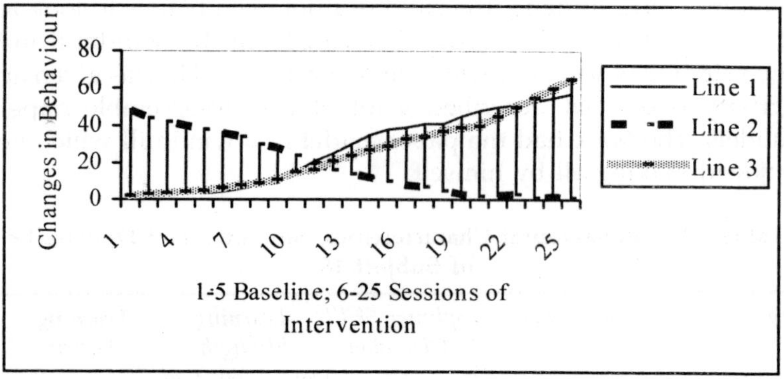

Figure 4.25: Experiment 16 — Subject 16

The positive behaviour changes were:

Line 1. The child's reading skills improved considerably.

Line 2. His anxiety and violent behaviour dwindled down considerably.

Line 3. He started expressing his needs, desires and happiness.

Experiment 17 — Subject 17

Experiment 17 was aimed at enhancing the motor skills and creativity through his passion for puzzles.

Subject 17 liked doing puzzles all the time and it was decided to reach out the child through his special love for puzzles. A lot of pictures were made and the child was asked to match the pictures such as 'socks and shoes', 'cup and saucer', 'spoon and fork', 'neck and tie', etc. He learnt several concepts through this picture and word matching games. Even though he was good in solving puzzles, when instructions were given to him directly, he had problems in understanding.

Table 4.18 : Behavioural Characteristics, Strengths and Drawbacks of Subject 17

Age	*Sex*	*Beh. Char*	*Splinter Skill/ Obsession*	*Learning Strength/ Dom. Intelligence*	*Learning Deficit*
7	M	Non-verbal; hypersensitive to sounds; poor social skills; echolalic.	Puzzles.	The ability to take in chunks of information; verbal-linguistic and visual-spatial intelligences.	Inability to follow directions and under-stand language.

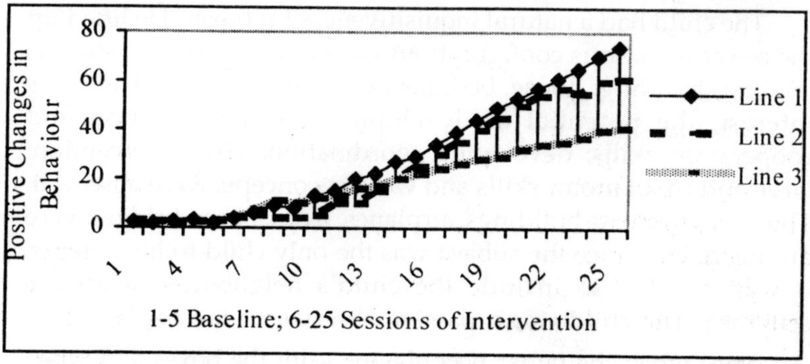

Figure 4.26 : Experiment 17 — Subject 17

The activities were further expaned by cutting greeting cards in the shapes of puzzles and the child was asked to put them together and glue them on a piece of paper. As the child was a visual learner, he relied on visual cues. He abhorred direct social contact, and direct instructions and directions. Several cue cards were prepared to give directions and instructions to the subject and this strategy paid off well. Reading to the child helped his parents to spend time with him. It helped the child to know that reading is very important. It also provided opportunities for the parents to share their knowledge and ideas with their child.

The child's keen interest in puzzles was further nurtured by introducing new games, and it was decided that teaching him chess would help him. As expected, he caught on to the game fast. He started playing in the local tournaments and won prizes.

The positive changes that took place in the child are given Figure 4.26.

The positive behavioural changes were:

Line 1. There was improvement in the subject's ability to follow instructions.

Line 2. His motor skills and creativity improved.

Line 3. He derived pleasure from his engagements.

Experiment 18 — Subject 18

Experiment 18 was aimed at developing oral language skills in the child and to improve his on-seat behaviour.

The child had a natural inquisitiveness for boxes. He lined up the boxes in various configurations for various purposes, such as bus, car, building, house, bed, kennel for his dog, etc. The boy's interest, the potential of developing social interaction and cooperation skills; developing coordination, visual perception, large and small motor skills and various concepts were observed. The boxes to create buildings, airplanes, jeeps, buses, bridges were arranged, etc. Since the subject was the only child to his parents, it was decided to include the child's neighbours in all the activities. The child was a passive observer in the beginning.

Once when the father was playing with the boxes and when he constructed a hospital, he forgot to put the sign 'Hospital' for the building he had constructed. Immediately, to his surprise, the child brought the sign and asked father to put the sign in a visible, conspicuous place. The child also learnt to use the same boxes for various purposes, such as sofa, doctor's table, television, hospital beds, etc. As an expanded experience, the child was taken to various construction sites, such as hospital, school, house, office, park, etc. This exposure widened his horizon of learning.

Table 4.19 : Behavioural Characteristics, Strengths and Drawbacks of Subject 18

Age	*Sex*	*Beh. Char*	*Splinter Skill/ Obsession*	*Learning Strength/ Dom. Intelligence*	*Learning Deficit*
13	M	Non-verbal; anxious; lack of eye contact; abhors social contact.	Boxes.	The ability to learn language without being taught; verbal-linguistic intelligence.	Engages in repetitive play and drifts aimlessly about.

The child, who was non-verbal all the while, started saying a few words such as 'two more boxes', 'box like this', 'long one', 'small one', etc., One day he built two tall structures. He crashed a plane over the structures and said 'World Trade Center'. He used new words such as 'crashing', 'screaming', 'burning', 'terror' etc. (After he played with the boxes, he was always reluctant to clean up the area and he refused to put back the boxes.) This was an opportunity to teach him to clean up and provide further learning experiences based on his demonstration of the World Trade Center tragedy. The child was taught new concepts such as 'debris', 'dirt', 'rescue', 'shelter', 'relief', 'life', 'injured', 'dead', 'first aid', etc.

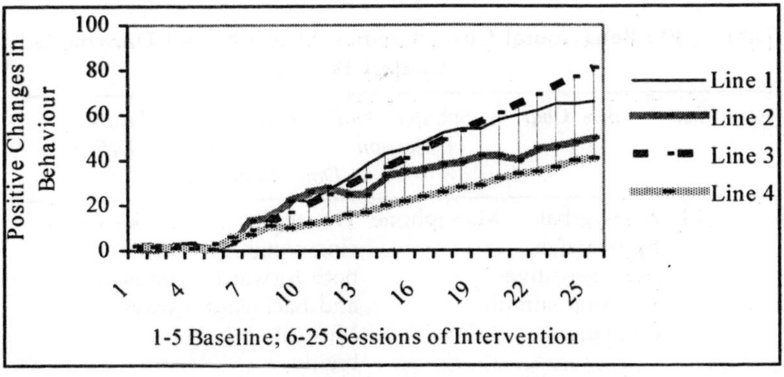

Figure 4.27: Experiment 18 — Subject 18

The graph given above illustrates the positive changes in the behaviour of the child.

The positive behaviour changes were:

Line 1. Developed oral language skills.

*Line 2.*Interacted cooperatively with others by sharing materials, objects, toys, etc.

— *Line 3.* Developed listening skills and vocabulary.

— *Line 4.* Learnt several new words and concepts through his play with boxes.

Experiment 19 — Subject 19

Experiment 19 was aimed at to enabling the child to focus on the given task through his exceptional musical intelligence.

Subject 19 had a fascination for microphones and he could be seen holding it all the time and singing songs. He could sing all the nursery rhymes, both forwards and backwards through his mike. But he would never sing without his mike. It was necessary to find out the underlying sensory feeling for his holding the mike. Soon, it was clear that the child wanted to hold something when he was singing. It was decided to reach out to him through his exceptional musical intelligence. The parents felt that he could learn instrumental music initially. As expected, he learnt violin very well. He liked attending concerts and he too wanted to give concerts when he grew up.

Table 4.20 : Behavioural Characteristics, Strengths and Drawbacks of Subject 19

Age	*Sex*	*Beh. Char*	*Splinter Skill/ Obsession*	*Learning Strength/ Dom. Intelligence*	*Learning Deficit*
8	M	Non-verbal; hyperactive; hypersensitive to visual stimuli; echolalic.	Microphone	The ability to sing songs both forward and backward; Musical and bodily-kinesthetic intelligences.	Seeks social contact in unusual ways.

When he was stressed, he often burrowed under heavy pillows and that comforted him. He avoided all moving and colourful objects and preferred dark; and he avoided bright and sunny spots as he was hypersensitive to visual stimulation. Listening to music calmed him, especially classical music and Beethoven's V symphony was his favourite. Whenever the child was restless, his favourite music was played were and he relaxed and could focus more on the given task. The changes that took place in the observable behaviour of the child are given below in the graph.

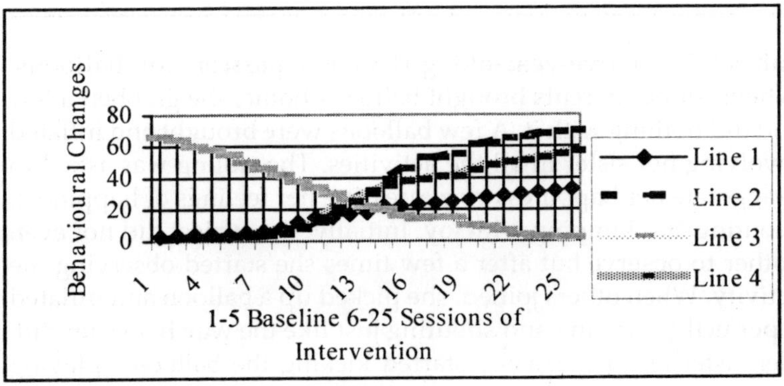

Figure 4.28 : Experiment 19 — Subject 19

The behavioural changes were:

Line 1. The subject' love for music helped him to relax and focus on the given task.

Line 2. His auditory discrimination and auditory memory improved. He could listen to Beethoven's symphony V.

Line 3. His hyperactivity diminished considerably.

Line 4. Making him listen to his favourite music reduced his hypersensitivity to visual stimuli that resulted in his restlessness.

Experiment 20 : Subject 20

Experiment 20 was aimed at providing learning experiences to improve various skills through her passion for balloons.

Table 4.21 : Behavioural Characteristics, Strengths and Drawbacks of Subject 20

Age	*Sex*	*Beh. Char*	*Splinter Skill/ Obsession*	*Learning Strength/ Dom. Intelligence*	*Learning Deficit*
5	F	Non-verbal; withdrawn; self-hurting; lack of eye contact; abhors social contact.	Balloons	The ability to persevere; visual-spatial and bodily-kinesthetic intelligences.	Inability to perceive and people around.

Subject 20, a five-year-old girl had a passion for balloons. Whenever her parents brought balloons home, she grabbed a few and did nothing with it. A few balloons were brought and inflated involving her sister in all the activities. The sibling was asked to exaggerate her happiness by expressing her feelings of happiness, shouting and jumping with joy. Initially, the subject did not even bother to observe but after a few times she started observing the activity. When others joined, she picked up a balloon and inflated it perfectly, jumping and shouting just like the way her sister did. Her sister and her friends started kicking the balloons, playing catch with the balloons, tying strings to the balloons, tossing and flying them. The children were asked to exaggerate their emotions and they followed the instructions given. The child ignored the other children for a few days and finally she made an attempt on the fifth day and from then on, she joined them in all their activities. As an extension of this activity, the children made flags and pennants, and she soon learnt to identify the national flags of different countries. It was decided to teach the child how to locate different countries, their capitals, weather, culture, lifestyle etc. An atlas was used teach her various places and she gained adequate mastery. But when she was asked to locate the places using a globe, she could not do so. This is an example of the inability to transfer skill from one area to another, a deficit that is quite common among children with autism.

The changes that occurred in the behaviour of the subject are given in the graph.

The positive changes in behaviour were:

Line 1. The child could frame sentences with a couple of words.

Line 2. She could identify the national flags of 2I countries.

Line 3. She could name several countries on the world map.

Line 4. Her self-hurting behaviour reduced considerably.

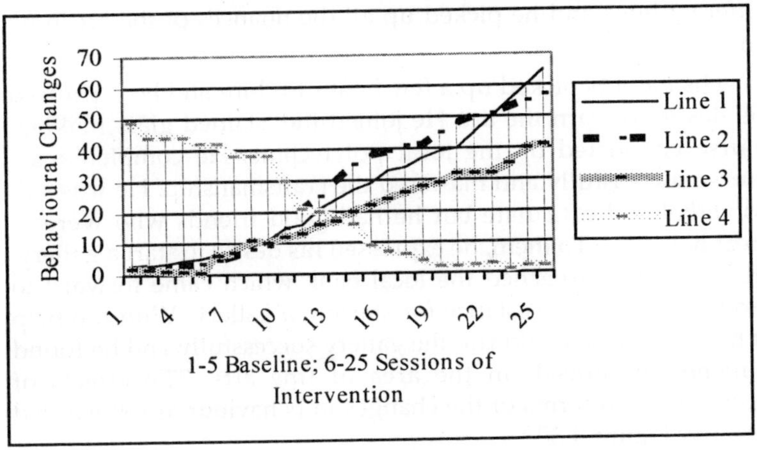

Figure 4.29: Experiment 20 — Subject 20

Experiment 21 — Subject 21

Experiment 21 was aimed at improving his span of attention and level of understanding through his love for stained glass.

Table 4.22 : Behavioural Characteristics, Strengths and Drawbacks of Subject 21

Age	*Sex*	*Beh.Char*	*Splinter skill/ Obsession*	*Learning Strength/ Dom. Intelligence*	*Learning Deficit*
19	M	Non-verbal; hypersensitive to sounds; socially withdrawn; lack of eye contact.	Stained glass.	The ability to perceive and present information visually; visual-spatial intelligence.	Inability to understand others' perspectives.

Subject 21 was seen observing and reproducing the intricate pattern of stained glass on the window of his house. It was quite clear from the exquisite work that he could reproduce from his memory whatever he saw only once or twice. He was given paper, pen, pencil, sketch pen, crayons, etc., and he could draw the stained glass design matching it with the exact colour given in the original picture even though he was non-verbal and could not name the colours. He was taught to mix different paints to get different hues and he picked up all the nuances of the art in no time.

His parents picked up a few books for him and he expressed his desire to learn the art. He joined the 'stained glass making' course conducted by the local polytechnic. He completed the course successfully and mastered the craftsmanship. He was still no-verbal and articulate but he had good friends who were of great help him. To them, he expressed his desire to start a gallery. His parents approached the local bank which came forward to provide financial assistance for starting a gallery. With the help of his friends, he could run the gallery successfully and he found a niche for himself in the area of fine arts. The effects of intervention in terms of the changes in behaviour are illustrated through Figure 4.30.

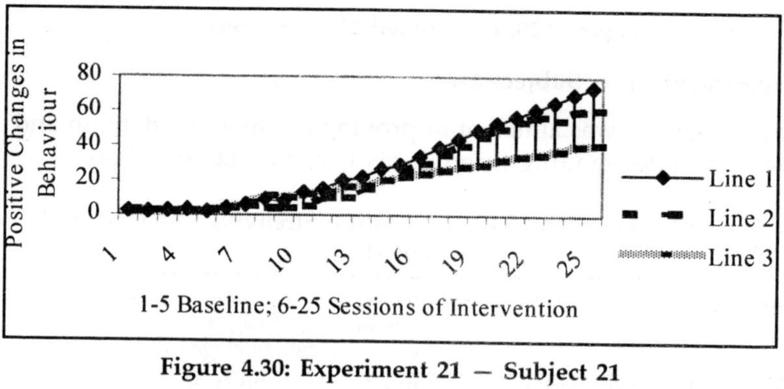

Figure 4.30: Experiment 21 — Subject 21

The positive changes in behaviour were:

Line 1.The child's attention span and listening ability improved significantly.

Line 2. He improved his level of understanding.

Line 3. He became more cooperative and friendly.

Experiment 22 : Subject 22

Experiment 22 was aimed at improving the subject's language skills and social engagement through his fondness for kitchen utensils.

Table 4.23 : Behavioural Characteristics, Strengths and Drawbacks of Subject 22

Age	*Sex*	*Beh. Char*	*Splinter Skill/ Obsession*	*Learning Strength/ Dom. Intelligence*	*Learning Deficit*
11	M	Non-verbal; non-compliant; impatient; has panic attacks.	Kitchen utensils.	Inter-personal intelligence.	Has poor gross motor skills; grasps things with his palm; has problems with motor imitation.

The child had a spontaneous liking for kitchen utensils. A treasure trove of learning activities was found in this passion of the child. He did not allow anyone to come near him except his father. He grasped objects with his palm and so he kept dropping the utensils. Soon, he learnt from his father to identify different utensils and the purposes for which they were used, such as skillet for dosa (pancakes), idli (rice cakes) plates for making idlis, pressure cooker for cooking rice, dal (lentils), various pulses, frying pan for making bajjis (stuffed vegetable fries), bondas (vegetable dumplings) and other fried items. He learnt the names of various things, food items and the recipes. He was also taught the nutrient values of the common food items.

He learnt to cook various food items and he enjoyed making different dishes. His culinary experiences and expertise taught him to describe the dishes that were prepared by him, to learn and identify different aromas and tastes, to be able to measure, and also small-muscle coordination. He became more and more observant as he observed the changes that were taking place when he cooked different vegetables, pulses, grains, cereals, etc. There was dramatic improvement in his language skills, problem-solving skills, decision-making skills, etc.

Activities involving food and cooking helped him to learn and grasp new information, gain new skills and gain control over the environment. These positive changes contributed significantly in the intellectual development of the child. He picked up several skills in cooking. His motor clumsiness diminished completely.

The positive changes in the behaviour of the subject are illustrated in Figure 4.31.

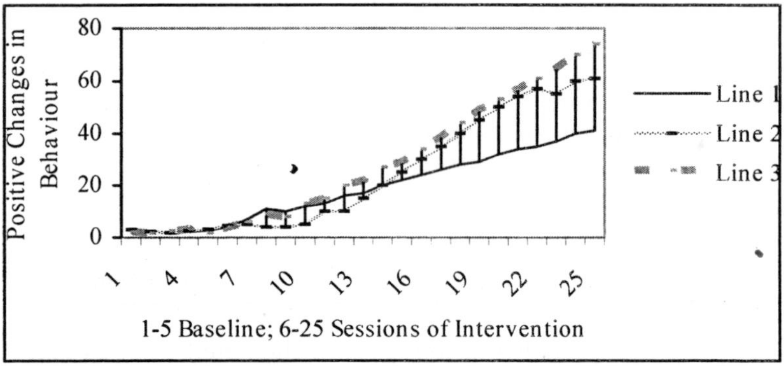

Figure 4.31: Experiment 22 — Subject 22

The positive behaviour changes were:

Line 1. Improvement in language skills, problem-solving skills, decision-making skills, etc.,

Line 2. Improvement in social engagement.

Line 3. Improvement in gross and fine motor skills.

Experiment 23 — Subject 23

Experiment 23 was aimed at to enabling the subject to improve her motor skills and social interaction through her splinter skill in making 'rangolis'.

Subject 23 had a keen interest in rangoli (floor decorations). Whenever her mother decorated the front-yard of their house with colour rangolis for festivals, she would help her mother in colouring it and decorating it with flowers. She had an innate ability to look at objects, to remember their size, shape and contour and to translate these into the appropriate motor patterns, which was quite different from that found in even the most gifted normal child.

Table 4.24 : Behavioural Characteristics, Strengths and Drawbacks of Subject 23

Age	*Sex*	*Beh. Char*	*Splinter Skill/ Obsession*	*Learning Strength/ Dom. Intelligence*	*Learning Deficit*
13	F	Non-verbal; withdrawn; abhors social contact.	Rangoli.	The ability to learn and repeat long routines, the ability to transfer visual world into motor patterns; visual-spatial and bodily-kinesthetic intelligences.	Inability to use and understand language; communicated with others by pointing.

The child's mother taught her to draw rangolis. This improved her fine motor skills, colour scheme, colour coordination, combinations, colour patterns, numerical skills, functional, social and communication skills, etc. As an extension of her ardent interest in rangoli, the mother taught her mehendi designs and she soon became an expert in it. The child also learnt 'vastu shastra' and she could become a vastu consultant, a rangoli expert and a mehendi designer. With her expertise in mehendi designing, she opened a small boutique at home and started doing bridal decorations, which paid her well. She enjoyed making money at such an early age and she was quite proud of her achievement.

Her mother opened a bank account for her and this enabled her to put her earnings as savings for her future, and it also gave her self-confidence. She learnt about interest rates; what type of account fetched her more interest and soon learnt to manage her money. Her parents were quite happy about her versatile interests and talents. The positive changes that occurred in the behaviour of the subject are given in Figure 4.32.

The positive behavioural changes were:

Line 1. The subject learnt to speak in meaningful sentences.

Line 2. She developed self-confidence.

Line 3. She learnt self-help skills.

Line 4. She learnt about interest rates and about which account fetched her more interest in the bank.

Line 5. Improvement in social interaction.

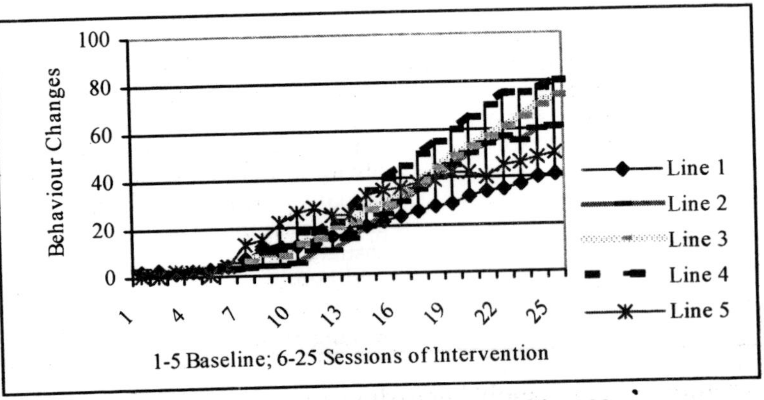

Figure 4.32 : Experiment 23 — Subject 23

Experiment 24 : Subject 24

Experiment 24 was aimed at improving him to talk coherently and meaningfully through his love for ships and sail-boats.

Table 4.25 : Behavioural Characteristics, Strengths and Drawbacks of Subject 24

Age	*Sex*	*Beh. Char*	*Splinter Skill/ Obsession*	*Learning Strength/ Dom. Intelligence*	*Learning Deficit*
12	M	Verbal; talks constantly and incoherently; echolalic.	Ships and sailboats.	The ability to take in chunks of information; verbal-linguistic and visual-spatial intelligences.	Inability to understand complex and idiomatic uses of language.

Subject 24 had an obsession for ships and he collected hundreds of pictures about ships. He could explain in detail how sailing ships used in ancient Egypt were propelled by simple paddles or *poles pushed into the riverbed. He referred the Encyclopedia Britannica,* collected all the details and noted down all the salient features of each and every type of ship, below the picture. His verbal-linguistic and writing skills were phenomenal.

He delineated in detail the cargo boats and galleys (fighting boats in battles) used by the Greeks and Romans. He described the differences between carracks and galleons that were capable of long ocean crossings. He could describe Viking boats, barques, clippers, etc., and gave detailed descriptions of steamships and luxury ocean liners.

He was also interested in stories related to voyages by ships such as 'Sindbad the Sailor', 'Robinson Crusoe', 'Gulliver's Travels', etc., He found the stories amazing. His knowledge and mastery of ships was phenomenal. He could make beautiful toy ships using shells of silk cotton and palm and coconut shells. He also created his own models of ships and he could pursue a career in ship designing. The changes in the behaviour of the subject are given in Figure 4.33.

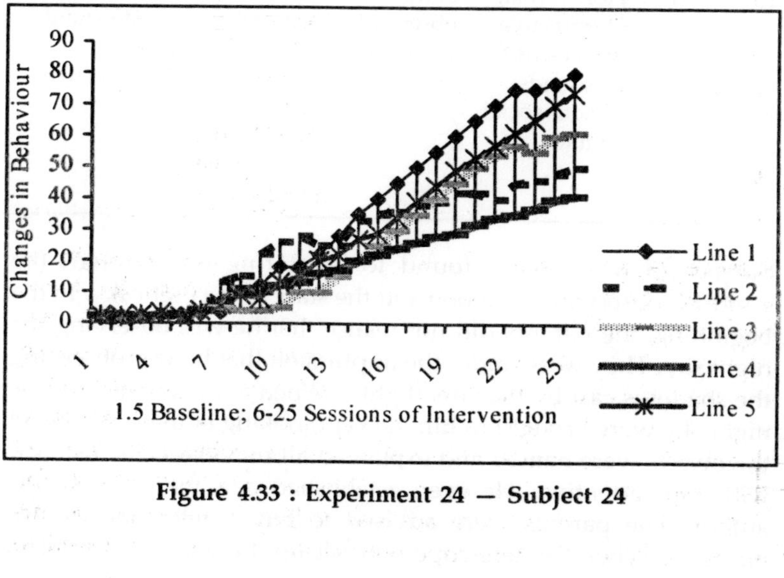

Figure 4.33 : Experiment 24 — Subject 24

The positive changes in behaviour were:

Line 1. He exhibited more interactive play with others.

Line 2. His vocabulary and enunciation improved greatly.

Line 3.His attention span and listening skills improved significantly.

Line 4. He could identify and differentiate various types of ships.

Line 5.He understood and enjoyed stories also.

Experiment 25 : Subject 25

The investigator's aim in Experiment 25 was to enable the subject become more organised and methodical through her splinter skill of observation.

Table 4.26 : Behavioural Characteristics, Strengths and Drawbacks of Subject 25

Age	*Sex*	*Beh. Char*	*Splinter Skill/ Obsession*	*Learning Strength/ Dom. Intelligence*	*Learning Deficit*
15	M	Non-verbal; hyperactive; hypersensitive to sounds; abhors social contact.	Stars; observing the night sky.	The ability to read and write volumes of materials; verbal-linguistic and visual-spatial intelligences.	Inability to understand the perspectives of others'

Subject 25 was always found to be staring out through the window, observing the moon and the stars in the night sky. In the beginning, the parents did not realise that he was observing the night sky. They were under the impression that he was observing the shadows cast by the streetlights. When a few pictures of the night sky were brought to him he kept looking at them. When all the objects were named and explained all the objects, he listened with rapt attention. He even established eye contact with the author. The parents were advised to buy a telescope for his birthday. When the telescope was set up, he was too scared to come anywhere near it. The investigator decided to desensitise the child and a paper roll was made for the child. This made him look at the night sky through it and he enjoyed this activity. One day, on his own, he picked up the telescope and started observing and shouting and yelling, out of happiness and excitement.

He was given newspaper clippings of the night sky and taught him the names of constellations, different stars and the planetary positions were taught to him. He even maintained a diary to note down all the points that he considered worth mentioning. He was, taught computer skills and how to access the internet. Soon, he was adept in it. He was interested in the biographies of famous astronomers, space scientists, etc., He could pursue his education and career in astronomy/space science. The positive changes that were observed in the behaviour of the subject are portrayed in the graph given below.

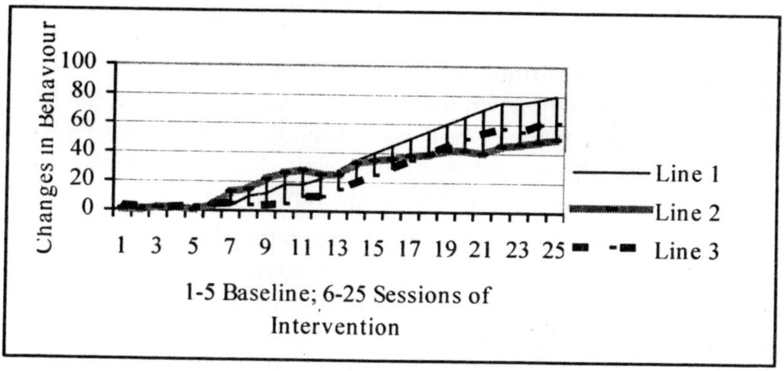

Figure 4.34 : Experiment 25 — Subject 25

The positive behavioural changes were:

Line 1. The subject became very organised and methodical.

Line 2. He exhibited more interactive play with others.

Line 3. He could develop vocational and functional skills.

Experiment 26 : Subject 26

Experiment 26 was aimed at enabling the child to eliminate his self-hurting behaviour and to improve his communicative skills.

Table 4.27 : Behavioural Characteristics, Strengths and Drawbacks of Subject 26

Age	*Sex*	*Beh. Char*	*Splinter Skill/ Obsession*	*Learning Strength/ Dom. Intelligence*	*Learning Deficit*
12	M	Non-verbal; self-hurting; has seizure disorders; lack of eye contact.	Block printing and vegetable dyeing.	The ability to transfer visual world into motor patterns; visual-spatial intelligence	Inability to do things consistently; can do sometimes and cannot at other times.

Subject 26 had an innate interest in block printing as he had observed his mother at work. His mother had her own home-based business - selling sarees and furnishings made with vegetable dyes and block printing. The child silently observed the mother quite a few times and soon started imitating her. He did the printing on whatever material that was in the vicinity. His mother further trained him by allowing him to experiment different patterns on different materials. From vegetables and fruits, he made dyes and this taught him about colours.

He soon mastered the art of vegetable dyeing and block printing. He picked up functional language skills. Apart from whatever words that were used in the area of vegetable dyeing and block printing, he did not know the names of other objects used in the house. He was still non-verbal but whenever his mother asked for a particular block, he would fetch it for her. But he could not verbalise his interests/needs/desires.

He could communicate with the members of his family and coworkers through gestures and signs. His mother, enrolled him in other classes, such as batik work and screen-printing. With his basic knowledge in vegetable dyeing and block printing, he soon picked up the nuances of batik printing. His eye contact was still fleeting; he used peripheral vision to look at people. The changes that took place in the observable behaviour of the child are given in the graph.

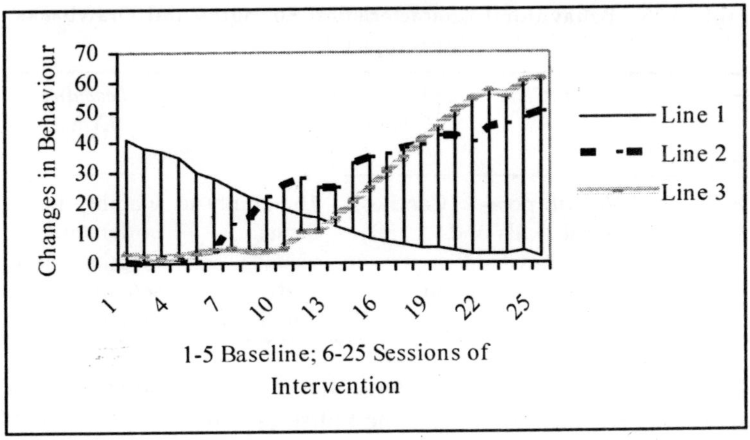

Figure 4.35 : Experiment 26 — Subject 26

The positive behavioural changes were:

Line 1. The subject's self-hurting behaviour diminished significantly.

Line 2. There was considerable improvement in his social engagement.

Line 3. He exhibited more interactive play with others.

Experiment 27 — Subject 27

Experiment 27 was aimed at enabling the subject to improve her oral language skills and social skills.

Subject 27 had a fascination for candles. The child was observed for a few days to know which sensory property provided stimulation to the child. She lit the candles from the main lamp that was burning in the pooja room. It was quite evident that the child liked the shadows created by the candlelight. It was decided to make use of the opportunities that this activity provided. The child was engaged in shadow making through hand positions of various animal shapes. She learnt to use vocabulary effectively, words such as 'The dog is barking' and 'The man is shouting like a dog', the difference between 'chocolate milk' and 'milk chocolate', etc.

Table 4.28 : Behavioural Characteristics, Strengths and Drawbacks of Subject 27

Age	*Sex*	*Beh. Char*	*Splinter Skill/ Obsession*	*Learning Strength/ Dom. Intelligence*	*Learning Deficit*
13	F	Verbal; poor social skills and lack of eye-hand coordination.	Candles.	The ability to focus; visual-spatial intelligence.	Inability to understand language and semantics of language.

The child was made to understand that it was not safe for her to carry a lighted candle all over the house. She was taught to turn the incandescent light on and carry on this activity. She was also taught concepts such as 'combustible' and 'non-combustible' items and also what supports 'burning'.

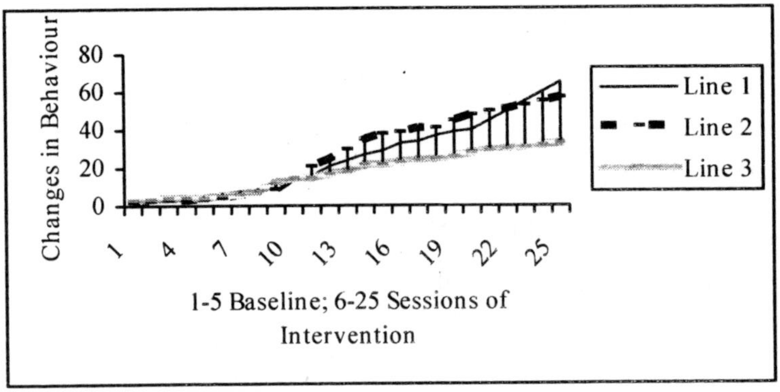

Figure 4.36 : Experiment 27 – Subject 27

As an extension, the child was taught to make candles. She also learnt to make designer candles for exclusive customers. She learnt to make various objects and gift items based on candle or wax, such as shell-lamps, earthen or terracotta lamps, which were received well by her clients. The changes that took place in the behaviour of the subject are given in the graph.

The positive changes in behaviour were:

Line 1. Dramatic improvement in semantics and pragmatics of the language.

Line 2. Considerable improvement in social interaction and engagement.

Line 3. Improvement in eye-hand coordination.

Experiment 28 : Subject 28

Experiment 28 was aimed at capitalising on the subject's splinter skill in paper craft to improve his perceptual skills, such as body awareness and body control.

Table 4.29 : Behavioural Characteristics, Strengths and Drawbacks of Subject 28

Age	*Sex*	*Beh. Char*	*Splinter Skill/ Obsession*	*Learning Strength/ Dom. Intelligence*	*Learning Deficit*
8	M	Non-verbal; withdrawn; has seizure disorders; lack of eye contact; abhors social contact.	Paper craft.	The ability to transfer visual world into; motor patterns visual-spatial intelligence.	Lack of body awareness, body control and perceptual control.

Taking advantage of the subject's splinter skill in paper craft, various activities were devised using all the intervention strategies that were devised. The child was taught to make several paper sculptures, such as springs, cones, steps, parapet walls and various three-dimensional shapes with construction paper and paper scraps. He was also taught to make paper fans, paper chains, stuffed animals, finger puppets, paper cut outs, pin wheels, etc., and he enjoyed these activities thoroughly. This activity enabled him to learn body awareness, body control and perceptual control.

The child had continence problem that he would run out of the room and sometimes, he urinated in the classroom. The child was diabetic and he needed to use the bathroom quite frequently. He was taught to use a visual cue card to indicate his need to use the bathroom. The synthesis of all the intervention strategies that were developed helped in better management and care of the subject. The changes that occurred in the behaviour of the subject are illustrated with the help of a graph given below.

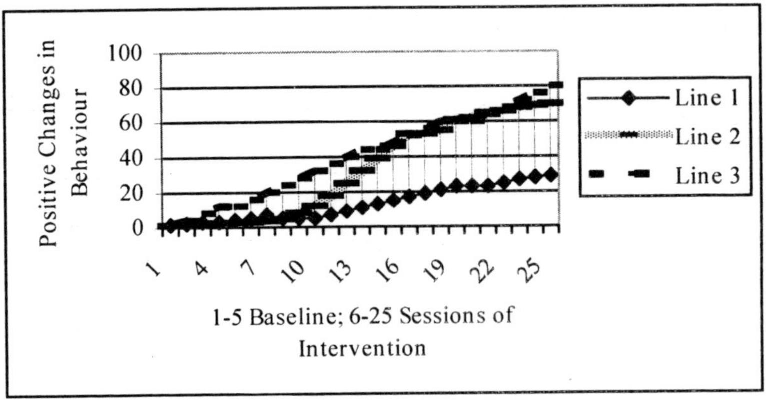

Figure 4.37 : Experiment 28 – Subject 28

The positive changes in beahviour were:

Line 1. The subject derived sensory pleasure from cutting and using the paper for different craft items.

Line 2. He planned his motor activities better and worked cooperatively.

Line 3. He improved his perceptual control, body awareness and body control.

Experiment 29 : Subject 29

Experiment 29 was aimed in helping the child eliminate his aggressiveness and to use his skill in a productive way.

Subject 29 could always be seen with a camera. He would not play with or pretend to take pictures with it but he could be seen meddling with it all the time. A Polaroid camera took instant pictures of the child and there were handed over to him. He kept staring at his pictures making 'ga-ga' sounds expressing happiness. Otherwise, he was totally non-communicative. If he did not meddle with the camera, he was biting his wrist or banging his head on the wall. Soon, it was clear that he indulged in self-hurting behaviour because of boredom. The child was approached and told hand over the camera so that pictures of him could be taken. As his personal space was invaded and he thought that the author was taking his camera away, he hit her.

Table 4.30 : Behavioural Characteristics, Strengths and Drawbacks of Subject 29

Age	*Sex*	*Beh. Char*	*Splinter Skill/ Obsession*	*Learning Strength/ Dom. Intelligence*	*Learning Deficit*
7	M	Non-verbal; wringing hands; self-hurting.	Camera.	The ability to concentrate on narrow topics of interest; visual-spatial intelligence.	Inability to imitate and understand language.

For a few more days, pictures of the child were taken and handed over to him immediately. Slowly, the child started associating pictures with the camera. One day, as his father was trying to take pictures, the child put his camera in his father's hands and said 'chee' for 'cheese', to his surprise. He pretended to take pictures with his camera. He was taught to use the camera. He learnt the different parts of the camera, their functions, etc., and he started enjoying this activity. He used the camera very effectively and shot beautiful pictures. He took pictures of his family members and knew who was who. He could remember their names and understand the relationships.

He could name the different objects that he took pictures of. He learnt to adjust the light, the colour, focus, etc., He still could not understand the moods and feelings expressed by people. By looking at a picture, he could not say whether the person was happy or sad or angry. The changes in his behaviour are given in the graph below.

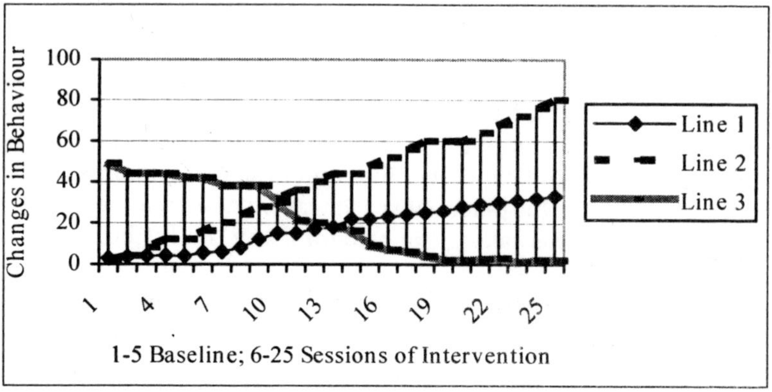

Figure 4.38: Experiment 29 — Subject 29

The positive behaviour changes were

Line 1. He started making sentences with one or two words.

Line 2. He learnt to spend his time in a productive manner.

Line 3. His anxiety and self-hurting behaviour dwindled down

Experiment 30 : Subject 30

Experiment 30 was aimed at capitalising on the child's proclivity in sand play to learn various concepts and to improve his skills.

Table 4.31 : Behavioural Characteristics, Strengths and Drawbacks of Subject 30

Age	*Sex*	*Beh.Char*	*Splinter skill/ Obsession*	*Learning Strength/ Dom.Intelligence*	*Learning Deficit*
11	M	Non-verbal; hypersensitive to sounds; self-hurting.	Sandplay.	The ability to transfer visual world into motor patterns; bodily-kinesthetic and visual-spatial intelligences.	Inability to perceive and organise events in time and understand language; uses adult's hands as tools.

Subject 30 indulged only in one independent leisure activity - playing in the sand and sifting the sand through his fingers. The child was observed for a few days to find out what was stimulating him. It was quite evident in a few days that his indulgence in this activity was reinforced by the visual aspect of the sand sifting through his fingers rather than the feel of the material. Several activities were planned and added to provide visual stimulation, such as planting seeds, cleaning and raking flowerbeds, measuring the sand with cups while playing in the sand, sorting and packaging seeds, etc.,

Variations were slowly incorporated in conjunction with the intervention strategies so as to keep up the optimum level of stimulation and to maintain the pace of learning. The variations increased flexibility and enabled the child to avoid any rigidity in interaction. Theses variations increased the child's level of tolerance for new and novel situations and information.

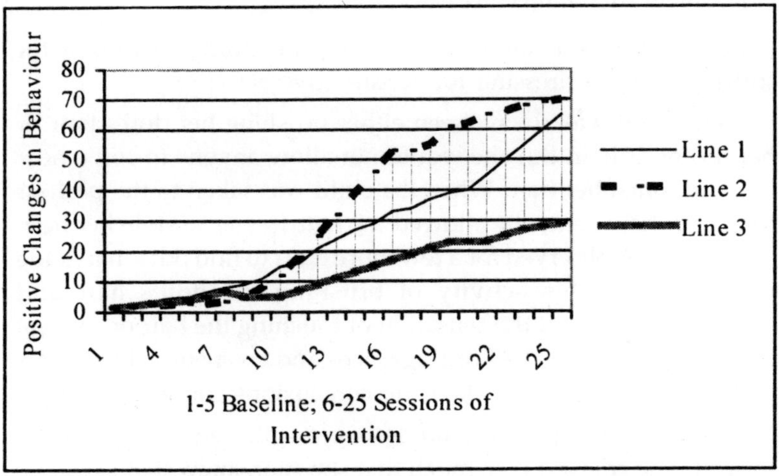

Figure 4.39 : Experiment 30 — Subject 30

Various activities were planned well in advance and contexts were created to encourage interaction. The author sat next to the child in the sand pit and sifted the dirt, measured the sand with the cup, filled up the mug and dumped it in a different place. The child observed the activities through his peripheral vision and started imitating it after a long time. This is an example of delayed praxis. The child used the author's hands as tools to play with sand.

The mother drew lines on the sand, made sand cakes and smoothed out the patterns. The child enjoyed this activity and he imitated the activity of the mother. He wanted his mother to make more cakes so that she could flatten them. This interactive activity enabled him to pick up a few words, learn new concepts and communication skills. The changes that took place in his behaviour are represented in the graph.

The positive changes in behaviour were

Line 1. The child picked up a few words and improved his communications skills.

Line 2. He initiated social interaction and play activities.

Line 3. He engaged himself in imaginative play.

Experiment 31 : Subject 31

Experiment 31 was aimed at utilising the child's obsession for sniffing and hairdressing for constructive activities.

The child was always seen either brushing her doll's hair or her mother's hair. But she would not allow anyone to come near her and touch her hair. When the child was taken to the parlour to get her hair done, she allowed the hairdresser to style her hair. The child was observed for a few more days to find out what made the her enjoy this activity of brushing the doll's hair and shampooing - was it the sensation of touching the hair or the feel of shampoo or the smell of fragrances and cosmetics? Even after observing her for a few days, no conclusions could be drawn.

A few empty perfume bottles were collected for the subject to sniff. She enjoyed it so much that she soon knew that each one was different and produced by different designers, and that each one had a brand name. She could soon identify different perfumes, the brand name and the designer. She could also delineate the salient features of each and every perfume that she came across. It was decided to expand the horizon of experiences for the child by teaching her hairdressing.

Table 4.32 : Behavioural Characteristics, Strengths and Drawbacks of Subject 31

Age	*Sex*	*Beh. Char*	*Splinter Skill/ Obsession*	*Learning Strength/ Dom. Intelligence*	*Learning Deficit*
17	F	Non-verbal; withdrawn; anxious; self-hurting.	Hairdressing.	The ability to transfer visual world into motor patterns; bodily-kinesthetic and visual-spatial intelligences.	Pulls away when touched; inability to perceive and organise events in time and understand language.

She was put in a short-term 'hairdressing course' but she did not do well and she did not enjoy it much. Then she attended a short-term course in cosmetology and she also interned in a cosmetics unit, which she found interesting. Her autism presented specific challenges, particularly in the development of social relationships. The changes that occurred in the behaviour of the child are shown in the graph given below.

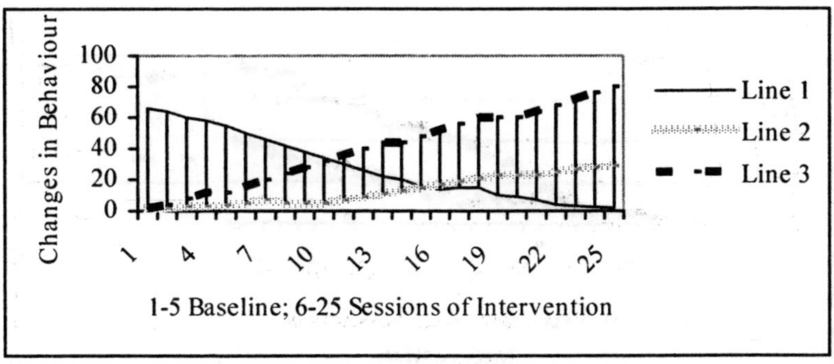

Figure 4.40: Experiment 31—Subject 31

The positive changes in behaviour were:

Line 1. The child engaged less in obsessional and ritualistic activities.

Line 2. She could direct her attention to more meaningful features of the environment.

Line 3. She could engage in social reciprocity and interaction.

Experiment 32 : Subject 32

Experiment 32 was aimed at utilising the subject's passion for dolphins for constructive activities.

Table 4.33 : Behavioural Characteristics, Strengths and Drawbacks of Subject 32

Age	*Sex*	*Beh. Char*	*Splinter Skill/ Obsession*	*Learning Strength/ Dom. Intelligence*	*Learning Deficit*
18	M	Non-verbal; withdrawn; has seizure disorders; lack of eye contact; abhors social contact.	Dolphins.	The ability to transfer visual world into motor patterns; visual-spatial intelligence.	Inability to attach meaning to visual information.

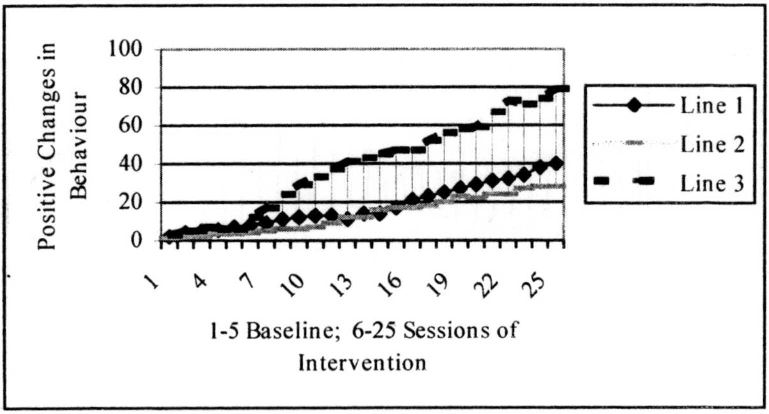

Figure 4.41 : Experiment 32 — Subject 32

Subject 32 had an obsession for dolphins and this obsession was capitalised on to teach him various concepts. He was taught to cut chart paper in the shape of dolphins and letters of the alphabet were taught through this. He collected a lot of pictures and figures of dolphins. He watched television and his favourite channel was 'Animal Kingdom'. His interest in watching television was expanded further by teaching him computer skills. Soon, he was adept in using the Internet and downloading information that he wanted. He was still non-verbal but his reading and writing skills improved dramatically.

Through his manipulation of Internet, he could access vast amount of information about dolphins. He created several files and he drew pictures of the dolphin. He wrote several stories and poems based on them. He drew several pictures and he collected a lot of graphics. So he wanted to open an exclusive museum or gallery dedicated to the study of dolphins; he also learnt a lot about marine biology. The parents consulted the local rotary club and other voluntary organisations for help, and they extended their help. He also secured bank loan and opened a small kiosk where he sold dolphin figurines and jewellery; he enjoyed it thoroughly. The positive changes that occurred in the overt behaviour of the child are given in Figure 4.41.

The positive changes in behaviour were:

Line 1. The subject's skill in reading and writing improved significantly.

Line 2. His interest in 'dolphins' helped him to widen his horizon and learn other skills effectively.

Line 3. He could make use of his interest to his vocational role.

Experiment 33: Subject 33

Experiment 33 was aimed at expanding the cognitive latitude of the child through his obsession for 'coconuts'.

Subject 33 was fond of coconuts. After eating the flesh, he never threw away the shells. He had a huge collection of coconut shells and he would not spare that to anyone. His mother approached the author to suggest some useful activities that he could be engaged in using the shells. Human faces were drawn on the shells - happy face, sad face, surprised face, angry face, etc., and the child was asked to identify the feeling expressed by the face. It took him more than a month to identify the feelings and from time to time he was asked to point out the face that represented the particular feeling that he experienced at that time.

Table 4.34 Behavioural Characteristics, Strengths and Drawbacks of Subject 33

Age	*Sex*	*Beh. Char*	*Splinter Skill/ Obsession*	*Learning Strength/ Dom. Intelligence*	*Learning Deficit*
17	M	Non-verbal; self-hurting; lack of eye contact; abhors social contact.	Coconuts.	The ability to use advanced splinter skill to learn new information; visual-spatial intelligence.	Inability to recognise human emotions and characteristics.

He was taught several objects that could be made with coconut shells, such as huts, houses, merry-go-round, etc. The child learnt to identify different types of dwellings and buildings. He learnt to craft several items with coconut shells, such as umbrella, boats, catamarans.

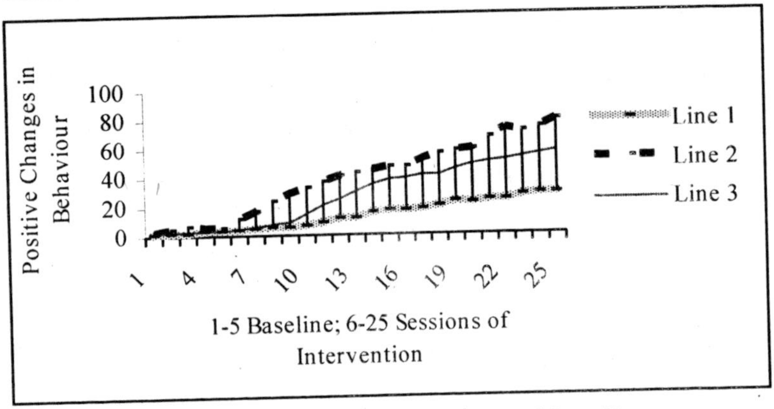

Figure 4.42 : Experiment 33 — Subject 33

The cognitive latitude of the child could be improved upon by showing the child other nuts and which particular nut is derived from which tree and the type of soil in which it grows, etc. He collected a lot of information about various nuts and the multifarious uses of the nuts, shells, leaves, barks, etc. He was fascinated by areca nut tree and how the bark can be used to make eco-friendly plates, cups and bowls that could replace plastic and styrofoam products. He evinced a keen interest in it and it was decided that he could start a cottage industry where he could make eco-friendly products based on barks and nuts which would otherwise go to waste. The positive changes in the behaviour of the child are given in the graph above.

The positive changes in behaviour were

Line 1. The subject could identify human feelings and characteristics.

Line 2. The subject directed his attention to meaningful features of information and environment.

Line 3. The subject could determine his vocational choice.

Experiment 34: Subject 34

The aim in this case was to reach out to him through his visual-spatial intelligence.

Table 4.35 : Behavioural Characteristics, Strengths and Drawbacks of Subject 34

Age	*Sex*	*Beh. Char*	*Splinter Skill/ Obsession*	*Learning Strength/ Dom. Intelligence*	*Learning Deficit*
14	M	Non-verbal; hyperactive and poor social skills.	Yarn.	The ability to transfer visual world into motor patterns; visual-spatial intelligence.	Inability to work within boundary.

Subject 34 was seen playing with yarn and ropes all the time. It was decided to capitalise on this interest of the child by teaching him to thread or string beads to make garlands, necklaces, to glue yarn over some patterns, doing embroidery with different types of yarn, knitting and crocheting. Large letters of the alphabet were drawn on a paper. The child dipped a length of yarn into a bowl of liquid starch and placed the yarn on the letter configuration. When it dried, a tactile letter was formed and he was thrilled and amazed by his artwork.

Different types of yarns, and the child were collected was taught different uses of the materials. He used jute to make beautiful bags, baskets and wall hangings. He was also taken to a coir industry where the coconut fibre was made into yarn and woven into doormats and carpets. He was taught to make necklaces with beads, cardboard tubes and styrofoam scraps. He made beautiful curtains using all the items. He also learnt to make bangles, belts, bracelets, anklets, etc. The yarn also was used to draw boundary for the child. He played skipping with the rope and he enjoyed it very much. The observable changes in the overt behaviour of the child are illustrated graphically as in Figure 4.43.

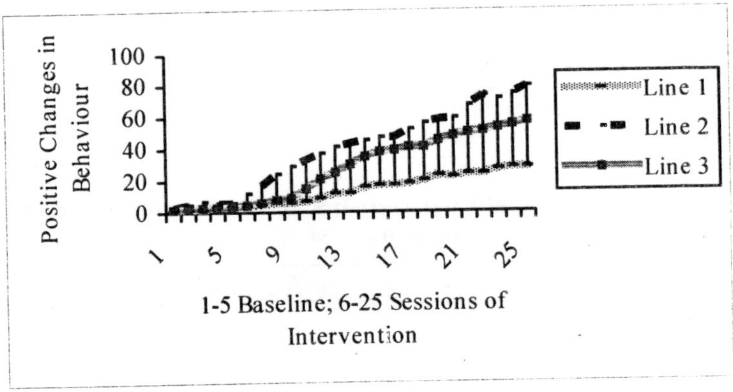

Figure 4.43: Experiment — Subject 34

The positive changes in behaviour were

Line 1. The subject learnt to work within a boundary.

Line 2. The subject developed vocational skills.

Line 3. He developed creativity and aesthetic sense.

Experiment 35 : Subject 35

Experiment 35 was aimed at helping the subject control his outbursts of anger and defiance, and to improve his gross and fine motor skills.

Banking on the child's natural inquisitiveness for computers, the vast potential of teaching him various concepts and skills was observed. But the child was using the computer to play various games. He knew the hardware of the computer so well that he knew the functions of each and every part. He was taught the basic skills in computer such as word processing, Microsoft office, paint options, etc. It was decided to expose the child to various softwares of the computer but he did not find it fascinating. When the service person came to repair the computer, he was found keenly observing. Even though he was non-verbal, he could type his doubts, queries and ideas on the computer. After the service person left, he opened the computer and he observed the mechanism and learnt to do minor repairs. He was recommended a course in 'Hardware' technology of the computer and he also learnt to service a television, a refrigerator and other appliances. A short-term certificate course helped him to open up a service centre and he could earn his living though he still lacked numeral skills and interpersonal skills. His mother took care of the shop as far as other issues were concerned so that he could focus on his job.

Table 4.36 : Behavioural Characteristics, Strengths and Drawbakcs of Subject 35

Age	*Sex*	*Beh. Char*	*Splinter Skill/ Obsession*	*Learning Strength/ Dom. Intelligence*	*Learning Deficit*
16	M	Non-verbal; had outbursts of anger and defiance; poor gross and fine motor skills.	Computers.	The ability to focus on narrow topics of interest; visual-spatial intelligence.	Inability to generalise or transfer information from one situation to the other.

He used a variety of strategies to help him maintain his focus on tasks and organise materials. These strategies allowed him to work more effectively and efficiently to achieve the relative goals and objectives.

The positive behaviour changes were:

Line 1. The subject's outbursts of anger and defiance dwindled down considerably.

Line 2. His gross and fine motor skills improved as he developed manual dexterity through his fixation for computers.

Line 3. He could engage in constructive activities and could develop vocational skills.

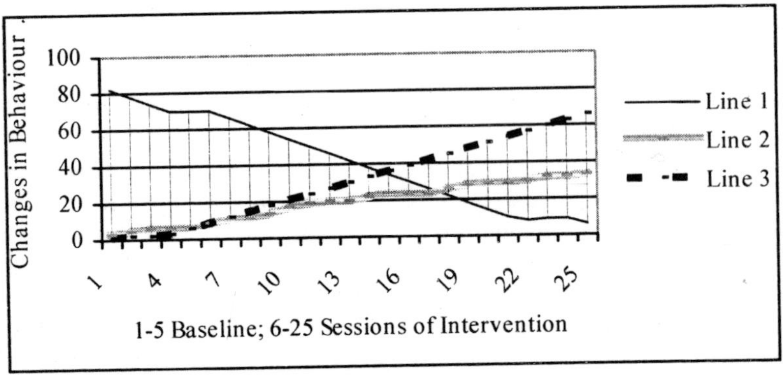

Figure 4.44: Experiment 35 — Subject 35

Experiment 36 : Subject 36

Experiment 36 was aimed at capitalising on the child's fixation for buttons to help him learn various concepts and skills.

The child had an unusual fancy for buttons. He could arrange them in different configurations to create different patterns, designs and figures. He lacked numerical skills totally. He was taught to count the number of buttons in each strip, at hand or in the box. This helped him to count the number of buttons accurately and he was asked to note them down. He was taught to maintain a 'button inventory'. He was also taught to make use of buttons for multifarious purposes such as decorating dresses, sticking buttons on different materials, making fancy belts, wall hangings and other craft items.

Table 4.37 : Behavioural Characteristics, Strengths and Drawbacks of Subject 36

Age	*Sex*	*Beh. Char*	*Splinter Skill/ Obsession*	*Learning Strength/ Dom. Intelligence*	*Learning Deficit*
11	M	Verbal; lack of social smile; limited language skills.	Buttons.	The ability to transfer visual world into motor patterns; visual-spatial intelligence.	Deficiency in understanding everyday situations; is overly anxious when asked to complete even simple tasks.

The child also learnt to name the colours and shown which type of button would go with certain dresses. He also learnt different values of attributes, such as size, colour and material. He was taught to decorate dresses with colour buttons. He learnt to make dresses. He attended sewing and tailoring classes and enjoyed this very much. He could pursue this as a vocation. A slight nasal speech pattern made him reluctant to communicate with others. The changes that occurred in the overt behaviour of the child are graphically presented in Figure 4.45.

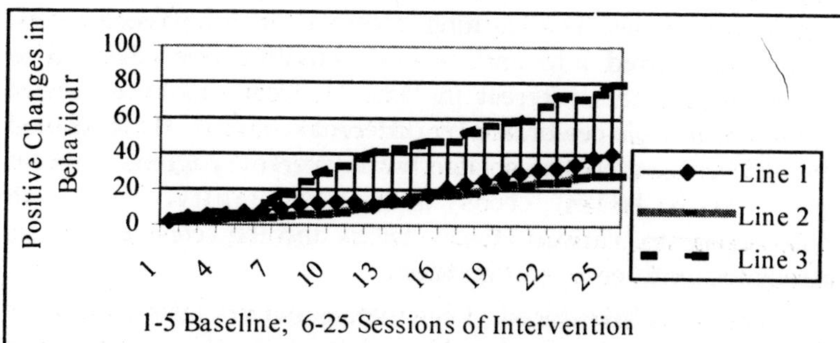

Figure 4.45: Experiment 36 — Subject 36

The positive behavioural changes were

Line 1. His understanding of everyday situations improved, as the child was observant.

Line 2. His anxiety and frustration decreased and he could focus on any given task.

Line 3. His vocabulary and enunciation improved greatly.

Experiment 37 — Subject 37

The aim in this case was to improve the child's ability to focus.

Table 4.38 : Behavioural Characteristics, Strengths and Drawbakcs of Subject 37

Age	*Sex*	*Beh. Char*	*Splinter Skill/ Obsession*	*Learning Strength/ Dom. Intelligence*	*Learning Deficit*
14	M	Verbal; has seizure disorders; lack of eye contact; abhors social contact.	Mythological figures.	The ability to organise information methodically and systematically; verbal-linguistic skills; visual-spatial intelligence	Inability to focus on relevant information.

The child was fond of mythological figures, icons, figurines of angels and fairies. The learning potential of this passion in the child was looked into and several activities weer devised to accommodate this interest in him. He came to know about different festivals celebrated by different religions. He identified the different symbols associated with different religions: crescent moon with Islam, cross with Christianity, fire with Zoroastrianism, various Hindu deities and the celestial vehicles associated with each god/goddess.

The child also evinced a keen interest in fairy tales and stories in general. He had exceptional linguistic skills. He was also good in writing. When instructions and directions were given to him in the form of stories, he understood them better. He was taught various social skills through social stories. An important part of reading and listening to stories is learning that they have endings. Sometimes the end of a story is a surprise, and sometimes it is not. Once the child became familiar with stories, he could create his own ending to a story.

The intervention team read a story to the child and when they came to the end of the story, they stopped reading. The child was asked to complete the story. Talking about the story's ending and the child's ending were compared. This activity enabled the child to make his own stories or give a different ending to other stories.

The combination of visual-spatial and verbal-linguistic intelligences in the child helped him to learn various skills quite effectively. He also made up his own stories and wrote them down. The positive changes in the behaviour of the subject are given in Figure 4.46.

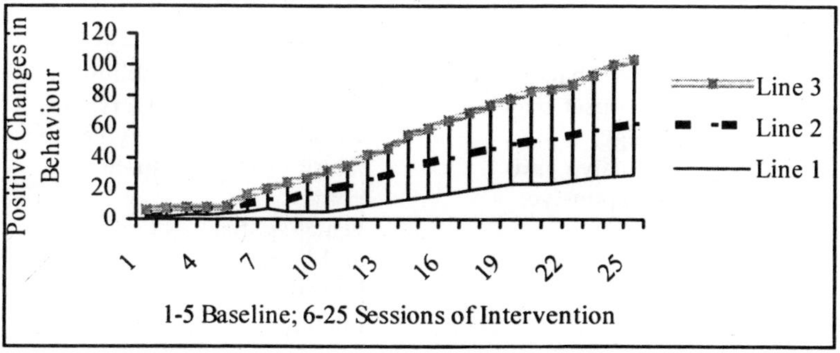

Figure 4.46 : Experiment 37 — Subject 37

The positive changes in behaviour were:

Line 1. He showed considerable progress in language and communications skills.

Line 2. His attention span and listening ability improved considerably.

Line 3. He was calm and more focused.

Experiment 38 : Subject 38

Experiment 38 was aimed at enabling the child to gain understanding of everyday situations through his fixation for cars.

The child would line up the cars and clap his hands after this was done. It was decided to add some visual clues and make the play interesting and purposeful. Roads were made with black poster paper and his sister placed a few cars on the road. She moved the cars on the road and after a few times, he started imitating this action. She also taught him a few words, such as the colour, model of the car, headlight, dashboard, glove box, brakes, accelerator, etc. Soon, he picked up the words and they even had a car race, which he enjoyed very much.

Table 4.39: Behavioural Characteristics, Strengths and Drawbacks of Subject 38

Age	*Sex*	*Beh. Char*	*Splinter Skill/ Obsession*	*Learning Strength/ Dom. Intelligence*	*Learning Deficit*
10	M	Non-verbal; gets upset by change; impulsive and unresponsive.	Cars	The ability to transfer visual world into motor patterns; visual-spatial and bodily-kinesthetic intelligences.	Inability to understand everyday life situations.

To make the activity more interesting, houses, gas station, theatre, shops were placed along the road. A car shed was also built for his house and more roads and road signs were added. For the festival of Navaratri (festival of dolls), when the dolls, are displayed, he put up a beautiful road with signs and landmarks for which he sought the help of his sister to glue some of the signs. He put his favourite doll in the car and he pretended that he was driving the car with the baby in the back seat. But he soon realised that the doll was bigger than the car and he asked his sister whether she could make or find a bigger car so that the doll could be made to sit in the back. His sister, with the help of her parents, made a car with a cardboard box; now he could put the doll in the back seat. While driving, he stopped the car in the middle and pretended to stop at a gas station to fill up the car with gas. He also learnt pretend play. He dashed the car against another car and said that he had a wreck.

His interest and fascination were not restricted to cars alone. He was also taught different types of transport. He expressed his desire to fly, and when his parents said that it costs a lot of money to buy air ticket, he brought his piggy bank and told his parents that the money in the piggy bank could be used to buy the air ticket. As an extension of this activity, he was taught to count money and thus his mathematical skills were developed. The changes that were observed in the subject are given in 4.47.

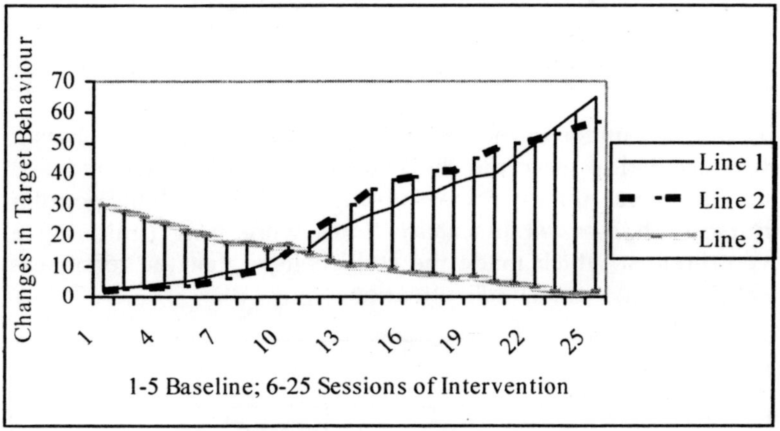

Figure 4.47: Experiment 38 — Subject 38

The positive behavioural changes were:

Line 1.The subject became more receptive and gained more understanding of everyday situations.

Line 2.He started paying attention to learning tasks.

Line 3. He was less impulsive and more responsive.

Experiment 39 : Subject 39

Capitalising on the subject's fixation for robots, he was taught social skills and control over the environment.

Table 4.40 : Behavioural Characteristics, Strengths and Drawbakcs of Subject 39

Age	*Sex*	*Beh. Char*	*Splinter Skill/ Obsession*	*Learning Strength/ Dom. Intelligence*	*Learning Deficit*
8	M	Non-verbal; anxious; physically aggressive; lack of eye contact; abhors social contact; echolalic.	Robots.	The ability to transfer visual world into motor patterns; musical and visual-spatial intelligences.	Inability to control motor and verbal responses.

Taking advantage of the subject's spontaneous love for robots it was decided to teach the child various concepts. The child was taught several nursery rhymes through the robot. All the popular nursery rhymes set in catchy tunes were sung (imitating a ventriloquist which made the child believe that the robot was singing) to get the child's attention.

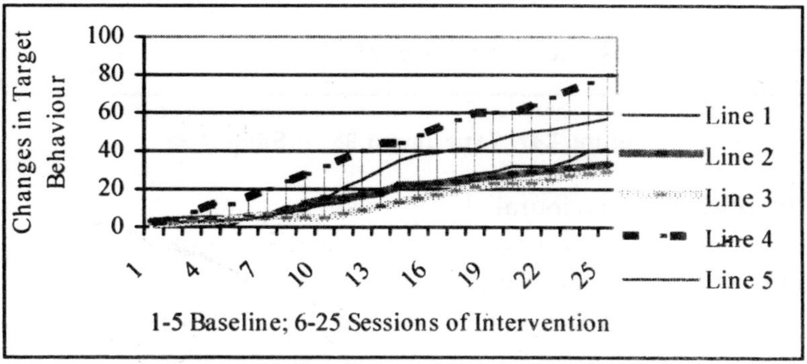

Figure 4.48 : Experiment 39 — Subject 39

The voice was modulated by exaggerating the high and low sounds as well as loud and soft sounds. This helped the child to develop listening skills and auditory awareness. Several pictures and models of birds and animals were also brought in to show the child how a bird sings in high pitch and a bear growls in low pitch. This enabled him to learn the names of various bird and animals. He soon learnt to imitate not only the sounds made by animals and birds but also the movements, such as flying like a bird, swimming like a fish, galloping like a horse and hopping like a bunny/kangaroo.

The child enjoyed all the activities and he started making several musical instruments with empty coconut shells, twigs, rubber bands, lids of cans, etc. He knew nothing about his personal space and boundaries and in order to teach him these concepts, a skipping rope, masking tapes and marked lines on the floors with chalk piece were used. The positive changes in the behaviour of the subject are given in Figure 4.48

The Positive changes in behaviour were:

Line 1. He developed listening skills and auditory awareness.

Line 2. With the help of robots and musical intelligence, he could improve his bodily-kinesthetic intelligence.

Line 3. He developed both large motor skills and small motor skills.

Line 4. He learnt social interaction and cooperation.

Line 5. His ablutions behaviour improved.

Experiment 40 — Subject 40

Experiment 40 was aimed at enabling the subject to utilise her passion for quilting and to teach innumerable skills.

Table 4.41: Behavioural Characteristics, Strengths and Drawbacks of Subject 40

Age	*Sex*	*Beh. Char*	*Splinter Skill/ Obsession*	*Learning Strength/ Dom. Intelligence*	*Learning Deficit*
8	M	Non-verbal; anxious; physically aggressive; lack of eye contact; abhors social contact; echolalic.	Robots.	The ability to transfer visual world into motor patterns; musical and visual-spatial intelligences.	Inability to control motor and verbal responses.

Subject 40 had a strong passion for quilts and quilting. As the first step, the child was asked to collect a variety of different textured and coloured fabric and was taught to cut them in different shapes and sizes. She was also taught the differences in materials, such as cotton, silk, nylon, polyester, rayon, etc. She was also taught to classify the materials according to prints such as plaid, solid, stripes, florals, etc.

Initially the child cut the fabric into different sizes and shapes and glued them on to paper and cardboard to create different geometrical patterns. The child's mathematical and visual-spatial skills were made use of. The subject had a special fascination for geometrical shapes and what was amazing about the child was that he could draw a perfect circle even without a compass. She was taught to make quilts and he enjoyed this activity. She could focus more on given task.

Quilting provided an excellent opportunity for her to develop and reinforce eye-hand coordination. She could also follow directions better. Quilting also enabled her to expand and reinforce her other learning activities, such as oral language skills, communications skills, numeral skills, social skills and functional skills. It also helped her to relax. The changes in her behaviour of the subject are depicted graphically in Figure 4.49.

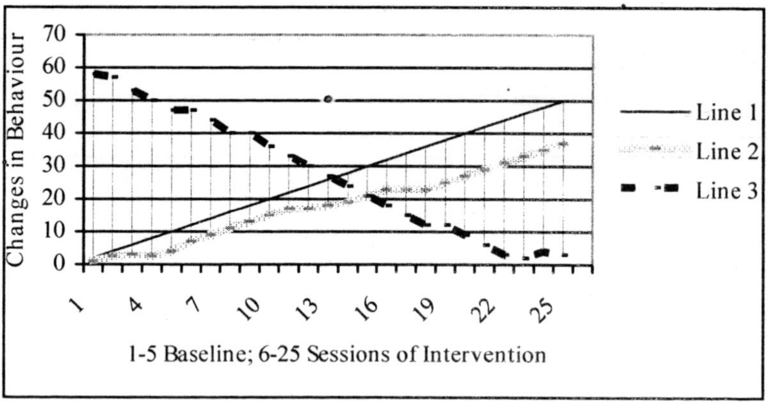

Figure 4.49: Experiment 40 — Subject 40

The positive behavioural changes were:

Line 1. Improvement in communications, numerical, social, language and functional skills.

Line 2. The child developed eye-hand coordination and fine motor skills.

Line 3. Her temper tantrums and aggressiveness reduced considerably.

Experiment 41: Subject 41

Experiment 41 was aimed at utilising the subject's organisational skills to help him learn functional skills.

Table 4.42: Behavioural Characteristics, Strengths and Drawbacks of Subject 41

Age	*Sex*	*Beh.Char*	*Splinter Skill/ Obsession*	*Learning Strength/ Dom. Intelligence*	*Learning Deficit*
7	M	Verbal; hyperactive; physically aggressive; abhors social contact; motor clumsiness.	Airplanes/ helicopters	The ability to organise information methodically and systematically; visual-spatial intelligence.	Has motor planning difficulties; bumps into things.

Subject 41 was fond of airplanes. He was found playing with the models of airplane all the time. The parents were asked to buy books with pictures of airplanes in it. He was taught to make paper airplanes. He made them in various designs and his brother and sister and other children in the neighbourhood joined him. He enjoyed it so much that he could even tell which plane would go the 'farthest', the 'longest' and the 'highest'.

He collected pictures of airplanes. He could name the models and reel out the dates of major air crashes and the underlying reason behind the crashes. He even voiced his concern about terrorism. He was especially fond of concords and he expressed his desire to travel in a concord. He came up with his own models of aircraft and gave fancy names to his models.

He could describe the story of the first manned flight in Paris in 1783, in a hot-air balloon built by the French brothers Joseph and Etienne Montgolfier in glorious terms. He even named one of his aircrafts 'Monty' after his hero. His interest in aviation could be encouraged and developed further and this interest could be used to widen his horizon of learning. As he was quite good in verbal-linguistic skills, he helped his peers in their project work. He showed signs of aggressiveness every now and then when he did not have anything to do. Changes in behaviour brought forth by the implementation of intervention are delineated in Figure 4.50.

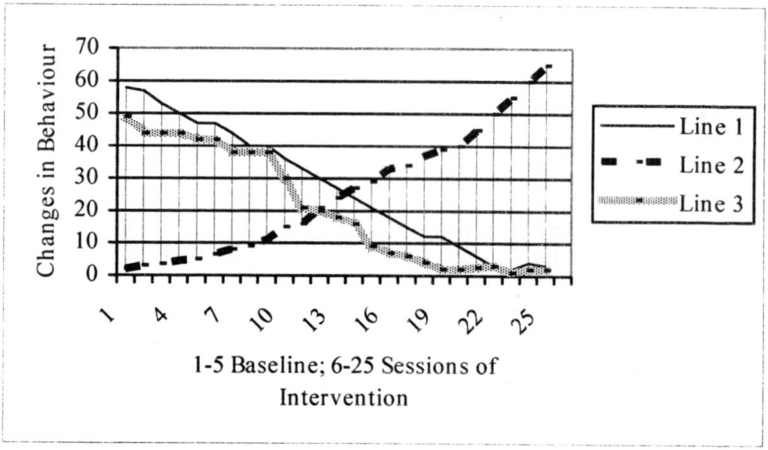

Figure 4.50 : Experiment 41 — Subject 41

The positive changes in behaviour were:

Line 1. He overcame his motor planning difficulties and clumsiness considerably.

Line 2. He made use of his splinter skill to help other children.

Line 3. His motor clumsiness dwindled down to a great extent.

Experiment 42 : Subject 42

Experiment 42 was aimed at enabling the subject to improve his social and language skills and to help him to understand changes in the environment.

Subject 42 had a fascination for spinning objects and as they lived in a neighbourhood where there were a lot of potters, he kept observing them for hours together. He was oversensitive to touch and sound, and he did not even touch play dough at school. However, when he was given an opportunity to work with the potter's wheel, he did not show any sign of aversion. He made a dish, which he kept very safe and he was proud to display it in the showcase. It was found that he responded better when people spoke to him in a low, soft voice.

Table 4.43: Behavioural Characteristics, Strengths and Drawbacks of Subject 42

Age	*Sex*	*Beh. Char*	*Splinter Skill/ Obsession*	*Learning Strength/ Dom. Intelligence*	*Learning Deficit*
13	M	Non-verbal; hypersensitive to touch; echolalic; abhors social contact.	Pottery.	Attachment to objects rather than people; musical and visual-spatial intelligences.	Resists change and gets upset by change.

He also focused more and was able to complete a task when melodious music was played in the background. He was put in a short-term course on 'ceramic designing' but he did not like the programme. He quit the course without completing it. He preferred the crude -type traditional wheel used by the potters. It was decided to give him more practice in this line. He showed signs of improvement in social skills but his language skills did not improve much and he was still echolalic. Changes in the overt behaviour of the subject are given in Figure 4.51.

The positive changes in behaviour were:

Line 1. The subject showed considerable progress in social skills.

Line 2. His hypersensitivity to touch dwindled down to a large extent.

Line 3. He initiated social interaction.

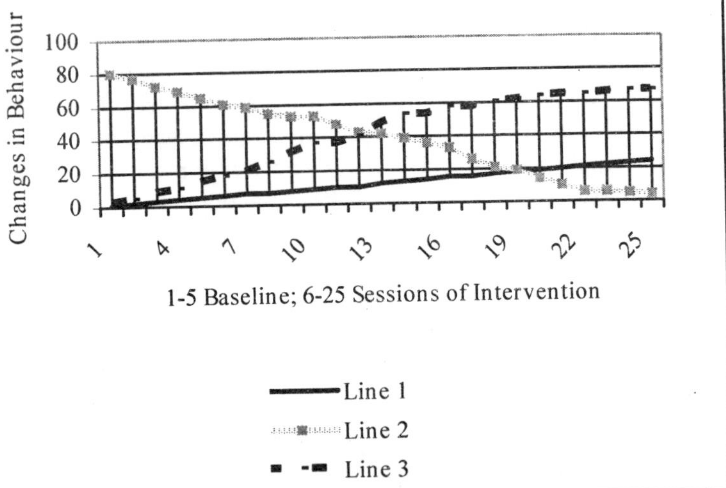

Figure 4.51 : Experiment 42 — Subject 42

Experiment 43 : Subject 43

Experiment 43 was aimed at providing appropriate visual cues and organisers and enable the child to understand things in proper perspectives or in totality.

Table 4.44 : Behavioural Characteristics, Strengths and Drawbacks of Subject 43

Age	*Sex*	*Beh. Char*	*Splinter Skill/ Obsession*	*Learning Strength/ Dom. Intelligence*	*Learning Deficit*
18	M	Non-verbal; aggressive; has seizure disorders; lack of eye contact; abhors social contact.	Shoes, sandals, footwear.	The ability to rely on visual cues and visual organisers; visual-spatial intelligence order.	Inability to retrieve information in a logical and sequential

Subject 43 had a fascination for shoes and sandals. When someone visited their house, he was found playing with the footwear and hiding them. It was embarrassing for his parents. But he did not know what type of footwear he should wear whenever he went out. He did not understand the differences among them. A semantic map were prepared to show him different types of footwear.

With the help of the semantic map, he knew the different types of footwear. He was also given pictures of them and was asked to match a particular shoe with its pair. He could do this perfectly well but when he was given real shoes, he had problems. He had problems with left and right shoes and he always put it on the wrong foot. He was asked to put the shoes on dummies and soon he learnt to put them on the appropriate foot. Pictures of footwear were made in different colours and the child was asked to match the pairs appropriately.

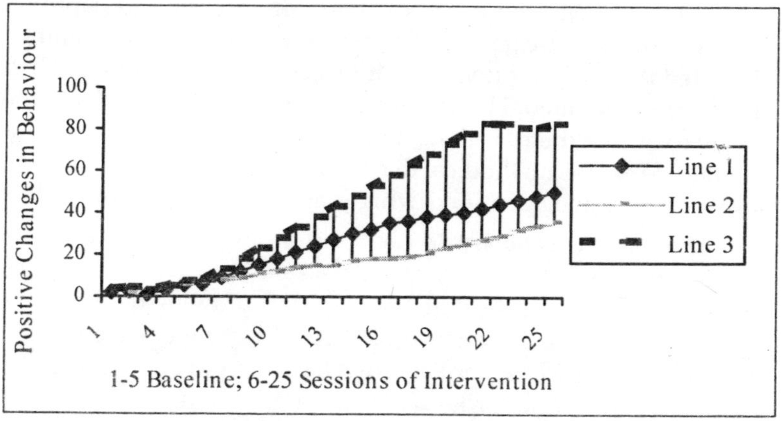

Figure 4.52 : Experiment 43 — Subject 43

He was also taught different materials that were used to make different types of footwear, such as leather, rubber, plastic, acrylic, canvas, etc. He learnt to identify the materials, and the merits and demerits of each material. He also learnt to polish and maintain the footwear properly.

The parents were advised to put in either Leather Technology or in Footwear Designing courses offered by polytechnics. The child underwent six-month course in Footwear Designing and completed the course successfully. Positive changes observed in the behaviour of the child are given in Figure 4.52.

The positive changes in behaviour were:

Line 1. The subject's obsession for shoes was capitalised on to teach him vocational skills.

Line 2. He learnt to analyse, organise and integrate information to derive meaning.

Line 3. He learnt to focus on important information and to visualise different things and perspectives in totality.

Experiment 44 : Subject 44

The aim of the experiment in this case was to enhance the subject's social skills and to reach him out through his fascination for trees and plants.

Subject 44 was fond of trees and plants and he was happy to play outdoors in the garden. The bird-song fascinated him and he imitated the birdcall often, even though he did not respond when his name was called. He was even taught to throw crumbs to the birds to attract them. He was taught to plant, grow and care for plants. He was so methodical that he even documented the growth of the plants and identified what plants needed to grow.

The child was taught to carry out an experiment with bean seeds. He could draw pictures of trees and plants. He had such exceptional visual skills that he could start drawing the tip of the leaf and complete the picture of a tree. Even though he did not have to draw in the sequential order, he could put pictures of plant growth in sequential order. He was taught the different parts of the plants that people eat: leaves such as cabbage, greens; roots such as beet, potato; flowers such as cauliflower, plantain; seeds and pods such as beans, corns, nuts; fruits such as oranges, bananas. He could identify different trees such as neem, mango, coconut, palm, etc. His knowledge and interest in trees was so amazing that he could identify plants that grow in different habitats such as cactus in the desert and water hyacinth, lilies, lotus in the lake. Positive changes in the behaviour of the subject are given in Figure 4.53.

Table 4.45 :Behavioural Characteristics, Strengths and Drawbacks of Subject 44

Age	*Sex*	*Beh. Char*	*Splinter Skill/ Obsession*	*Learning Strength/ Dom. Intelligence*	*Learning Deficit*
9	M	Verbal; hypersensitive to sounds; echolalic; abhors social contact.	Trees and plants.	The ability to control and scan important and relevant information; Visual-spatial intelligence	Inability to generalise or transfer information from one situation to other.

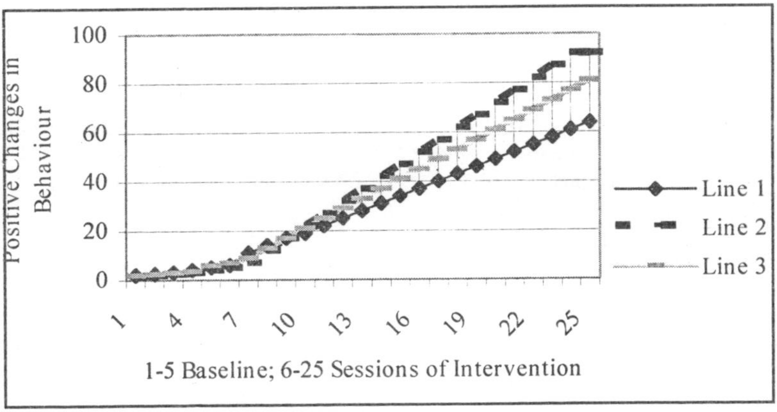

Figure 4.53 : Experiment 4.44 Subject 4.44

The positive changes in behaviour were:

Line 1. The subject's ability to retrieve information in a sequential order improved.

Line 2. He became more methodical and improved his documentation skills.

Line 3. The activities and learning experiences enhanced his visual-spatial, logical and bodily kinesthetic intelligences.

Experiment 45 : Subject 45

The subject had a fixation for furniture. He was fond of wood sculpting that at the time of construction of their house, he obtained small pieces of lumber. He glued various pieces together and arranged them in different ways to create a doll house furniture. Various learning situations and opportunities were provided. The child was given boxes of varying sizes, from a jewellery box to a shoebox, and he created his own unique configurations; he used bits of cloth, ribbon and sparklers to decorate the furniture. He even used sewing spools to create new designs of furniture.

Table 4.46 : Behavioural Characteristics, Strengths and Drawbacks of Subject 45

Age	*Sex*	*Beh. Char*	*Splinter Skill/ Obsession*	*Learning Strength/ Dom. Intelligence*	*Learning Deficit*
13	M	Non-verbal; hyperactive; lack of eye contact; abhors social contact.	Furniture designing; carpentry.	The ability to use visual information meaningfully; visual-spatial intelligence.	Inability to initiate communication.

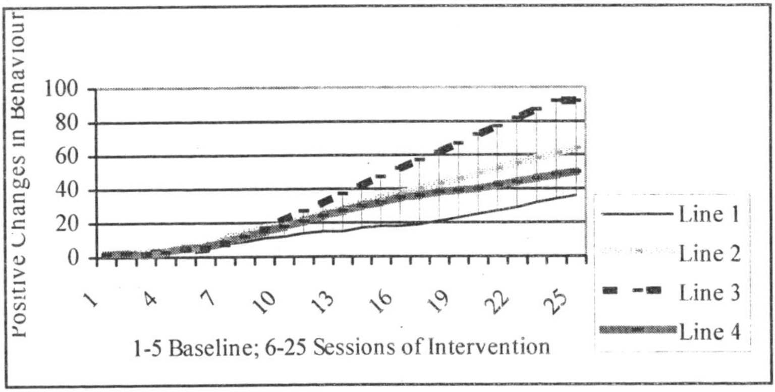

Figure 4.54 : Experiment 45 — Subject 45

The child was so innovative in his uses of boxes that he used boxes and crates made of deal-wood as a playhouse by cutting doors and windows in it. He even taped curtains on the windows and flowers outside. He used the same box as an aircraft and a spaceship. In the beginning, he was so possessive that he did not allow anyone to come near there objects. But later on, he enjoyed sharing them with other children and allowed them to decorate and modify his playhouse also. Positive changes observed in the child are given in Figure 4.54.

The positive changes in behaviour were:

Line 1. The subject initiated communication and understood turn taking.

Line 2. He learnt to be more creative and innovative.

Line 3. He learnt to generate alternatives and solve problems.

Line 4. He himself to new and novel situations.

Experiment 46 : Subject 46

Experiment 46 was aimed at enabling the child to develop social skills and to talk coherently.

Subject 46 was always seen wringing her hands and it was soon clear that she derived sensory stimulation and pleasure in this activity. It was decided to channelise this into a socially acceptable and useful activity. As a first step, the subject was taught basket making with plastic wires. As expected, she enjoyed this activity and she learnt to make wire baskets in various designs. She was also taught knitting and crocheting but her favourite pastime was to make fancy baskets in different configurations.

Table 4.47 : Behavioural Characteristics, Strengths and Drawbacks of Subject 46

Age	*Sex*	*Beh. Char*	*Splinter Skill/ Obsession*	*Learning Strength/ Dom. Intelligence*	*Learning Deficit*
8	F	Verbal; talks incoherently; poor social skills.	Hand wringing.	The ability to concentrate on narrow topics of interest; visual-spatial intelligence.	Inability to process information and modulate or integrate sensory information.

The child was also taught embroidery and she liked animal motif in embroidery. She learnt different types of stitches and also different types of materials that could be used for embroidery. She was also taught machine embroidery and she picked it up very soon. She also learnt a lot about the nuances of embroidery, colour scheme, designs and patterns and she traced all the patterns and designs in a notebook. She was very methodical in her work. Figure 4.55 gives a vignette of the changes in the behaviour of the subject.

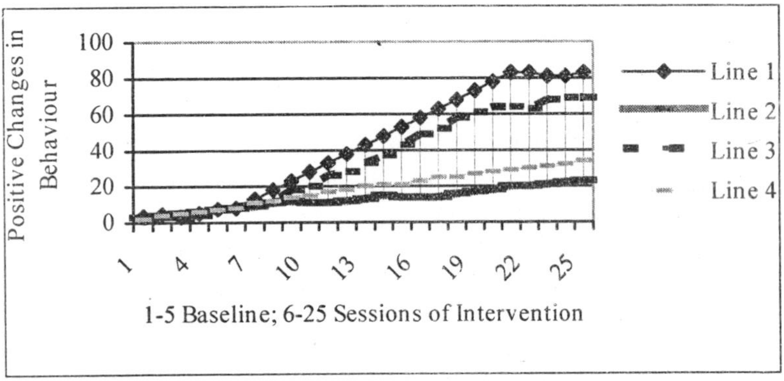

Figure 4.55: Experiment 46 — Subject 46

The positive changes in behaviour were:

Line 1. The subject learnt about colours, colour scheme, designs etc.

Line 2. She could change unacceptable behaviour to constructive behaviour.

Line 3. She also learnt to talk coherently.

Line 4. The activities provided to her helped her to enhance her social and functional skills.

Experiment 47 : Subject 47

Experiment 47 was aimed at providing structure and visual cues to help the child learn new concepts.

Table 4.48 : Behavioural Characteristics, Strengths and Drawbacks of Subject 47

Age	*Sex*	*Beh. Char*	*Splinter Skill/ Obsession*	*Learning Strength/ Dom. Intelligence*	*Learning Deficit*
10	M	Non-verbal; anxious; has seizure disorders; lack of eye contact; abhors social contact.	Telephone directory.	The ability to rely on concrete, visual cues; phenomenal memory; visual-spatial intelligence	Inability to perceive and organise events in time and understand language.

Subject 47 had such a phenomenal memory that he remembered all the telephone numbers in the first five pages of the telephone directory. It was decided to teach him numerical skills, functional skills and communication skills through this splinter skill in him. The moment he got up in the morning, he was seen totally engrossed in memorising the numbers.

As soon as he came to school, he would get restless when he was asked to line up for assembly. He would throw tantrums half way through the prayers and when the teacher gave him the directory, he calmed down. To modify this behaviour, he was told before he went to assembly that as soon as the prayer was over, he could come to class and read the directory. He continued throwing tantrums even after this. The underlying reason for his tantrums needed to be investigated. It was found that he did not understand the concept 'over' and he wanted some concrete pointers. It was specified to him that after singing the national anthem, he could come to class, along with his classmates and read the directory. This helped him to understand the instruction and he stopped throwing tantrums.

He was also given instructions to memorise 10 numbers from the telephone directory, and then continue with his regular class work,such as learning numbers, letters of the alphabet and other skills. This provided the structure to his activities and he became more focused. Figure 4.56 delineates the positive changes in his behaviour.

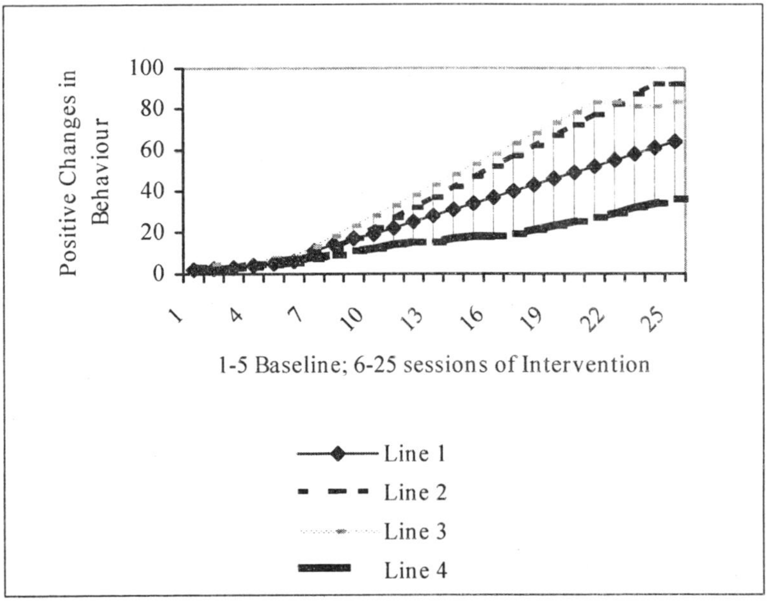

Figure 4.56: Experiment 47 — Subject 47

The positive changes in behaviour were:

Line 1. Improvement in language and numerical skills.

Line 2. Improvement in his level of understanding.

Line 3. Improvement in social engagement.

Line 4. Concrete, visual cues enabled him to perceive and organise events in time.

Experiment 48 : Subject 48

Experiment 48 was aimed at enabling the child to learn concepts through his fondness for marbles.

Subject 48 had a huge collection of marbles and it was decided to teach him various concepts through his passion for marbles. He learnt to count the number of marbles and sorted them according to size and colour. He also named and identified the colours. He could also play various games with his marbles. Playing with marbles enhanced his numerical skills, functional skills, and communications skills. He was taught addition and subtraction. He soon became adept in abacus. He also learnt to make unique mosaic patterns using the marbles.

Table 4.49: Behavioural Characteristics, Strengths and Drawbacks of Subject 48

Age	*Sex*	*Beh. Char*	*Splinter Skill/ Obsession*	*Learning Strength/ Dom. Intelligence*	*Learning Deficit*
7	M	Non-verbal; hypersensitive to sounds; lack of eye contact; stressful; lacked direction and focus.	Marbles.	The ability to learn and repeat long routines; visual-spatial intelligence.	Is upset by any change in routine; responds unpredictably to noise.

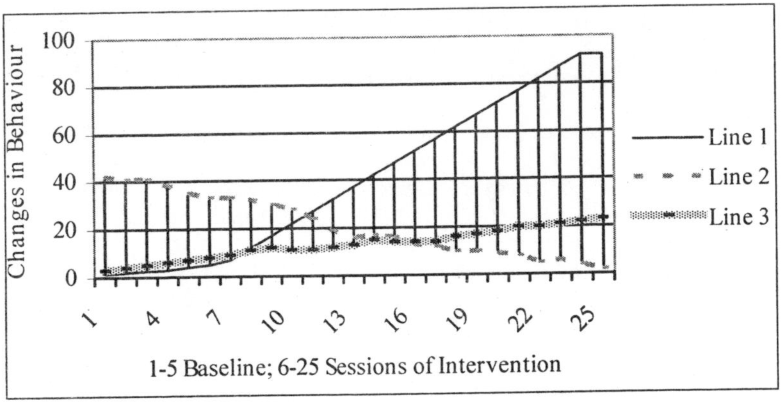

Figure 4.57 : Experiment 48 — Subject 48

The child learned to get ready for school by looking at a sequence of drawings that explained step by step various things he had to do. When he put pn his uniform his mother sat on the bed to make sure that he was following all the steps. She was admitted in the hospital for delivery of her second child and the child threw tantrums; it was difficult to understand why he was behaving thus. When the father explained to the mother the events and when the tantrums occurred, the mother could understand the underlying reason. She explained to him when he came to see her that she would come home in five days and she told him that his father would watch over him until she returned. The change in routine, when it was explained to him, put him at ease and he could follow the instructions. Figure 4.57 provides details about the changes in the behaviour of the subject.

The positive changes in behaviour were:

Line 1. When opportunities were provided, the child learnt to follow directions and self-management.

Line 2. Stress was reduced when changes in routine were explained clearly to him.

Line 3. He learnt to be more creative and self-directed.

Experiment 49 : Subject 49

Experiment 49 was aimed at enabling the child to improve and integrate reading, writing and spelling.

Table 4.50 : Behavioural Characteristics, Strengths and Drawbacks of Subject 49

Age	*Sex*	*Beh.Char*	*Splinter Skill/ Obsession*	*Learning Strength/ Dom. Intelligence*	*Learning Deficit*
8	M	Verbal; anxious; lack of eye contact; abhors social contact.	Newspaper	The ability to transfer visual world into motor patterns; exceptional reading skills in English; visual-spatial intelligence.	Inability to speak and write in English

Subject 49 had a fascination for newspaper and he also often tore them to pieces. He was able to glean the main points in texts if they were highlighted. He was given old magazines and newspapers and asked to glue the torn pieces on to a paper in different shapes to create various patterns. When the motions were channelised in a positive way, he found himself occupied in a useful manner.

A word bank was developed New words, as the child learnt them, were added and filed in a box. Frequent experiences were provided for the child to search for a specific word. The child was helped to make sets of word cards and games and language games were played with him. The child cut strips of words from the newspaper and the small word strips were filed in the word bank. The child was encouraged to pull the strips from the bank and use the words in meaningful sentences.

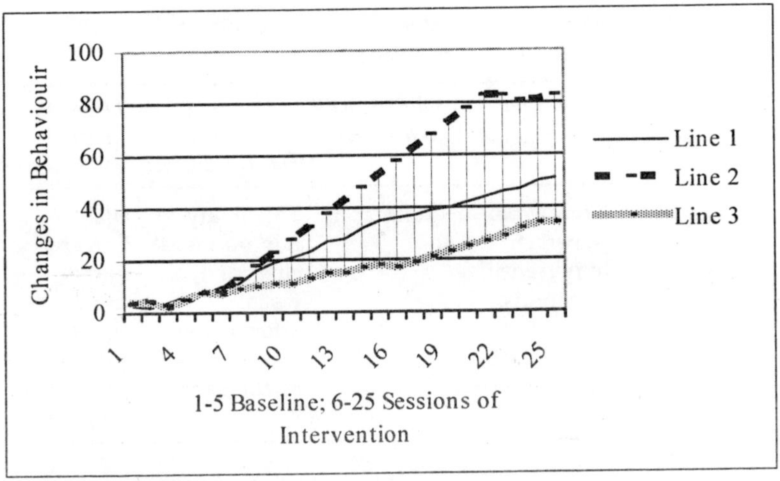

Figure 4.58 : Experiment 49 — Subject 49

Even though the subject was good at writing, he did not know how to initiate the writing process. When, he was provided physical assistance by the author placing her middle and fourth fingers under the his palm (of the dominant hand), he could write easier. But often he did not know where to begin. A cross was put and he was asked to use it as a starting point, thus he could write. This type of 'cognitive visual strategies' enabled him to improve his writing skills.

The changes that took place in the subject are given in Figure 4.58.

The positive behavioural changes were

Line 1. The subject learnt most basic language concepts systematically.

Line 2. He understood the visual motor integration process that is involved in writing.

Line 3. He developed fine motor skills and he learnt where to start on a paper without being prompted.

Experiment 50 : Subject 50

Experiment 50 was aimed at teaching new skills and concepts by providing alternatives to the subject.

Table 4.51: Behavioural Characteristics, Strengths and Drawbacks of Subject 50

Age	*Sex*	*Beh. Char*	*Splinter Skill/ Obsession*	*Learning Strength/ Dom. Intelligence*	*Learning Deficit*
12	M	Non-verbal; hyperactive; hypersensitive to sounds; screaming and shouting; self-destructive.	Calligraphy.	The ability to rely on visual clues and visual information; visual-spatial intelligence.	Inability to perceive and organise events in time and understand language.

As the subject was hypersensitive to sounds, he screamed many times a day, closing his ears and nothing could be done to make him stop. It was discovered later on that he screamed when he wanted to work on his calligraphy or when he had a sore throat. He often caught cold often and when some soothers were given or when he was given an opportunity to work on his calligraphy, he stopped screaming. Screaming was the only way by which he could communicate his needs, his desires and problems.

The intervention plan was elaborate and included several visual cue cards. The child had to point out the body part that was hurting. As the child did not know where his throat was, as it was not marked and visible in the picture, he could not indicate that he had a sore throat. A concrete visual clue was needed. The picture of the medicine bottle with the name of the medicine as it is printed on the bottle were drawn. The child learnt to associate his sore throat with the picture of the medicine that he pointed out the picture whenever he had a sore throat.

Variations were also added. The child joined other kids in the neighbourhood in playing 'blindman's bluff' and at that time, he understood that it was all right to scream. So whenever the child wanted to scream, he would ask someone to blindfold him so that he could scream. He enjoyed this game very much. This game provided the legitimate way for him to scream, make noise and release his stress and tension. Whenever he wanted to work on the calligraphy, he was asked to bring his notebook, special pen and other supplies, instead of screaming. Figure 4.59 highlights the changes in his behaviour.

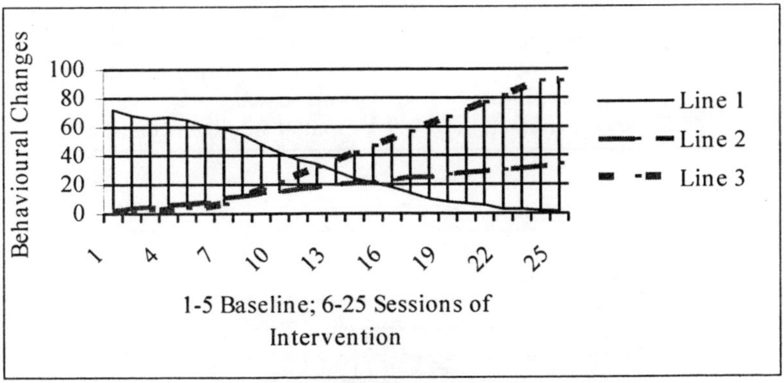

Figure 4.59 : Experiment 50 — Subject 50

The positive behaviour changes were:

Line 1. His screaming behaviour dwindled down.

Line 2. Organising and structuring the activities helped him to eliminate his screaming behaviour.

Line 3. He also learnt new concepts, skills and rules.

Experiment 51 : Subject 51

Experiment 51 was aimed at enabling the subject to develop social and functional skills.

The subject had a fixation for coins; she put them in her piggy bank but was always removing all the coins and playing. What reinforced this activity in the child was the stimulation of handling the coins. The child was first taught to sort out the coins according to different denominations. Though the child had problems initially, she soon learnt to sort them out. The next step in the process was to identify the value that is etched on the coins. She soon learnt the value of the coins.

Table 4.52 : Behavioural Characteristics, Strengths and Drawbacks of Subject 51

Age	*Sex*	*Beh. Char*	*Splinter Skill/ Obsession*	*Learning Strength/ Dom. Intelligence*	*Learning Deficit*
7	F	Non-verbal; withdrawn; self-hurting; lack of eye contact; abhors social contact.	Coins.	The ability to take in chunks of information; verbal-linguistic and visual-spatial intelligences.	Inability to follow even simple commands.

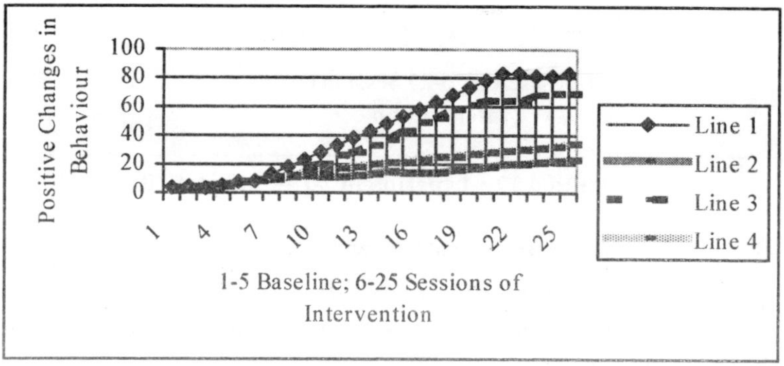

Figure 4.60 : Experiment 51 — Subject 51

The subject was taught to add up the coins that she sorted out into different denominations. This activity taught her the computational skills and she learnt all these in a natural environment. She was fond of hard candies and her father helped her to get them from the petty shop. She was asked to find out the number of candies that she would be getting for a particular amount. Each time she came up with the right answer, she was rewarded; this reinforced her mathematical skills and she learnt addition and subtraction very easily.

As the child enjoyed social stories, several stories were made to teach and to reinforce her numeral, mathematical skills and she was also provided enough opportunities and experiences where she could put the skill to practical use. Figure 4.60 sheds light on the changes that took place in her behaviour.

The positive changes in behaviour were:

*Line 1.*The fixation of the child was utilised to teach her numerical and computational skills.

*Line 2.*The subject also learnt that money is required to 'buy' things.

*Line 3.*The child learnt the practical uses of money.

*Line 4.*The subject also learnt several social skills and concepts.

Experiment 52 : Subject 52

Experiment 52 was aimed at enabling the child develop new skills through his fascination for crayons.

Table 4.53 : Behavioural Characteristics, Strengths and Drawbacks of Subject 52

Age	*Sex*	*Beh. Char*	*Splinter Skill/ Obsession*	*Learning Strength/ Dom. Intelligence*	*Learning Deficit*
9	M	Non-verbal; hypersensitive to sounds; socially withdrawn.	Crayons.	The ability to remember information for a long time; visual-spatial intelligence	Inability to control thoughts, movements and responses.

The child had a special fascination for crayons. He would not use them for drawing or colouring but he would them in his mouth and he would chew on them. A few cookies, finger fries, French fries etc. were given to him to chew on. Various pictures were drawn and colouring done. The child observed these activities for a few days and on the seventh day he offered his crayons with which draw. He used the author's hands to draw; this is an example of a unique characteristic in children with autism - using adult's hands as tools.

When he was given a paper and a few crayons to draw, he did not know what to do with them; he started crying and he again resorted to chewing the crayon. But when his hand was held to help him to draw, he did well. The next day when the he was given paper with crayons, he started drawing and colouring the figures he drew.

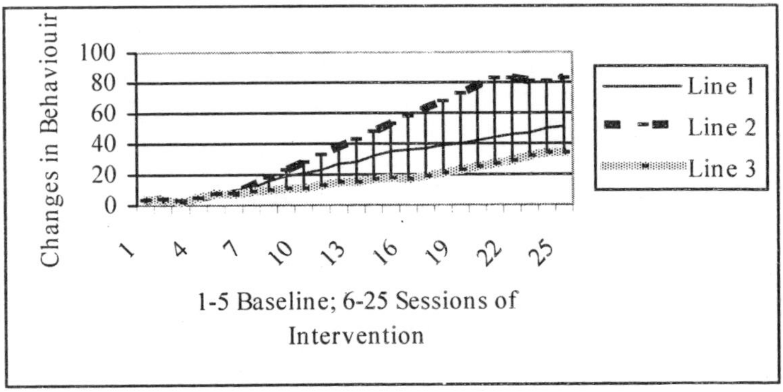

Figure 4.61 : Experiment 52 — Subject 52

The child was taught several activities that he could do with crayons, such as ironing the crayon shavings on a wax paper and creating designs, making self-portraits with crayons, tracing various shapes, playing dot-to-dot with them, etc. The child was soon quite adept in his usage of crayons that he could create fancy greeting cards with crayon shavings. Figure 4.61 portrays the positive behavioural changes of the subject.

The positive behaviour changes were:

Line 1. The child developed small motor control.

Line 2. His eye-hand coordination improved.

Line 3. His language skills improved.

Experiment 53 : Subject 53

The aim in this case was to enhance the play and communications skills in the subject.

Table 4.54 : Behavioural Characteristics, Strengths and Drawbacks of Subject 53

Age	*Sex*	*Beh. Char*	*Splinter Skill/ Obsession*	*Learning Strength/ Dom. Intelligence*	*Learning Deficit*
12	M	Non-verbal; anxious; physically aggressive.	Match-boxes.	The ability to understand concrete, context-based information; visual-spatial intelligence.	Inability to indulge in parallel play.

Capitalising on the child's interest in matchboxs, a number of activities and games were devised to teach various skills and concepts to the subject. The reinforcer in this activity was first identified and it was found that the noise made by the matchsticks in the matchbox was the stimulating factor. As the child was musically inclined, the the child was helped to make rattles. The child found an old tin and filled it up with pebbles, seeds, marbles, etc. He was also taught to make a gong by attaching a rope to a metal plate and striking the plate with a spoon. The child enjoyed these activities and he made several musical instruments making use of the materials that were available to him in the environment.

The child was taught to make a drum by making holes on each side of a round tin, threading a thick piece of string through each hole and making a knot on it on the inside to hold it in place. He tied a bead on the other end of the string. When the tin was swung from side to side, the beads made a sound against the tin. The child experimented and explored with various instruments and identified the different sounds made by different instruments. He was also taught to find out the different kinds of sounds he could make with his body, such as clapping his hands, snapping his fingers, tapping with toes, stamping his feet, whistling and singing. Figure 4.62 describes the positive changes in the observable behaviour of the subject.

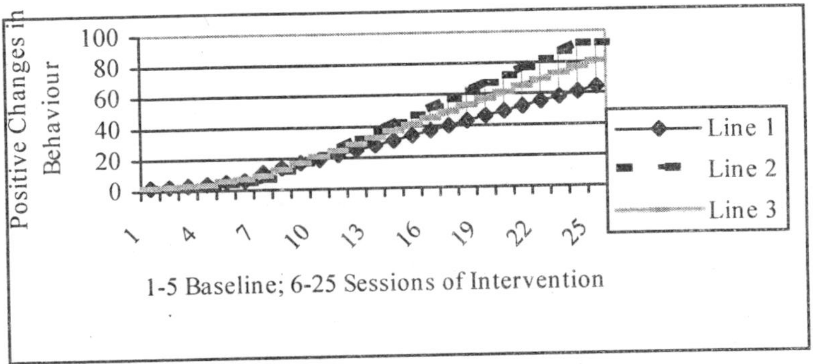

Figure 4.62 : Experiment 53 — Subject 53

The positive behaviour changes were:

Line 1. His listening skills and auditory awareness improved dramatically.

Line 2. Music contributed to the speech and language development in him.

Line 3. Music also encouraged his creative expression and provided a release for his feelings and frustrations.

Line 4. Music also provided him opportunities for social interaction and cooperation.

Experiment 54 : Subject 54

Experiment 54 was aimed at enabling the child to develop social and communication skills.

Subject 54 had a huge collection of toothpicks and this interest in the child was utilised as a teaching agent. Her Down syndrome has resulted in a significant cognitive disability. She enjoys being with her peers and has benefited from integrated experiences in the past. The intervention team has developed an Individual Transition Plan (ITP) that focuses on improving computational and social interaction skills (key skills in the work environment). The child can benefit much by cooperative learning, peer interaction and group work.

Table 4.55: Behavioural Characteristics, Strengths and Drawbacks of Subject 54

Age	*Sex*	*Beh. Char*	*Splinter Skill/ Obsession*	*Learning Strength/ Dom. Intelligence*	*Learning Deficit*
11	F	Non-verbal; has down syndrome; withdrawn; lack of eye contact; abhors social contact.	Toothpicks.	The ability to remember information for a long time; rote memory; visual-spatial intelligence.	Inability to generalise information.

The child was taught computational skills by counting the number of toothpicks, and she was asked to divide them into bundles of hundreds. She was able to do this slowly but later she picked up accuracy and speed. She was asked to find appropriate boxes to put them in. Initially she brought huge boxes but later she collected empty boxes of uniform size to put the toothpicks in the was also given opportunities to draw something on the box and colour it. She made little happy faces and glued them on to the toothpicks.

The subject learnt to count, sort, compare and put them together. These activities helped her to establish one-to-one correspondence, to learn patterning, counting, number meaning and recognition, addition and subtraction, etc. Manipulative materials, such as toothpicks, provided the concrete experiences for her. Familiar objects made the learning experiences more enjoyable. The positive changes that were observed in her behaviour are given in Figure 4.63.

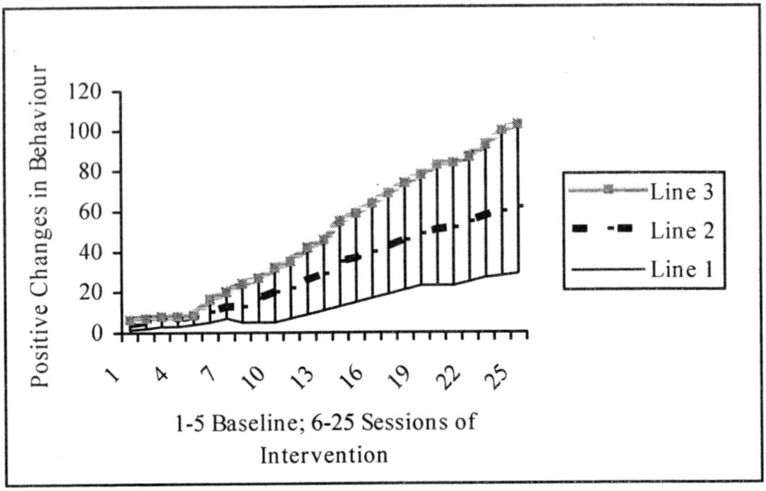

Figure 4.63 : Experiment 54 — Subject 54

The positive changes in behaviour were:

Line 1. The hands-on experiences provided enjoyable learning experiences to the subject.

Line 2. She learnt various mathematical concepts such as counting, sorting, comparing, matching, etc.

Line 3. She developed social skills and functional skills.

Experiment 55 : Subject 55

Experiment 55 was aimed at enabling the child to improve communication and social skills.

The child was so fond of driving that he always indulged in imaginative play by pretending to drive a car even when he was sitting in a chair. Very bright neon lights fascinated him. Combining these two splinter skills of the child, he was, taught traffic rules, traffic lights, road signs etc. First was taught to prepare green, yellow and red circles and what each light meant was discussed with him. He learnt very soon that 'green' means 'go', 'yellow' means 'watch out' and 'red' means 'stop'. He pasted the circles in a shoebox lid in the order simulating real traffic signals and he pretended to drive around in his car.

Table 4.56 : Behavioural Characteristics, Strengths and Drawbacks of Subject 55

Age	*Sex*	*Beh. Char*	*Splinter Skill/ Obsession*	*Learning Strength/ Dom. Intelligence*	*Learning Deficit*
13	M	Verbal; talks constantly but incoherently; neologisms; indulged in meaningless and incoherent talk.	Lights and driving.	The ability to process and integrate sensory stimulation; visual-spatial intelligence.	Inability to perceive and organise events in time & understand language.

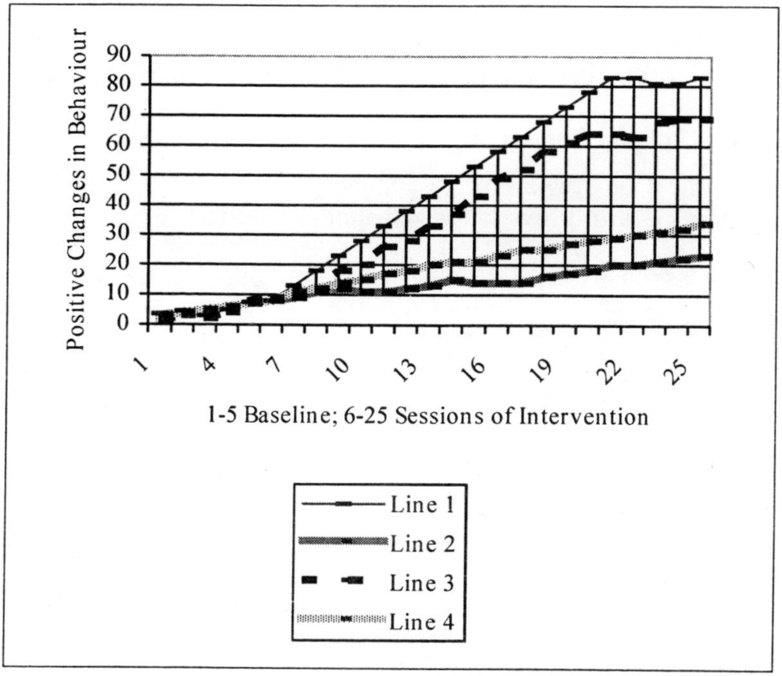

Figure 4.64 : Experiment 55 — Subject 55

He also prepared various road signs using construction paper. He learnt to extend the activity further and also to transfer the skill to different areas. He used road signs as props with tricycle traffic. To reinforce this skill, he was asked to count the number of road signs and traffic lights from home to school and back. He also observed that one has to keep left while driving. Whenever he required the sensory stimulation, he was allowed to play with a flashlight in a darkened room and to follow a rhyme. This activity helped him to relax too. The positive changes that occurred in his behaviour are shown in Figure 4.64.

The positive behavioural changes were:

Line 1. The subject's fixation for lights enabled him to learn new concepts.

Line 2. The activities that made him use a flashlight helped him to relax.

Line 3. His playing and communicative skills improved to a great extent.

Line 4. He was able to speak coherently and meaningfully.

Experiment 56 : Subject 56

Experiment 56 was aimed at enabling the child to express his emotions and improve his visual-spatial intelligence.

Table 4.57: Behavioural Characteristics, Strengths and Drawbacks of Subject 56

Age	*Sex*	*Beh. Char*	*Splinter Skill/ Obsession*	*Learning Strength/ Dom. Intelligence*	*Learning Deficit*
10	M	Non-verbal; hyperactive & hyper-sensitive to sounds.	Caterpillars/ Worms.	The ability to transfer visual world into motor patterns; visual-spatial intelligence	Inability to perceive & organise events in time and understand language.

Subject 56 was fond of caterpillars and worms. Alphabet worm and number worm were made so that he learnt the letters of the alphabet and numbers from 1 to 100 in a month's time. He was also shown the birth cycle of butterfly and the child collected pictures of butterflies in different colours. He learnt the names of colours and he could also identify the different colours. He also learnt the different varieties of butterflies and how they suck nectar from flowers and how they help in the propagation of plants. He learnt a lot about biology, and flora and fauna in particular.

As an extension of this activity, he was taken to a sericulture farm and was shown how silk fibre was extracted from silkworms. He did not like the worms being boiled in thousands and he expressed his sympathy often by saying 'poor worms'. He even told his mother not to wear silk saris as thousands of worms are killed for making a sari. He evinced more interest in butterflies and he wanted to draw and paint them in various colour combinations; he enhanced his skill in drawing and painting. Figure 4.65 provides a clear picture of the positive changes in his behaviour.

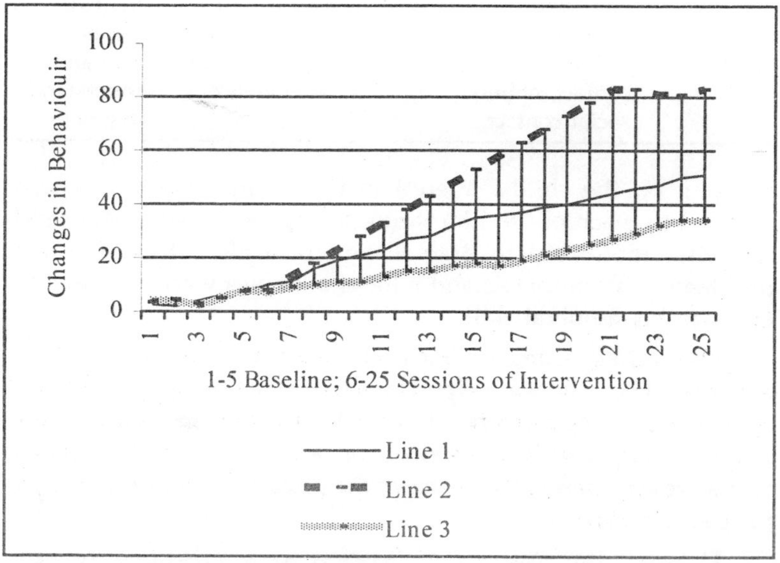

Figure 4.65: Experiment 56 — Subject 56

The positive changes in behaviour were

Line 1. Improvement in visual-spatial skills - drawing, colouring and painting.

Line 2. He expressed his emotions such as happiness, sorrow, sympathy, kindness, etc.

Line 3. He developed numerical skills and language skills.

Experiment 57 : Subject 57

Experiment 57 was aimed at enhancing other intelligences in the subject by utilising his visual-spatial intelligence as a channel.

Table 4.58: Behavioural Characteristics, Strengths and Drawbacks of Subject 57

Age	*Sex*	*Beh. Char*	*Splinter Skill/ Obsession*	*Learning Strength/ Dom. Intelligence*	*Learning Deficit*
8	M	Non-verbal; withdrawn; has seizure disorders; lack of eye contact; abhors social contact.	Clock.	The ability to transfer visual world into motor patterns; visual-spatial intelligence.	Inability to perceive and organise events in time and understand language.

Banking on the child's interest in clocks and watches, it was decided to reach out to him through this special skill. The child was first motivated to draw the picture of a clock. He had problems with numerals and a lot of activities were designed to enhance his numeral skills.

The child's younger sibling was made to join him in all the activities. The child was helped to make a clock from a paper plate. After learning the numerals, he could trace them in crayon on the plate. A long hand and a short hand were cut from chart paper and were attached to the centre of the plate. The child was taught to read the time.

Through the strategy of 'associated acquisition', several activities that were carried out at different hours were highlighted. For instance, the child was asked what activity he was reminded of if the time was 1 p.m. In the beginning, it was difficult for him to perceive and organise events in time and understand language related to time. Very soon he learnt to associate each hour with a particular activity and he learnt various concepts. Along with it he developed time-related anxiety, so he was taught relaxation techniques that helped him to gain more self-control. The changes that took place in the overt behaviour of the subject due to intervention are given in Figure 4.66.

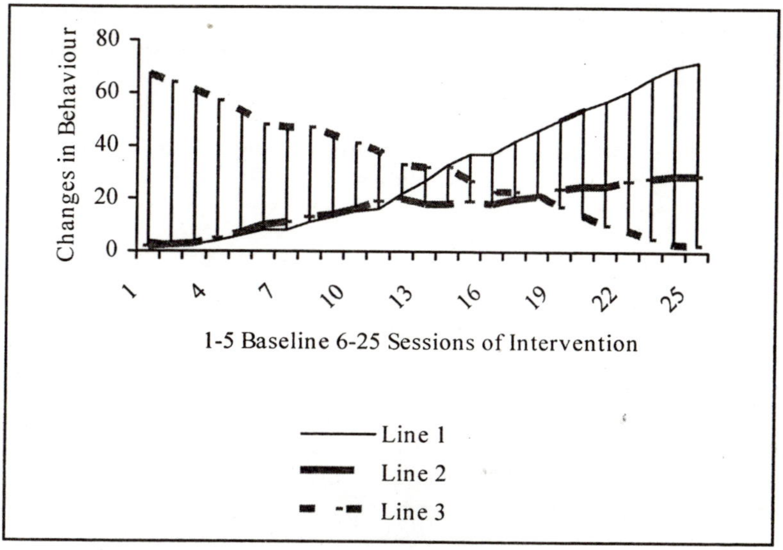

Figure 4.66: Experiment 57 — Subject 57

The positive changes in behaviour were:

Line 1. Various activities pursued by the child enhanced his logical numerical intelligence.

Line 2. He also gained self-control and relaxation.

Line 3. His time-related anxiety reduced considerably

Experiment 58 : Subject 58

Experiment 58 was aimed at teaching new concepts and skills to the subject.

Subject 58 liked to play with straw all the time; so it was decided to teach her various concepts and skills through this liking of the child. She was also fond of animals. The child was taught the to cut shapes of animals on construction paper and to staple them on to straws to make several puppets. The sounds and movements of various animals were initiated. She was also taught to make swinging animals. She drew the animal with crayon on construction paper adding an extra inch to the arms or tail. She coloured the shapes and cut them out. Bending the arms or tail over a straw, she stapled them and the animal was ready to swing. She made swinging monkeys and opossums. The children in the neighbourhood flocked into her house to buy the 'swinging animals'.

Table 4.59 : Behavioural Characteristics, Strengths and Drawbacks of Subject 58

Age	*Sex*	*Beh. Char*	*Splinter Skill/ Obsession*	*Learning Strength/ Dom. Intelligence*	*Learning Deficit*
10	F	Verbal; withdrawn; lack of eye contact; abhors social contact.	Straws.	The ability to use visual information meaningfully; visual-spatial intelligence.	Inability to modulate and process sensory stimulation & information.

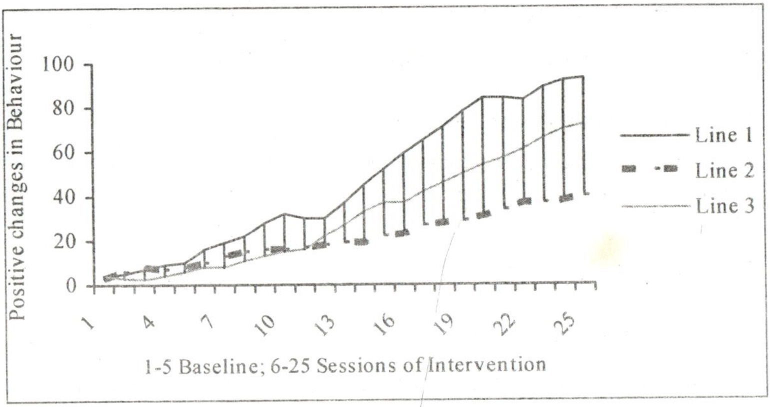

Figure 5.67 : Experiment 58 — Subject 58

This exceptional skill in the child was encouraged and enhanced further by teaching her to count the money she earned through the sale of her products. She cut straws of different colours into small pieces and threaded them together in different colour combinations to make necklaces for small children and dolls. She strung beads together to make necklaces in different materials and she also made bead jewellery as per the choices and demands of the customers. The children in the neighbourhood encouraged her by buying her creations. Figure 5.67 depicts the positive changes in the behaviour of the subject.

The positive changes in behaviour were:

Line 1. The subject learnt colour recognition and colour scheme.

Line 2. She developed vocational and avocational skills.

Line 3. She used her splinter skill productively and constructively.

Experiment 59 : Subject 59

Experiment 59 was aimed at improving social skills in the child and to help him to enjoy the activities that he engaged in.

Table 4.60 L Behavioural Characteristics, Strengths and Drawbacks of Subject 59

Age	*Sex*	*Beh. Char*	*Splinter Skill/ Obsession*	*Learning Strength/ Dom. Intelligence*	*Learning Deficit*
8	M	Non-verbal; withdrawn; has seizure disorders; lack of eye contact; abhors social contact.	Cards/ playing cards.	The ability to concentrate on narrow topics of interest; visual-spatial intelligence.	Inability to focus on relevant information.

Subject 59 had an exceptional splinter skill in playing card games. The potential of teaching the child, different concepts through his interestwee explored. Alphabet cards were prepared and this, the child mastered soon. As an extension of this activity, word matching and picture matching cards were created and the child could match the appropriate words and pictures successfully.

He knew every card of the deck, but when he was asked to identify pictures of queen, king, joker etc. he had problems, even though he could identify the 'queen' card. On the whole, he exhibited a jagged cognitive profile, a typical characteristic in autism. His fascination for animals was used here as it provided valuable learning experiences for him. He was asked to make a deck of cards with pictures of birds. He enjoyed it and he could play interactively with his peers. He also devised a game of his own. He enjoyed the 'fortune teller' using parrots to choose the cards so much that he prepared a set of cards and he made his toy parrot to choose cards for his friends. Figure 4.68 portrays the positive changes in the behaviour of the subject.

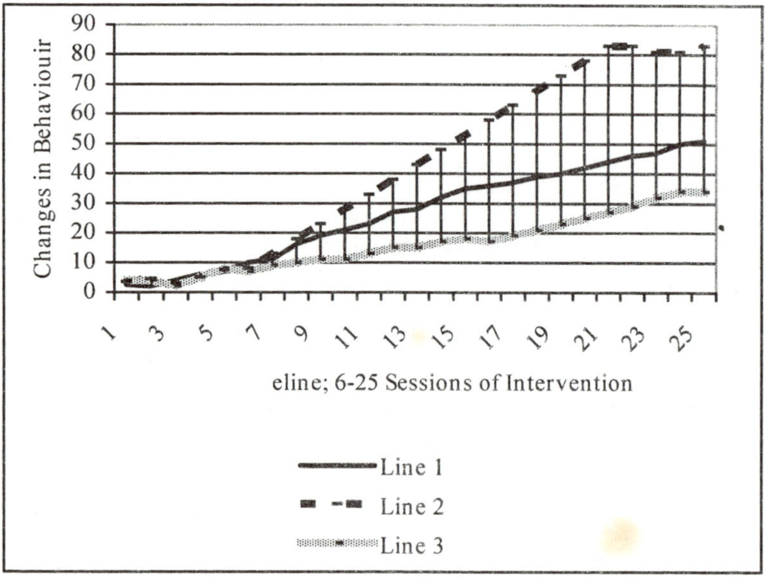

Figure 4.68: Experiment 59 — Subject 59

The positive changes in behaviour were:

Line 1. The subject initiated and engaged in social interaction.

Line 2. He improved his oral and written language skills.

Line 3. He derived pleasure by engaging himself in various activities.

Experiment 60 : Subject 60

In this case the experiment was used to utilise the subject's exceptional visual-spatial intelligence as a channel to reach out to him.

Table 4.61: Behavioural Characteristics, Strengths and Drawbacks of Subject 60

Age	*Sex*	*Beh. Char*	*Splinter Skill/ Obsession*	*Learning Strength/ Dom. Intelligence*	*Learning Deficit*
7	M	Non-verbal; anxious; self-hurting.	Umbrella.	The ability to transfer visual world into motor patterns; visual-spatial intelligence	Inability to organise and integrate information.

Subject 60 had a fascination for umbrellas and he could be seen holding one all the time and playing with it. He was taught the concept of colour and the use of umbrella. Parachutes were introduced and the child took an instant liking for them. The child was helped make toy parachutes by tying the four corners of a handkerchief with strings and attaching that to a sewing spool. He was asked to throw the parachute up into the air. He did not understand the instructions and he did not want to part with his chutes either. He did not understand that he could play with it. His sibling and the children in the neighbourhood were included in the activity. After observing the other children for a while, he was also drawn into it. He also learnt to make parachutes.

He enjoyed this activity so much that he always wanted to play with it and he was quick to notice that his sister's parachute stayed in the air longer than his own. He was taught various concepts such as 'bigger', 'smaller', 'lighter', 'faster', 'polythene sheet', 'sewing spool' etc. He also understood that his sister's parachute was bigger and hence it stayed up longer in the air. He also understood various scientific concepts such as the direction in which the wind was blowing, gravity, measurement and weight. He also started drawing and colouring. The changes that occurred in his behaviour are given in Figure 4.69.

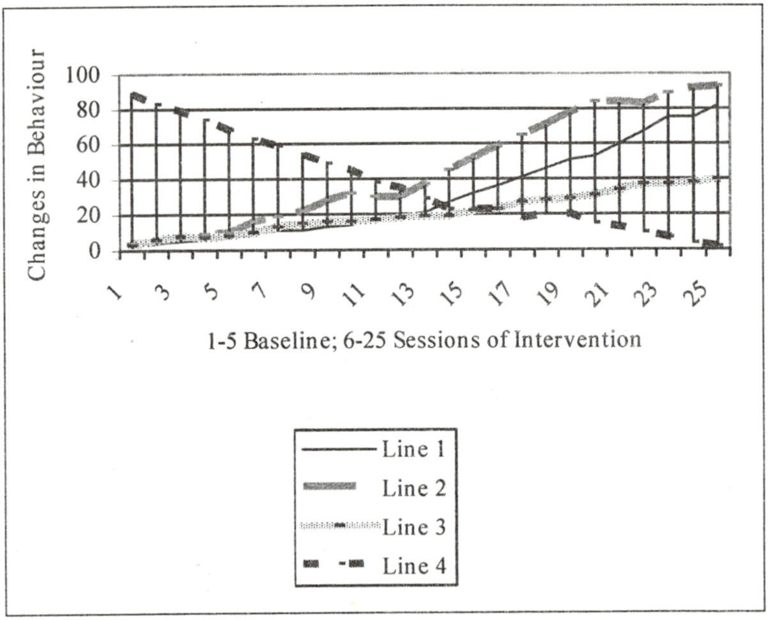

Figure 4.69 Experiment 60 - Subject 60

The positive changes in behaviour were:

Line 1. The subject developed and understood various scientific concepts.

Line 2. He enjoyed drawing and painting.

Line 3. He learnt colour recognition and colour scheme.

Line 4. His self-destructive behaviour decreased.

Experiment 61 : Subject 61

Experiment 61 was aimed at developing language and play skills in the subject.

Subject 61 had an obsession for locks and keys. Several activities were devised to capitalise on this obsession of the child. He was given paper cut outs of locks and keys with letters of the alphabet written on them. With his exceptional rote memory, he learnt all the letters of the alphabet. He was taught to cut construction paper in the shape of locks and keys and he was taught whole words. The child was able to take in chunks of information. He was even taught to frame complete sentences.

Table 4.62 : Behavioural Characteristics, Strengths and Drawbacks of Subject 61

Age	*Sex*	*Beh. Char*	*Splinter Skill/ Obsession*	*Learning Strength/ Dom. Intelligence*	*Learning Deficit*
10	M	Non-verbal; hypersensitive to sounds; self-hurting.	Locks and keys.	The ability to take in chunks of information; visual-spatial and bodily-kinesthetic intelligences.	Inability to engage in pretend play or imaginary play.

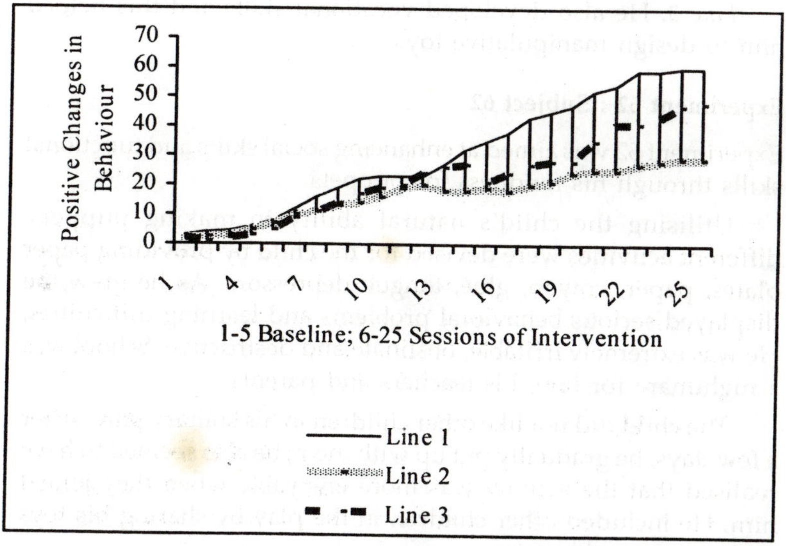

Figure 4.70 : Experiment 61 — Subject 61

Through this interest in the child, it was easier to develop his imaginative play. He played the role of the father who usually secures the door whenever they go out. The child was also given manipulative toys and he especially enjoyed wind up toys. The possibility of helping him to make or design wind-up toys were explored but apart from playing with the wind-up toys, he also evinced an interest in making them. With the help of a spring and a few items available at home, such as spoons, ladles, flashlight, etc., he made small manipulative toys. He mended the toys when they did not work. To extend and to expand this further, it was decided to teach him 'servicing' of small household appliances; he showed great interest in it and he picked up the skill soon. Figure 4.70 gives a vignette of the changes in the behaviour of the subject.

The positive changes in behaviour were:

Line 1. The subject's ability to take in chunks of information helped him to frame complete sentences using the words he learnt.

Line 2. He could play imaginatively.

Line 3. He also developed vocational skills and this helped him to design manipulative toys.

Experiment 62 : Subject 62

Experiment 62 was aimed at enhancing social skills and functional skills through his fondness for puppets.

Utilising the child's natural ability in making puppets, different activities were devised for the child by providing paper plates, paper, crayon, glue, tongue depressors. As he grew, he displayed serious behavioral problems and learning difficulties. He was extremely irritable, obstinate and destructive. School was a nightmare for him, his teachers and parents.

The child did not like other children in his solitary play. After a few days, he gradually put up with them; he also seemed to have realised that the activity was more enjoyable when they joined him. He included other children in the play by sharing his toys and puppets with them.

He gave chances for other children to draw faces on the plates and decorate them to create colourful puppets. He used the tongue depressor for handles and the children decided to have a puppet party. Children joined together in pairs and presented a show and they also prepared outfits for the puppets. They organised a puppet parade set to music. The child joined other children in imitating a temple festival and he made a toy chariot. He pulled the toy chariot in the pretended procession. He with his peers put up stalls as well. The changes observed in the overt behaviour of the child are given in Figure 4.71.

Table 4.63 : Behavioural Characteristics, Strengths and Drawbacks of Subject 62

Age	*Sex*	*Beh. Char*	*Splinter Skill/ Obsession*	*Learning Strength/ Dom. Intelligence*	*Learning Deficit*
12	M	Non-verbal; hyperactive; anxious; aloof and withdrawn.	Puppets.	Visual-spatial, bodily-kinesthetic and musical intelligences.	Inability to engage in social interaction & communication.

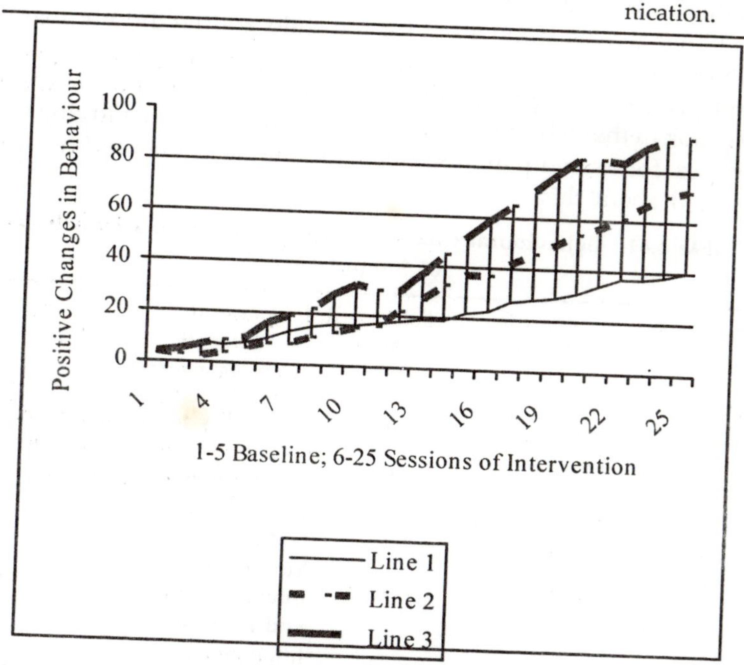

Figure 4.71 : Experiment 62 — Subject 62

The positive changes in behaviour were:

Line 1. Improvement in group-interaction.

Line 2. Transition from one activity to another was smooth.

Line 3. Playing with puppets enabled the child to form concepts and understand the skills necessary for successful social interaction.

Experiment 63 — Subject 63

Experiment 63 was aimed at reaching out the child through his multiple intelligences.

Subject 63 liked to play with sponges that he was always seen standing near the faucet and soaking them in water. Several activities were planned for the child to utilise his passion for productive activities. The sponge was cut into different shapes and attempts were made to teach him the shapes but he did not bother to look at them. It took a while for to understand that a wet sponge was stimulating for the child and he did not like it when it was dry. The cut shapes were dipped in tempera paint and pressed on a paper to get the cut out shapes and the child partook in this activity enthusiastically. He started identifying the shapes, forms and patterns. He made unique figures and he was excited about this.

Table 4.64 : Behavioural Characteristics, Strengths and Drawbacks of Subject 63

Age	*Sex*	*Beh. Char*	*Splinter Skill/ Obsession*	*Learning Strength/ Dom. Intelligence*	*Learning Deficit*
14	M	Non-verbal; hyperactive; anxious; self-hurting; has seizure disorders.	Sponge.	The ability to take in chunks of information; visual-spatial, bodily-kinesthetic, interspersonal and musical intelligence.	Inability to work within boundary.

It was necessary to capitalise on the exceptional bodily-kinesthetic intelligence of the child. A sponge was cut into long strips in the shape of human figures with eyes, eyebrows, nose, mouth drawn etc. The sponge was dipped in tempera paint and allowed to dance on the paper according to music, which the child particularly enjoyed. Different styles of music were played such as classical music, film songs, western pop and instrumental music. He was also taught to close his eyes and let the sponge dance on the paper. This helped him to work within boundaries. Figure 4.72 gives a vignette of the positive changes in the behaviour of the subject.

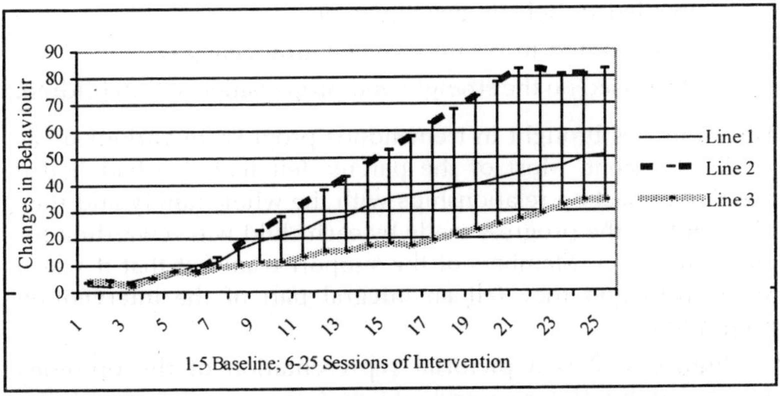

Figure 4.72 : Experiment 63 — Subject 63

The positive changes in behaviour were:

Line 1. The subject started identifying the shapes, forms and patterns.

Line 2. He made unique figures and was happy and excited about them.

Line 3. He learnt to work within boundaries.

To sum up, the views expressed by special teachers, parents and other members of the support team about the Strategic Intervention Paradigm (SIP) are given here. The responses given by the team members numbering 193 totally felt that the intervention strategies that were implemented in an eclectic manner brought about the desired changes in the behaviour of the children. All those associated with the implementation of intervention expressed positive views about the intervention and felt that the children had benefited a lot. Ninety-nine per cent of the respondents felt that the Strategic Intervention Paradigm was successful and they felt that:

- — it provided relevant and meaningful learning experiences.
- — multiple intelligences provided appropriate entry points.
- — splinter skills acted as natural reinforcers.
- — relevant functional and social skills were developed.
- — involvement of the family achieved positive outcomes.
- — this led to holistic development.
- — this resulted in positive behavioural changes.
- — it focused on the strength and propensities of the children.

The strategies brought in tremendous progress in various areas of development. Most of the parents felt that this had had a positive impact on relationships with the whole family and they also felt that the progress made by each child was rewarding for the entire team. Members of the support team felt that it was a team effort and they felt an integral part of the intervention programme.

Figure 4.72 is a pictorial representation of the opinions expressed by the respondents and the percentage of the respondents who conferred with the opinion.

Figure 4.73 portrays some of the positive changes in the behaviour of the children with autism brought forth by the Strategic Intervention Paradigm. As the feedback was received from the team members immediately after each session and the necessary modifications incorporated immediately, it was felt it would be redundant to repeat and it would not be possible to catalogue all the positive changes in behaviour in one or two pages. The pyramid illustrates only the changes that were observed in the majority of the children as the graph given for each individual deals with the changes found at each individual level.

The intervention team members were generally happy with the outcomes and the positive changes brought forth by the programme. There was a genuine sense of involvement and teamwork. All children have made a great deal of progress. The case studies provide examples of progress in detailed areas of development that were agreed upon by all observers.

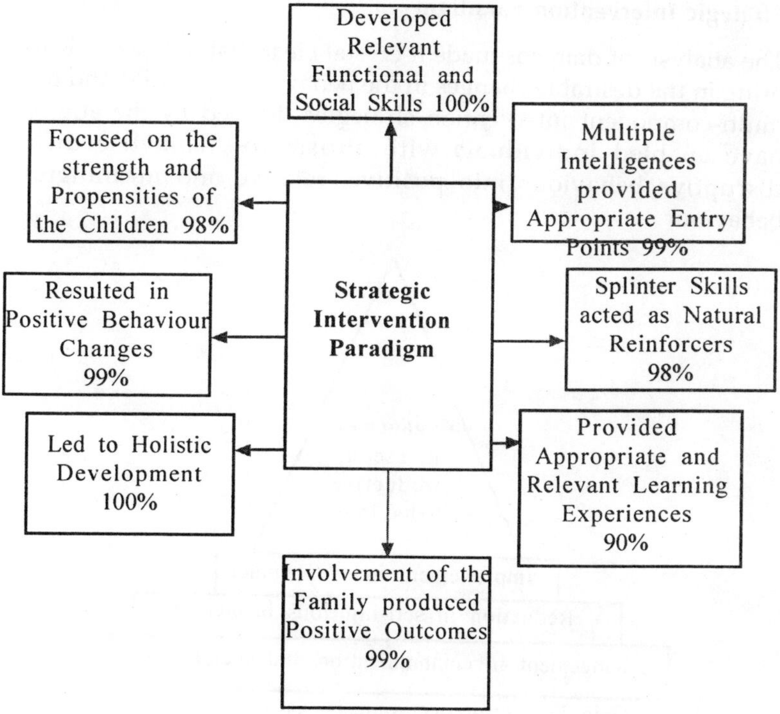

Figure 4.73 : Opinions of Special Teachers and Parents (Intervention Team Members) on Strategic Intervention Paradigm

The top of the pyramid illustrates the most important and the most desired learning outcome of the intervention – engaging the child in useful and productive activities. This was achieved through several strategies devised by the author. Learners with autism need information and instructions to be provided in a clear and understandable manner in order to contribute to the society like any other typical member of the society. The interpreter must have a clear understanding of the needs, issues and perspectives of these children, devise broad range of strategies and provide the necessary support or scaffolding.

Autism still remains an enigma, and primary caregivers should not straightjacket the child in any methodology. Right opportunities have to be provided to the learners in a variety of situations and ways.

Strategic Intervention Paradigm

The analysis of data has made it crystal clear that it is possible to bring in the desirable changes in the behaviour of a child and the multi-component intervention strategies devised by the author have enabled individuals with autism to channelise their disruptive behaviour into positive, relative and meaningful behaviour.

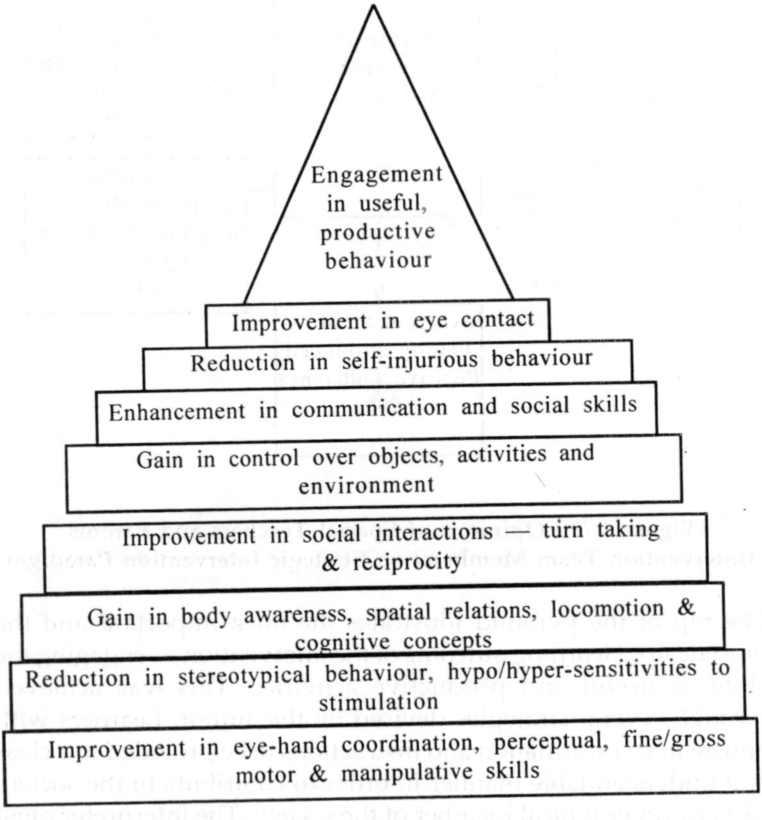

Figure 4.74: Positive Behaviour Changes Brought

5

Summary and Conclusions

The findings that have resulted from quantitative and qualitative analyses of the data are presented in this chapter. A detailed and profound enquiry helped in identifying the challenges involved and the efficacy of psychologically and pedagogically sound intervention strategies while dealing with children with autism. In the light of the findings of the study, recommendations and suggestions for improvement are provided. Suggestions for further research in the field of autism are also given.

Summary of the Findings

1. As children with autism live in cocoons, it is necessary to break the cocoons open and reach the core of the children. The theory of Multiple Intelligences was useful in understanding the dominant intelligence of each child and providing interventions based on that.
2. The current study has reinforced the fact that Multiple Intelligences provide insight into the different learning styles of children and enable the teacher to provide optimum learning environment and experiences for the pupils.
3. The results show that maintaining eye contact and keeping oneself at the eye level of the child with autism (Visual Comfort Zone, one of the intervention strategies) is an important factor in developing meaningful communication.

4. Embedded Communication Activities stresses on the importance of teaching functional, social and communication skills by exploiting functional routines.
5. In Toto Configuration enables both the child and the interventionist to consider the big picture or complete picture about the activities and also about the child.
6. The study sheds light on the need to provide opportunities for interaction, turn-taking, giving and receiving for children with autism, as in a ping pong game.
7. The study highlights the fact that children with autism depend on others to provide critical and seminal information to understand external structure (Topographical Organisers). Topographical organisers provide clarity, meaning, purpose and structure, and they also reduce anxiety from distractions.
8. Visual references prepared under Cognitive Visual Strategies facilitated and augmented communication.
9. The study has focused on making the learning situations and experiences more meaningful by expanding and enhancing various skills, strengths, intense interests, obsessions and fixations of children with autism. Propensity Enhancement, one of the strategies adopted, has broadened narrow and fixated interest of the child into constructive and purposeful activity.
10. The study has made it clear that children with autism rely on concrete visual references to organise information, to prepare for changes and transitions and to clarify time, concepts, ideas, events and structure. Visual references and organisers included in the strategy Visual Self-management Systems were calendars, mini-calendars, cue cards, semantic maps, cartoon strips, comic strips, flash cards, T-charts, thematic webs, social stories, etc.
11. The study emphasizes on the importance of holistic learning by integrating all therapies and services to teach useful and meaningful skills. Collaborative Teaching helped the children to develop holistically and enabled them to avoid unrelated splinter skills.

12. The study has brought to light the importance of hearing the language in natural contexts. The use of adaptations and positive language experiences such as 'parallel talking', 'exaggerated facial expressions', 'visual cues' and 'reflective listening' techniques has resulted in better and meaningful learning as given in the strategy, Adapted Language Experience.
13. The study has made it clear that children with autism learn better when these children are supported in their endeavours by responsible and thoughtful adults as delineated by the strategy, Adult Supported Endeavours.
14. It is quite palpable from the results obtained in the study that every activity that interests the child should be expanded further and channelled into functional skill as proved by the strategy, Expanded Experience.
15. The study has further confirmed that many types of activities and situations of home life provide opportunities for children to interact with people in real life as is given in the strategy, Daily Life Situations.
16. The study has encapsulated the fact that children with autism learn better when objects are presented while the child is taught different concepts instead of teaching the concepts in isolation, as proved by the strategy, Associated Acquisitions.
17. This investigation has illuminated that from the beginning the child needs structured environment at home and school. Children with autism often have varying degrees of intellectual disability, which impacts on the general level of function and educational abilities.
18. It is quite palpable that the involvement of the child's parents, the siblings and family is critical to the assessment process. Irrespective of the diagnosis, the parents' role in assisting their child's additional needs is paramount. Involvement of the family can be effective in helping to achieve positive outcomes for both the child and the family.
19. Parents report that early intervention programmes equip the family with skills that enable them to better manage their child in any setting.

20. The eclectic effect of various therapies with a distinct focus on behavioural therapy, which formed the basis of the Strategic Intervention Paradigm centred on positive reinforcement of desirable behaviour, has been shown to be successful in improving socially acceptable and appropriate behaviour, functional skills and communication and in reducing inappropriate behaviour such as violence, non-compliance, aggression, self-destructive and obsessional behaviour.

21. The effectiveness of the specific treatment and intervention techniques for an individual child depends on many factors. It is based on ongoing monitoring of progress and adaptation, and modification of specific techniques that are appropriate. Many behavioural strategies have been found to be effective in improving communication for young children with autism. Intervention strategies can be easily adapted to an individual child's situation.

22. The study suggests that the basic procedures for effective treatment have to be grounded on the proclivities of children, and these can be utilised in improving maladaptive behaviours, communication, and social interaction for children with autism.

23. Various social or educational strategies have been found to be effective in increasing spontaneous language and teaching communication skills.

24. Picture-enhanced Communication Competency Model for Children with Autism (in compact disc) has made it clear that children with autism will be able to make dramatic progress once they are able to communicate. Communication deficits and lack of social skills are core elements defining autism. Behavioural or educational intervention techniques to improve communication and social interactions are important components of intervention programmes for young children with autism. It is particularly important to concentrate on the functional aspects of language development (use of language in context and social aspects of communication—the compact disc stands testimony to that).

25. This study sheds light on the fact that various behavioural strategies have been found to be effective in increasing reciprocal social interactions between children with autism and other children. It is often useful to train peers with age appropriate development to interact with a child with autism.
26. It is quite obvious from the study that one useful method may be to train parents to focus on multiple cues from the child, and use natural reinforcers in response to the child's attempts. This more naturalistic approach may be more effective in reducing parent stress and increasing parent happiness than more directive methods that train parents to teach their child one response at a time in discrete trials.
27. The developmental model used in the Strategic Intervention Package formed the basis for a comprehensive intervention approach emphasizing the child's affect and relationships, developmental level, and individual differences.

Recommendations for Teachers, Parents and Other Para-professionals

Early intervention programmes equip the family with skills that enable them to better manage their child in any setting.

It is often useful to train peers with age appropriate development to interact with a child with autism.

The adult caregiver has to make sure that the developmentally delayed children are kept at the eye level of the caregiver. Eye contact helps to develop increased body awareness, attention to surroundings and perceptual motor coordination.

The basic procedures for effective treatment have to be grounded on the proclivities of children, and these can be utilised in improving maladaptive behaviours, communication, and social interaction for children with autism.

Functional routines, such as getting dressed, school interval or recess, lunch, play time, going to the doctor and leisure activity can be capitalised on to communicate with the child with autism.

While developing an effective Individualised Education Programme (IEP), it is important to consider the big picture or complete picture, the gestalt. The IEP is much like a travel plan or an itinerary. The plan for those with autism has to be drawn with great and elaborate details. Just like a travel plan, it should be developed with understanding the starting place (current level of functioning), places of stay (teaching strategies, interventions, modifications and adaptations) and final destination (the ultimate goal). The ultimate goal is to enable the child to lead an independent and meaningful life and to contribute to the society.

As the urge to interact and communicate is almost absent in autism, young children need many opportunities to interact and to communicate. The adult care giver/ sibling/ teacher/ therapist/ friend or anyone who interacts with a child with autism has to start an activity or imitation, matching the child's.

It is imperative to provide opportunities for interaction, turn-taking, giving and receiving. The activity or a game should be selected in such a way that it requires both players to interact with each other as in a ping-pong game.

Structured play-based strategies provide a context for spontaneous communication and social interaction.

The environment, the events, the space and the time should be organised and structured in such a way that optimal level of stimulation is maintained for effective learning to take place.

It is important to highlight on critical and seminal information, to provide clarity, meaning and purpose, and to reduce anxiety from distractions.

Pairing signs with speech are useful in teaching basic language concepts because some of the attributes of an object, such as shape, colour, size and movement, are graphic.

Planning and preparing visual references to augment and support communication are of paramount importance.

Activities, people and objects that are liked by the children with autism have to be enhanced and expanded further to provide meaningful learning situations. Obsessions, fixations and intense interests act as natural reinforcers and tremendous motivators. Teaching new skills through special interests serve as entry points through which the children can be reached. A narrow, fixated interest needs to be broadened into constructive activities.

In order to organise information, to prepare for changes and transitions and to clarify time, concepts and ideas the learner needs information in a concrete and visual format.

Visual references and organisers include calendars, mini calendars, cue cards, semantic maps, thematic webs, stories, etc. Visual instructional strategies provide new teaching skills and also enable to solve behaviour problems in children with autism.

Parents, special education teacher, therapists, siblings and friends should work together as a team to integrate all therapies and services to teach useful and meaningful skills in a holistic manner and to avoid confusion and to prevent the learning of unrelated splinter skills. Every member of the team has to collaborate, share information and expertise.

Hearing the language in natural contexts is a prerequisite for understanding and using the language for communication. Adaptations and positive language experiences such as 'parallel talking', 'exaggerated facial expressions', 'animated facial expressions', 'visual cues' and 'reflective listening' will result in better and more meaningful use.

Activities related to the subject of their interest ought to be explored in as much detail as time and enthusiasm allow. This sort of spontaneous learning does much to encourage a curious and questioning attitude in children. They are much more likely to continue to explore objects and ideas if they are supported in their endeavours by a thoughtful and responsible adult. The adults must be alert to provide assistance at the most optimal point for the child to communicate his needs.

While playing with a child with autism, every activity is to be treated as a form of interpersonal communication. Talking with children about their activities can clarify or confirm their understanding. An important part of this is asking questions. Novel actions added to the natural interaction and new dimensions of the actions increase flexibility and tolerance for new and complex information, and prevent rigid routines in children with autism.

Many types of activities and situations of home life provide opportunities for children to learn various concepts and to interact with people in real life. Focused and structured experiences that enable the children to develop communication and social skills, independence, positive self-concept and autonomy to make choices must be provided.

A child acquires language through cognition, generalisation, discrimination and classification of concepts. He perceives an object through his senses and adds meaning to his perception, and these two processes occur together. Two brain functions of joint attention and the ability to focus along with another person enable him to acquire language. It is of vital importance to provide a language-rich environment where the child can match or associate objects or activities with their names.

Engaging and involving parents in all the activities is important to provide meaningful learning experiences. To prevent rigidity it is vital not to follow any particular pattern but to be flexible, providing structure and support to help the child remain engaged, develop communication, leisure and social skills. Teaching social skills and social interactions specifically in a structured way enables a child with autism to prepare for situations and interactions.

Involving the child in turn taking, reciprocal interactive activities that require shared space and materials are prerequisites for fostering social skills.

Using pictures, visual cues, visual references/organisers and visual charts are vital to enable the child to understand various activities and transition from one activity or one situation to the other.

Encouraging the child to join a peer or engaging peers and neighbours in the favourite activity of the child with autism has produced favourable outcomes.

Devising any intervention for children with autism has to be built on the strengths and propensities, and any fixation or obsession has to be capitalised on.

Helping children with autism to function effectively in any situation, and enabling them to practise their skills in different situations are of vital importance.

Teaching skills to transfer or generalise skills they have learned in one setting and applying it to another setting is very important for children with autism.

Suggestions for Further Research

- Comprehensive studies covering more cities in India could be taken up to know the prevalence of Autism Spectrum Disorder and the services that are available.
- Future research should be conducted to assess the empirical support for interventions that provide individuals with skills to understand themselves and others.
- New and innovative treatment strategies through single case designs and smaller clinical trials have to be carried out.
- The more severe challenges of some children with autism may be best addressed by a structured education and behaviour program, which contains a one-on-one teacher-to- student ratio or small group environment
- In future research, it will be important to explore in detail the early neuropsychological impairments in autism.
- Studies on social and pragmatic deficits in autism can be carried out.
- Further research on the strategies evolved by the researcher can be done.
- Investigations on cognitive approach to the education of children with autism have to be done.
- A trans-disciplinary approach for early intervention is the crying need of the hour.
- Studies can be done on social and communicative development of children with autism. Language acquisition and communicative behaviour in autism have to be explored.
- Sensory impairment in autism deserves special focus and attention of the research community.

- Studies can be carried out on high functioning/ Asperger's syndrome children.
- The impact of physical exercise on disruptive behaviour in autism has to be investigated upon.
- Integrating creative art therapies and vocational skills deserve special attention of the research community.
- Future research should consider the prospects of including visual systems to teach functional and communication skills to children with autism.
- Treatment of social behaviour in autism through social skills has to be addressed.
- Future research should focus on self-management of problematic and disruptive social behaviour.
- Methods to enhance learning in children with autism have to be investigated upon.
- More studies have to be conducted to assess the therapeutic value of psycho-social, behavioural and educational interventions.
- Researches have to be done in future on numerous challenges in psychosocial interventions, especially from a methodological perspective, such as selecting the appropriate experimental design, comparison group, assessment instruments, and treatment fidelity measures.
- There is a need for further testing of widely used treatments and approaches.
- Further research is necessary to understand individual differences in treatment response, and for demonstrating effective ways to individualise treatment.
- More studies have to be done to balance, compare, and contrast one research approach with the other approaches.

Expansion of Limitations of the Study

The sample drawn for the study is restricted to 63 children with autism (only the children who met DSM IV Criteria were chosen for the study).

More number of children could not be included as the children in special schools who were thought of as 'autistic' or 'mentally retarded' by the special schools did not meet DSM IV Criteria.

1. Apart from this, the investigator had to meet several challenges. The major challenge was from the mother of the child with autism who did not want to accept the fact that her child has autism.
2. Contradictory reports and views expressed by family members,
3. Family members, especially parents believing in superstitions, astrology and horoscopes (some of the parents) believed and argued that their children would overcome all autistic features when they reach a particular age or after 7 ½-year phase of the planet Saturn is over.
4. Some of the parents had reservations about learning intervention strategies.
5. Some parents compared their child with their nephews and nieces who are so called 'normal', and argued that those children also behave in the same way as their 'autistic' child (for instance, they too do not answer when being called).
6. Non-compliance from school managements.
7. Professionals or teachers working in special schools did not like being interrupted by research scholars.

    — The areas covered for investigation are confined to the two cities of Chennai and Coimbatore.

      More number of cities in Tamil Nadu could not be included as the study would have become more elaborate and out of control. As autism is a complex disorder and the positive changes in a child are difficult to achieve, out the study was carried in two major metropolises in Tamil Nadu.

    — The sample was drawn only from special schools.

      A comprehensive, comparative study could have been carried out by including children who were 'mainstreamed' or by including children who were 'normal' or typical. But that did not fall under the purview of the study.

- The investigation focused only on children who fell under Autism Spectrum Disorder.

  A broad study would include children with other disabilities and disorders, such as cognitive and developmental disabilities, cerebral palsy or down syndrome but the investigator's objective was to concentrate only on Autism Spectrum Disorder and bring in positive changes in the children with autism as this itself was a formidable task and autism is a complex disorder. The investigator deliberately avoided other disabilities to make the present study more in-depth.

- One palpable limitation in this kind of study is the examiner's bias. To eliminate this bias and to ensure reliability of the study, all observations were recorded and inter-observer agreement was stuck firmly to.

Conclusion

This investigation addresses three major areas of importance: psychological, social and pedagogical spheres of the personality of children with autism. It provides relevant strategies and approaches for teaching any child with autism to function meaningfully and live as independently as possible. This investigation presents some of the key educational approaches and teaching techniques that can be drawn from strategies into the classroom.

This study supports the view that the key to achieving positive behaviour changes cannot be attributed to one particular strategy but eclectic amalgamation of all the strategies evolved by the author. The purpose of the present study was to reach the core of the children with autism through different entry points. These were explored and gained using the Theory of Multiple Intelligences. Once the dominant intelligence of the child and his/her learning style were understood, it paved the way for further enhancement and development all five domains of a child — the adaptive domain, the cognitive domain, the communication domain, the physical domain and the social or emotional domain— and cognitive competence, sensory competence, language/communication competence, social competence, educational competence, daily living skills, vocational competence recreation and leisure skills.

The importance of this type of research is underscored by evidence converging on the conclusion that outcomes for children with autism can be significantly enhanced by early intensive intervention. Although many questions remain (notably, for what intensity and duration? And whether a particular strategy is more effective than the other one), effective interventions, all target specific skills are characterised by carefully planned, delivered, and monitored individualised teaching, regardless of orientation.

The present study has reinforced the fact that has been stressed upon by experts that programmes that begin early in life are generally the most effective. Essential components of effective programmes for children and adolescents with autism include emphasis on chronological, developmental and age appropriate, functional and social skills that are required to be successful in the real world. The research also suggests that to be effective, any approach should be flexible and proactive in nature, rely on positive reinforcement, be re-evaluated on a regular basis and provide a smooth transition from home to school to community environments, from one environment to another, from one activity to another, and from one setting to another.

Children with autism should have training in vocational skills, social pragmatic skills, functional and community living skills at the earliest possible age. Learning to cross a street safely, to take part in a game or to go to a shop and make a simple purchase, or to ask for assistance when needed are critical skills, and may be difficult, even for those with average intelligence levels. Tasks that enhance the person's cognitive, language, social and pragmatic skills, independence and provide more opportunities for personal choice or allow more freedom in the community are important.

Intervention must address both the communication and the behavioural disorders, and must be systematic, intensive and individualised. A good intervention programme fosters normal development, develops learning, reduces rigid stereotypical behaviour patterns, eliminates behaviour problems and reduces family stress. A clear conclusion from the study is that children have made dramatic progress on all measures and this indicates that the programme has been successful in helping children achieve their potential. After all, self-actualisation is the sole aim of education.

Appendix-I

DSM IV Criteria for the Autistic Disorders

The full diagnostic criteria for the pervasive developmental disorders are outlined below. As mentioned above, the diagnostic criteria for the autistic (PDD) disorders are defined by the DSM IV criteria.

I. Childhood Autism

A. A total of six (or more) items from (1), (2), and (3), with at least two from (1), and one each from (2) and (3):

1. Qualitative impairment in social interaction, as manifested by at least two of the following:
   a) marked impairment in the use of multiple non-verbal behaviours, such as eye-to-eye gaze, facial expression, body postures, and gestures to regulate social interaction.
   b) failure to develop peer relationships appropriate to developmental level.
   c) a lack of spontaneous seeking to share enjoyment, interests, or achievements with other people (e.g., by a lack of showing, bringing, or pointing out objects of interest).
   d) lack of social or emotional reciprocity.
2. Qualitative impairments in communication as manifested by at least one of the following:
   a) delay in, or total lack of, the development of spoken language (not accompanied by an attempt to compensate through alternative modes of communication such as gesture or mime).
   b) in individuals with adequate speech, marked impairment in the ability to initiate or sustain a conversation with others.

c) stereotyped and repetitive use of language or idiosyncratic language.
d) lack of varied spontaneous make-believe play or social imitative play appropriate to developmental level.

3. Restricted, repetitive, and stereotyped patterns of behaviour, interests, and activities, as manifested by at least of one of the following:
   a) encompassing preoccupation with one or more stereotyped and restricted patterns of interest that is abnormal either in intensity or focus.
   b) apparently inflexible adherence to specific, nonfunctional routines or rituals.
   c) stereotyped and repetitive motor mannerisms (e.g., hand or finger flapping or twisting, or complex whole body movements).
   d) persistent preoccupation with parts of objects.

B. Delays or abnormal functioning in at least one of the following areas, with onset prior to age three years: (1) social interaction, (2) language as used in social communication, or (3) symbolic or imaginative play.

C. The disturbance is not better accounted for by Rett's disorder or childhood disintegrative disorder.

II. Asperger's Syndrome

A. Qualitative impairment in social interaction, as manifested by at least two of the following:
   1) Marked impairment in the use of multiple non-verbal behaviours such as eye-to-eye gaze, facial expression, body postures, and gestures to regulate social interaction.
   2) Failure to develop peer relationships appropriate to developmental level.
   3. A lack of spontaneous seeking to share enjoyment, interests, or achievements with other people (e.g., by a lack of showing, bringing, or pointing out objects of interest).
   4. lack of social or emotional reciprocity.

B. Restricted, repetitive, and stereotyped patterns of behaviour, interests, and activities, as manifested by at least of one of the following:

1. Encompassing preoccupation with one or more stereotyped and restricted patterns of interest that is abnormal either in intensity or focus.
2. Apparently inflexible adherence to specific, nonfunctional routines or rituals.
3. Stereotyped and repetitive motor mannerisms (e.g., hand or finger flapping or twisting, or complex whole body movements).
4. Persistent preoccupation with parts of objects.

C. The disturbance causes clinically significant impairment in social, occupational, or other important areas of functioning.

D. There is no clinically significant delay in language (e.g., single words used by age two years, communicative phrases used by age three years).

E. There is no clinically significant delay in cognitive development or in the development of age-appropriate self-help skills, adaptive behaviour (other than in social interaction), and curiosity about the environment in childhood.

F. Criteria are not met for another specific pervasive developmental disorder or schizophrenia.

III. Rett's Disorder

A. All of the following:
1. apparently normal prenatal and perinatal development.
2. apparently normal psychomotor development through the first five months after birth.
3. normal head circumference at birth.

B. Onset of all of the following after the period of normal development:
1. Deceleration of head growth between ages 48 months and five years.
2. Loss of previously acquired purposeful hand skills between ages 30 months and five with the subsequent development of stereotyped hand movements (e.g., handwringing or handwashing).
3. Loss of social engagement early in the course (although often social interaction develops later).
4. Appearance of poorly coordinated gait or trunk movements.

5. Severely impaired expressive and receptive language development with severe psychomotor retardation.

IV. Childhood Disintegrative Disorder

A. Apparently normal development for at least the first two years after birth as manifested by the presence of age-appropriate verbal and non-verbal communication, social relationships, play, and adaptive behaviour.

B. Clinically significant loss of previously acquired skills (before age 10 years) in at least two of the following areas:
   1. Expressive or receptive language.
   2. Social skills or adaptive behaviour.
   3. Bowel or bladder control. 4. Play. 5. Motor skills.

C. Abnormalities of functioning in at least two of the following areas:
   1. Qualitative impairment in social interaction (e.g., impairment in non-verbal behaviours, failure to develop peer relationships, lack of social or emotional reciprocity).
   2. Qualitative impairments in communication (e.g., delay or lack of spoken language, inability to initiate or sustain a conversation, stereotyped and repetitive use of language, lack of varied make-believe play).
   3. Restricted, repetitive, and stereotyped patterns of behaviour, interests, and activities, including motor stereotypies and mannerisms).

D. The disturbance is not better accounted for by another specific pervasive developmental disorder or by schizophrenia.

V. PDD NOS

This category should be used when there is a severe and pervasive impairment in the development of reciprocal social interaction or verbal and non-verbal communication skills or when stereotyped behaviour, interests, and activities are present but the criteria are not met for a specific pervasive developmental disorder, schizophrenia, schizotypal personality disorder, or avoidant personality disorder. For example, this category includes "atypical autism" — presentations that do not meet the criteria for autistic disorder because of late age at onset, atypical symptomatology, or sub-threshold symptomatology, or all of these.

Appendix-II

Autism Research: Institute Autism Treatment Evaluation Checklist (ATEC) Internet Scoring Programme

The Autism Research Institute (ARI) has developed this simple Internet scoring procedure that will calculate subscale scores and a summary score from the ATEC. The scores are weighted according to the response and the corresponding subscale. The higher the subscale and total scores, the more impaired the subject.

Click here to view the ATEC. Click here to download and print a clean copy of the ATEC using Adobe Acrobat (pdf file). If you would like to receive a copy of the ATEC in the mail to use for research purposes, send us a stamped self-addressed envelope to: ATEC Request c/o Autism Research Institute, 4182 Adams Avenue, San Diego, CA 92116. We will send you a high quality copy of the ATEC.

Click here to read our recent letter to practitioners and researchers.

A. Information About Researcher and Project

Last Name / First Name of Researcher: [ ] / [ ]

Name of data entry person [if different from above]: [ ]

Address1: [ ]

Address2: [ ]

City: [ ] , State: [ ] Zipcode: [ ]

Country [if outside U.S.]: [ ]

Telephone: [ ] Fax: [ ]

E-mail: [ ] <==Please enter your e-mail address

Intervention, if any, Being Evaluated [optional]: [ ]

B. Information Specific to Each ATEC/Person (Research Subject)

Assessment Period [e.g., baseline,
1 week post, 1 month post, etc.]: [ ]

Diagnosis: You may check more than one diagnosis.

☐ Autism ☐ Asperger Syndrome ☐ PDD-NOS ☐ Landau-Kleffner Syndrome ☐ Other

If you checked 'Other,' please specify: [ ]

ATEC

Last Name / First Name of Child [or identification code]:

[ ] / [ ]

Sex of Child: ○Male ○Female

Age: [ ]

Date of Birth [format: mo/da/yr; e.g., 09/25/98]: [ ]

Today's Date [same format as above]: [ ]

Form Completed By: [first and last name] [ ]

Relationship: [e.g., mother, teacher] [ ]

Please Click the Appropriate 'Radio Button'

I. Speech/Language/Communication

N = Not true S=Somewhat true V=Very true

1. Knows own name	○N	○S	○V
2. Responds to 'No' or 'Stop'	○N	○S	○V

3. Can follow some commands	○N	○S	○V
4. Can use one word at a time	○N	○S	○V
5. Can use 2 words at a time	○N	○S	○V
6. Can use 3 words at a time	○N	○S	○V
7. Knows 10 or more words	○N	○S	○V
8. Can use sentences with 4 or more words	○N	○S	○V
9. Explains what he/she wants	○N	○S	○V
10. Asks meaningful questions	○N	○S	○V
11. Speech tends to be meaningful/relevant	○N	○S	○V
12. Often uses several successive sentences	○N	○S	○V
13. Carries on a fairly good conversation	○N	○S	○V
14. Has normal ability to communicate for his/her age	○N	○S	○V

II. Sociability

N = Not descriptive S=Somewhat descriptive V=Very descriptive

1. Seems to be in a shell - you cannot reach out to him/her	○N	○S	○V
2. Ignores other people	○N	○S	○V
3. Pays little or no attention when addressed	○N	○S	○V
4. Uncooperative and resistant	○N	○S	○V
5. No eye contact	○N	○S	○V
6. Prefers to be left alone	○N	○S	○V
7. Shows no affection	○N	○S	○V
8. Fails to greet parents	○N	○S	○V
9. Avoids contact with others	○N	○S	○V
10. Does not imitate	○N	○S	○V
11. Dislikes being held/cuddled	○N	○S	○V
12. Does not share or show	○N	○S	○V

13. Does not wave 'bye bye'	❍N	❍S	❍V
14. Disagreeable/not compliant	❍N	❍S	❍V
15. Temper tantrums	❍N	❍S	❍V
16. Lacks friends/companions	❍N	❍S	❍V
17. Rarely smiles	❍N	❍S	❍V
18. Insensitive to other's feelings	❍N	❍S	❍V
19. Indifferent to being liked	❍N	❍S	❍V
20. Indifferent if parent(s) leave	❍N	❍S	❍V

III. Sensory/Cognitive Awareness

N = Not descriptive S=Somewhat descriptive V=Very descriptive

1. Responds to own name	❍N	❍S	❍V
2. Responds to praise	❍N	❍S	❍V
3. Looks at people and animals	❍N	❍S	❍V
4. Looks at pictures (and T.V.)	❍N	❍S	❍V
5. Does drawing, colouring, art	❍N	❍S	❍V
6. Plays with toys appropriately	❍N	❍S	❍V
7. Appropriate facial expression	❍N	❍S	❍V
8. Understands stories on T.V.	❍N	❍S	❍V
9. Understands explanations	❍N	❍S	❍V
10. Aware of environment	❍N	❍S	❍V
11. Aware of danger	❍N	❍S	❍V
12. Shows imagination	❍N	❍S	❍V
13. Initiates activities	❍N	❍S	❍V
14. Dresses self	❍N	❍S	❍V
15. Curious, interested	❍N	❍S	❍V
16. Venturesome - explores	❍N	❍S	❍V
17. "Tuned in" - Not spacey	❍N	❍S	❍V
18. Looks where others are looking	❍N	❍S	❍V

IV. Health/Physical/Behaviour

N = Not a Problem MI=Minor Problem MO=Moderate Problem S=Serious Problem

1.	Bed-wetting	N	MI	MO	S
2.	Wets pants/diapers	N	MI	MO	S
3.	Soils pants/diapers	N	MI	MO	S
4.	Diarrhoea	N	MI	MO	S
5.	Constipation	N	MI	MO	S
6.	Sleep problems	N	MI	MO	S
7.	Eats too much/too little	N	MI	MO	S
8.	Extremely limited diet	N	MI	MO	S
9.	Hyperactive	N	MI	MO	S
10.	Lethargic	N	MI	MO	S
11.	Hits or injures self	N	MI	MO	S
12.	Hits or injures others	N	MI	MO	S
13.	Destructive	N	MI	MO	S
14.	Sound-sensitive	N	MI	MO	S
15.	Anxious/fearful	N	MI	MO	S
16.	Unhappy/crying	N	MI	MO	S
17.	Seizures	N	MI	MO	S
18.	Obsessive speech	N	MI	MO	S
19.	Rigid routines	N	MI	MO	S
20.	Shouts or screams	N	MI	MO	S
21.	Demands sameness	N	MI	MO	S
22.	Often agitated	N	MI	MO	S
23.	Not sensitive to pain	N	MI	MO	S
24.	"Hooked" or fixated on certain objects/topics	N	MI	MO	S
25.	Repetitive movements	N	MI	MO	S

Enter data for scoring *Start over*

Classification/Diagnosis: Gender (Circle one): Male Female

Behavioural Support Plan

Name:	Date of Birth:
Parent or Guardian:	Team Contact:
	School Address:
Home Address:	Phone:
Phone:	Fax: E-mail:

List challenging behaviours, definition, and summary of data in order of priority, from highest to lowest priority for change:

Behaviour	*Definition*	*Approximate Frequency*	*Severity (1-5) 1=mild concern 5=life threatening*
1.			
2.			
3.			

Identify intervention target(s) from above list:
Rationale for priority decision:

Team Members

List persons to be involved in student's programme planning:

	Who	*Role*	*Relationship to Student*
1.			
2.			
3.			
4.			
5.			
6.			
7.			
8.			

Student Strengths:

Relevant History (e.g., social factors, health conditions, medications, previous treatments):

Functional Assessment

List the assessments conducted for each behaviour, and the general conclusions (i.e., what is motivating these behaviours) drawn from these data:

Behaviour	*Assessments*	*Conclusions*
1.	1.	
	2.	
	3.	
2.	1.	
	2.	
	3.	
3.	1.	
	2.	
	3.	

Hypothesis: [Provide a summary hypothesis stated in terms that under these conditions a specific behaviour occurs that results in these outcomes.]

Implementation Plan

1. Prevention Strategies

Are short-term prevention procedures needed (e.g., temporarily changing schedules, tasks)? If so, describe what should be changed, and how it fits in given the assessment information. Be sure to include who is responsible for each procedure.

At School:

At Home:

2. Environmental and Instructional Enhancements

Do long-term changes need to be made in goals or activities? If so, describe what needs to be changed and how these accommodations are consistent with prevention strategies. Be sure to include who is responsible for each procedure.

3. Immediate Consequences

Based on the assessment information, describe how people should react to the challenging behaviour each time it occurs. Is a crisis plan needed for severe outbursts? If so, describe this plan.

At School:

At Home:

Crisis Plan (if needed):

4. Teaching Alternative Behaviours

A. School:

a) Which behaviour is the team going to target for skills training?

b) How will this alternative behaviour serve as a functionally equivalent replacement for the problem behaviour?

c) In what situations will training occur?

d) Who will be responsible for conducting the training sessions?

e) Describe how the team will evaluate whether and when the student uses the new response:

B. Home:

a) Which behaviour is the team going to target for skills training?

b) How will this alternative behaviour serve as a functionally equivalent replacement for the problem behaviour?

c) In what situations will training occur?

d) Who will be responsible for conducting the training sessions?

e) Describe how the team will evaluate whether and when the student uses the new response.

Appendix-III

Form I. Demographic Details of the Child

Name :
Sex :
Age :
Name and address of the school :
Locality : Rural
: Urban

Details of the family

S.No	*Name*	*Relationship to the head of the family*	*Sex*	*Age*	*Qualification*	*Occupation*	*Monthly Income Rs*

Form II. Open-structured Interview Schedule

Name of the child :

Age of the child :

Relationship of the interviewee to the child :

Onset of autism :

What triggered autism in the child? :

What treatment was given? :

How long do you know the child? :

Any other detail worth mentioning :

Form III. Note-taking for Observation

Name of the Child :

Date :

Setting :

Place of observation :

Beginning time :

Ending time :

Observations :

Form IV. Matrix for Assessing Intervention Strategies

Criteria for evaluation	*Strategies for intervention*	*Target behaviour*	*Feasibility*	*Implement-ability*	*Positive changes n the nehaviour*

Form V. Opinionairre on Strategic Intervention Paradigm

(Special Teachers, Parents, Intervention Team Members)

Name :

Relationship to the child :

Age :

Gender :

Qualification :

Home Address :

Do you find the instructional materials used in this study suitable to the level of pupils?

Are the instructional materials used in this study effective?

Are the instructional strategies followed in this study effective?

What are the positive changes observed in the behaviour of the child?

Have you yourself initiated any form of intervention strategy? If so, please specify.

Please feel free to add any comments or suggestions on the Strategic Intervention Paradigm.

Family Priorities: Weekday Schedule

Student:—————————————————Age:——Date:————-----

Directions: Ask family members to describe what the student does or is helped to do at home (from getting up, going to school; and from arriving home until going to bed). Identify routines that are age-appropriate and those that are family priorities, to be included in the student's IEP.

Approximate time	*Routine*	*Environ/ ment area*	*How does this happen now? How much help is needed?*	*Age appropriate Y/N*	*Priority Y/N*	*Comments*

(*Project QUEST Inservice Manual,* (Falco et al, 1990)

Assessment of Social Skills

Student:------------------------------

Routine:---Environment:-------------------

Component	*Natural cues*	*Skills*	*+/0*	*Quality/ Tempo*	*Y/N*	*Need assist/Errors*	*What to do*
Initiate							
Prepare							
Perform							
Terminate							
Problem solve							
Enrichment social							
Communication							
Choice							

(*Project QUEST Inservice Manual,* Falco et al., 1990).

Social Skills Assessment: Informant Interview

Student:-------------------------------

Date----------Informant:---------------------

Rating Code: 0 = No opportunity to do it, or never observed

4 = Does it consistently and appropriately.

2 = Gets it done, but does it inappropriately in a variety of situations

3 = Does it occasionally or if prompted

NA = Not Applicable

Directions: Read the definitions for social skills 1-10 (page 4 of this form). For each situation below, rate your child's performance in each social skill. Give examples of what your child does in each situation.

(*Project QUEST Inservice Manual,* Falco et al., 1990).

Assessment of Daily Activities

Student: ——————————————Date—————————

Directions: This form is used to structure an interview to determine the relationship of various conditions to problem behaviour. First, parents and/or staff members make notes on a copy of the form prior to the interview. The interviewer then structures questions to clarify the details and enlarge on the examples. When making comments, given details such as: types of possible perspective of the student when problems occur.

Time	*Activity location/ supervisor and croup size*	*Age appro- priate activity?*	*Meaning- ful activity?*	*Liked activity?*	*Does the individuals have Choice/ Control?*	*Problems?*	*Comments*

(*Project QUEST Inservice Manual,* Falco et al., 1990).

Preferences Survey

Student——————————————————————————

—Date——————————

Likes What people, objects or activities are liked a lot or selected during free time?	*Tolerates* What is done when asked, but never done if not asked?	*Dislikes* What people, objects or activites are resisted, avoided or rejected?

Strategic Intervention Paradigm Significance and Usage

(Manual for Parents, Special Teachers, Speech and Occupational Therapists and other Interventionists)

Strategic Intervention Paradigm addresses the critical needs and goals of individuals with autism and SIP manual is a compendium of the intervention strategies devised by the author. The interventions are designed to increase appropriate behaviours and decrease destructive and negative behaviours. Strategic Intervention Paradigm has been developed based on six dynamic and interrelated processes of intervention.

1. Identification, Analysis and Evaluation of Problems
2. Determination of Interventions & Adaptations
3. Refinement & Organisation of Structure
4. Design & Construction of Space, Time & Events
5. Providing Visual Support, Visual Adaptations & Developing Visual and Verbal Instructional Strategies
6. Developing New Skills & Expanding Communication, Self-management and Independence.

The manual elaborately explains the Theory of Multiple Intelligences and its relevance in this study. The manual elucidates all the fourteen strategies evolved by the author in detail and each strategy and each dimension of intelligence is enhanced by clip art figures and illustrations. Extensive use of clip art has been made as clip art figures have universal acceptability, access and recognition and they represent ethnic and cultural diversity of the people of the globe. People who use computers in any part of the world have accessibility to clip art and it is used to portray a wide range of situations, events and human emotions. The manual serves as a guideline for parents, special teachers, therapists, paraprofessionals and interventionists.

Picture-Enhanced Communication Competency Model for Children with Autism

(Compact Disc Prepared to Improve Communication Skills in Children with Autism)

The UN Convention on the Rights of the Child (1989) established the principle that all children should enjoy "freedom to seek, receive and impart information and ideas of all kinds". To enable children to enjoy this right, they need to be supported to communicate spontaneously, that is, to initiate interactions with others in order to convey their wishes and feelings, needs and wants. All teachers believe that communication is the key curricular area for the children and argue that there should be more freedom to concentrate on this aspect of the curriculum. For children with severe autism who use little or no speech, therefore, there is a strong argument that communication should be established as the core curricular area. Children with severe autism and minimal speech form one of the most communicatively deprived groups in our society. The issue of enabling them to communicate spontaneously is a crucial one — and one that deserves to be recognised as a key educational goal.

One of the major areas of difficulty for students with autism spectrum disorders is the development of social and communication skills. They have difficulty in initiating and sustaining conversations and understanding how communication works. Many also have language difficulties, either being non-verbal throughout their lives or having delayed speech. Some children use language in unusual ways, such as repeating the words or sentences said to them (echolalia) or using only single words to communicate. Language difficulties may contribute to behavioural problems. Unable to use language to communicate his or her needs, a child with autism may resort to screaming and shouting and indulge in self-injury.

Communication breakdowns can be a "root" cause of problems in social interaction, educational performance, and behavior. While it is common for educational programming to focus on developing communication skills, that focus in most settings tends to be directed toward developing the student's expressive communication. Comparatively little attention is directed toward increasing the student's ability to understand the communication in his life.

Common misconceptions about the communication and interaction abilities of children with autism and little or no speech can mean that these children are not receiving the professional support they need to learn how to initiate communication. This is often compounded where the children's communication environment does not enable spontaneous communication. In order to enhance the communication skills, a compact disc that contains photographs that were favourites among children with autism has been prepared. Children with autism were found gazing at these pictures often and hence these photographs were chosen for the compact disc. These photographs evoked responses from the children and some of them answered all the questions asked by the investigator.

This study supports the view that the key to achieving this is the creation of communication enabling environments, communication embedded activities within school and home settings, using strategies and approaches that are designed to enhance children's own role as spontaneous communicators. It is time to shift the focus away from talking about individual communication 'deficits', to looking at how we can develop environments, attitudes and curricula that are more communication enabling and empowering for these children.

Bibliography

The format of the references is based on WEAPAS (Web Extension to American Psychological Association Style (Revision 2.0) (2001)

Aarons, M. and Gittens, T. (1994) *Autism a guide for Parents and Professionals.* London and New York: Routledge.

Acta Psychiatrica [et Neurological] Scandinavica, "Autism: not an extremely rare disorder". "Autism: not an extremely rare disorder", Vol. 99, no. 6, June 1999, pp. 399-406.

Aggleton, K. (1992). Social Cognition in Developmental Language Disorders and High Level, *Developmental Medicine and Child Neurology,* 1996, 38, 487-495.

Akogiounoglou , D. (1990). The ability of autistic children to orient themselves and respond to familiar and novel auditory stimuli: Environmental, vocal, and musical sounds. Unpublished master's thesis, Michigan State University, Lansing.

Arendt, R.E., Maclean, W.E, Jr., & Baumeister, A.A. (1988). Critique of sensory integration therapy and its applications in mental retardation. *American Journal on Mental Retardation,* 92, 401 - 411.

Attwood A. (1998) *Asperger's Syndrome:A Guide for Parents and Professionals,* London, Kingsley Publishers.

Ayres, A. Jean, *Sensory Integration and the Child.* Western Psychological Services: Los Angeles, 1979.

Baron-Cohen, S., , Leslie, A. M., & Frith, U. (1985). Does the autistic child have a "theory of mind"? *Cognition, 21,* 37-46.

_______________, Leslie, A. M., & Frith, U. (1986). Mechanical, behavioural and intentional understanding of picture stories in autistic children. *British Journal of Developmental Psychology, 4,* 113-125.

_______________ , (1987). Autism and symbolic play. *British Journal of DevelopmentalPsychology,* 5, 139-148.

_______________ (1988). Social and pragmatic deficits in autism: Cognitive or affective? *Journal of Autism and Developmental Disorders,* 18(3), 379-402.

_______________ (1989). The autistic child's theory of mind: A case of specific developmental delay. *Journal of Child Psychology and Psychiatry 30,* 285-297.

_______________ and Bolton, P. (1993) *Autism The Facts.* Oxford: Oxford University Press.

_______________ Tager-Flusberg, H., Cohen, D.J. (Eds.), (1993). *Understanding Other Minds: Perspectives From Autism.* Oxford University Press, Oxford.

_______________ (1994). How to build a baby that can read minds. *British Journal of Developmental Psychology,* 9, 33-51.

_______________ Ring, H., Moriarty, J., Schmitz, B., Costa, D., Ell, P. (1994). The brain basis of theory of mind: the role of the orbitofrontal region. *British Journal of Psychiatry,* 165, pp. 640–649.

_______________ (1995). *Mindblindness.* Cambridge MA: MIT Press.

_______________ Jolliffe, T., Mortimore, C., Robertson, M. (1997). Another advanced test of theory of mind: Evidence from very high functioning adults with autism or Asperger syndrome. *Journal of Child Psychology and Psychiatry,* 38 (7), pp. 813-822.

_______________ (in press). Are autistic children "Behaviorists"? An examination of their mental-physical and appearance-reality distinctions. *Journal of Autism and Developmental Disorders.*

Barth, C., Fein D., & Waterhouse, L. (1995). Delayed match to sample performance in autistic children. *Developmental Neuropsychology,* 11, 53-69.

Bauman, M.L., & Kemper,T., (1994) *The Neurobiology of Autism,* Johns Hopkins Press, pp.30-31.

Binstock, T., (1993). *Research in Developmental & Behavioural Neuroanatomy.*

_______________, (1997) *Autism: a Novel Form of Mercury Poisoning.*

Bishop, D.V.M. and Rosenbloom,L.(1987). Classification of Childhood Language Disorders in W.Yule & M.Rutter. Language Development and Disorders. Double Issue (No.s 101, 102) of *Clinics in Developmental Medicine,* pp 16-41, London, Mackeith.

_______________, (1998). Development of the children's communication checklist (CCC): a method for assessing qualitative aspects of communicative impairment in children. *Journal of Child Psychology and Psychiatry,* 39, 879-892.

Bretherton, I., & Beeghly, M. (1982). Talking about internal states: The acquisition of an explicit theory of mind. *Developmental Psychology,* 18(6), 906-921.

Brook & Bowler, D. (1992), Autsim by another name? Semantic and Pragmatic Impairments in Children, *Journal of Autism and Developmental Disorders*, 22, 66-81.

Brothers L. (1990),The social brain: a project for integrating primate behaviour and neuropsychology in a new domain. *Concepts in Neuroscience* 1: 27-51.

_______________ Ring,B., King,A. (1990). Response of Neurons in the Macaque amygdala to complex social stimuli, *Behavioral Research.* 21, 41(3), pp 199-213.

Buitelaar, I.K. & Vandergaar, R.J. (1998) Diagnostic Rules for children with PDD-NOS and Multiple Complex Developmental Disorder. *Journal of Child Psychology and Psychiatry*, 39 (6), 911-20.

Calhoun, M., Rose, T., Hangt, B., and Sturky. C. (1991). Social reciprocity interventions: Implications for developmental therapists. *Physical and Occupational Therapy in Pediatrics*, 11, 45-56.

California Department of Developmental Services recently produced *A Report to the Legislature: Changes in the Population of Persons with Autism and Pervasive Developmental Disorders in California's Developmental Services System: 1987 through 1998.*

Cammisa, K.M. & Hobbe, S.H., (1993) 'Etiology of Autism: A Review of Recent Biogenic Theories and Research'. *Occupational Therapy in Mental Health* (39), Volume 12, Issue 2, pp 39-67.

Cardoza, I. (2000). The National Trust for Welfare of Persons with Autism, Cerebral Palsy, Mental Retardation and Multiple Disabilities Act. *Update on Legal Issues: Autism in India.* Retrieved May 7, 2001, from http://www.autism-india.org/.

Case-Smith J., Miller H. Occupational therapy with children with pervasive developmental disorders. *American Journal of Occupational Therapy*, September-October 1999, 53(5):506-13

_______________ Bryan,T. (1999). The Effects of Occupational Therapy with Sensory Integration Emphasis on Preschool Age Children with Autism. *The American Journal of Occupational Therapy* (443), Volume 53, Issue 5, pp 189-505.

Clauss, E. L. (1995). Effects of music on attention and self-stimulatory behaviors in autistic people. Unpublished doctoral dissertation. [On-line]. Retrieved November 17, 1999 from PsycInfo Online database on the World Wide Web: web4.infotrac.galegroup.com.

Cohen and Volkmar, (1997), eds., *Handbook of Autism and the Pervasive Developmental Disorders*, 2nd edition, 1997: Chapter 18, *MEDICAL CONDITIONS[:]* Infections…Immunological Association*[:]pp 398-400.*

Comi, M., Zimmerman, A.W., Frye, V.H., Law, P.A. & Peeden J.N. (1999). "Familial clustering of autoimmune disorders and evaluation of medical risk factors in autism", *Journal of Child Neurology*, vol. 14, no. 6, June 1999, pp. 388-94.

Cook, D. (1991). A sensory approach to the treatment and management of children with autism. *Focus on Autistic Behavior*, 5 (6): 1 - 19.

Cook, T.D. & Campbell, D.T. (1979). *Quasi-experimental design and analysis issues for field settings*. Boston, MA: Houghton Mifflin.

Crawford, C.C. (1928). *The Techniques of Research in Education*. Los Angeles: CA.

Daly, E., Witt J. Martens,B., & Dool, E.(1997). A Model for conducting a functional analysis of academic performance problems. *School Psychology Review*, 26, 554-574.

Davies, S., Bishop, D., Manstead, A., & Tantam, D. (1994). Face perception in autistic children. *Journal of Child Psychology and Psychiatry and Allied Disciplines*, 35, 1033-1058.

Dawson, G., & Fernald, M. (1987). Perspective-taking ability and its relationship to the social behavior of autistic children. *Journal of Autism and Developmental Disorders*, 17(4), 487-498.

Diagnostic and Statistical Manual of Mental Disorders: DSM-IV, fourth edition (1994). Washington, DC: American Psychiatric Association, pp 66-69.

Duncan J. 1986 Disorganisation of Behaviour after Frontal Lobe Damage. *Cognitive Neuropsychology* 3 271-290.

Dunn, R. & Dunn, K. (1978). *Teaching Students Through Their Individual Learning Styles: A Practical Approach*. Reston Publishing Company, Reston, VA.

Edgerton, C. L. (1993). The effect of improvisational music therapy on the communicative behaviors of autistic children. Unpublished masterís thesis, Michigan State University, Lansing.

Elder, J. H. (1997a). Defining parent training for practice and research. *Journal of the American Psychiatric Nurses Association*, 3,103-110.

_______________ (1997b). Single subject experimentation for psychiatric nursing. *Archives of Psychiatric Nursing*, 11(3), 133-8.

Ermann, J., & Fathman, C.G. (2001) "Autoimmune Diseases: Genes, Bugs and Failed Regulation", *Nature Immunology*, Vol. 2, no. 9, 2001, September 2001, pp. 759-761.

Ermer, J. and Dunn, W. (1998) The Sensory Profile: A discriminant analysis of children with and without disabilities. *The American Journal of Occupational Therapy* (443), Volume 52, Issue 4, pp 283-290.

Falco, R., Janzen, J. Arick, K., Wilgus and M. De Boer.1990. *Project QUEST inservice manual: Functional assessment of student needs and functional instructions for communication, social interactions, self-management and choice.* Portland, OR: Department of Special and Counselor Education, Portland State University.

Fenske, E. C., Zalenski, S., Krantz, P. J. & McClannahan, L. E. (1985). Age at intervention and treatment outcome for autistic children in a comprehensive intervention program. *Analysis and Intervention in. Developmental Disabilities,* 5, 49-58.

Fombonne, E., (1998). Diagnostic assessment in a sample of autistic and developmentally impaired adolescents. *Journalism of Autism and Developmental Disorders,* 22, 563-582.

Frith U. (1994). *The Cognitive Neuropsychology of Schizophrenia.* Hove: Eribaum.

_______________ . Morton J., and Leslie A. (1992). The cognitive basis of a biological disorder: Autism. *Trends in Neuroscience* 14 433-438.

_______________ , (1988). Autism: Possible clues to the underlying pathology: Psychological facts. In L. Wing (Ed.), *Aspects of Autism: Biological Research* (pp. 19-30). London: Gaskell, Royal College of Psychiatrists.

_______________ (1989). *Autism: Explaining the Enigma.* Oxford, England: Blackwell.

Frith, C. D., Frith, U. (1999). Interacting minds, a biological basis. *Science,* 286, pp. 1692–1695.

Fudenberg, H.H. (1998). NeuroImmuno Therapeutics Research Foundation, *Classic Infantile Onset Autism is an Autoimmune Disease.*

Gagnon, L., Motron, L. & Joanette, V. (1997). Questioning the validity of the Semantic Syndrome Diagnosis, *Autism* (1):37-55.

Gallagher, H.L., Happe, F., Brunswick, N., Fletcher, P.C., Frith, U., Frith, C.D. (2000) Reading the mind in cartoons and stories: an fMRI study of 'theory of mind' in verbal and nonverbal tasks. *Neuropsychologia* 38, pp. 11–21.

Gardner, H. (1983). *Frames of mind: The theory of multiple intelligences.* NY: Basic Books.

_______________ & Blythe, T. (1990) 'A School for All Intelligences', *Educational Leadership.*

Garrett, H.E. (1973), *Statistics in Psychology and Education,* Bombay, Vakils, Feffers and Simons Pvt Ltd, pp.58.

Geller E. 1998. An investigation of communication breakdowns and repairs in verbal autistic children. *The British Journal of Developmental Disabilities* 44(2) 71-85.

Gent, T.V., Heijnen, C.J. & Treffers, P.D. (1997) Autism and the Immune System. *Journal of Child Psychology & Psychiatry,* Vol 38, pp. 337-349.

Gillberg, C. & Coleman, M., (1992) *The Biology of the Autistic Syndromes—* second edition, pp. 222-224.

Grandin, T. (1996). *Thinking in Pictures and Other Reports from my Life with Autism.* Vintage Books.

Hairston, M. J. P. (1984). Analyses of responses of mentally retarded autistic and mentally retarded non-autistic children to art therapy and music therapy. Unpublished doctoral dissertation, University of Georgia. [On-line]. Retrieved November 17, 1999 from Dissertations Abstracts Online database (Dissertations Abstracts Online, No. AAG48421116) on the World Wide Web: firstsearch.oclc.org.

Happe, F. (1994) *Autism: An Introduction to Psychological Theory,* UCL Press: London.

_______________ Ehler, S., Fletcher, P., Frith, U., Johansson, M., Gillberg, C., Dolan, R., Frachowiak, R. & Frith, C. (1996) Theory of mind in autism: evidence from a PET scan study of Asperger's syndrome, *Neuroreport,* 8, 197-201.

_______________ Brownell, H., Winner, E. (1999). Acquired 'theory of mind' impairments following stroke. *Cognition* 70, pp. 211–240.

Hatch-Rasmussen, C., (1995) *Sensory Integration* http://www.autism.org/si.html.

Hersen, M., & Barlow, D. (1987). *Single-case experimental design: Strategies for studying behavior change.* New York, NW: Pergamon Press.

Heubner, R.A. (1992). 'Autistic Disorder: A Neuropsychological Enigma'.*The American Journal of Occupational Therapy* (443), Volume 46, Issue 6, pp 487-501.

_______________ , (1986 a). The autistic child's appraisal of expressions of emotion. *Journal of Child Psychology and Psychiatry,* 27(3), 321-342.

_______________ , (1986 b). The autistic child's appraisal of expressions of emotion: A further study. *Journal of Child Psychology and Psychiatry,* 27(5), 671-680.

_______________ Ouston, J., & Lee, A. (1988a). Emotion recognition in autism: Coordinating faces and voices. *Psychological Medicine, 18,* 911-923.

_______________ Ouston, J., & Lee, A. (1988 b). What's in a face? The case of autism. *British Journal of Psychology, 79, 441-453.*

Hornig, M. & Lipkin, W.I., (1999). "An Infection-based Model of Neurodevelopmental Damage," *Proceedings of the National Academy of Sciences,* vol. 96,no.21,pp.12102-12107,Oct.12,1999.

_______________ & Lipkin, W.I., (2001). "Infectious and Immune Factors in the Pathogenesis of Neurodevelopmental Disorders: Epidemiology, Hypotheses, and Animal Models", *Mental Retardation and Developmental Disabilities Research Reviews,* vol. 7, no. 3, 2001,pp.200-210.

Hughes C. 1998. Executive function in pre-schoolers: links with theory of mind and verbal ability. *British Journal of Developmental Psychology* ,16, 233-253.

_______________ Russell, J. & Robbins, T.W. (1993). Evidence for executive dysfunction in autism. *Neuropsychologia,* 32, 477-492.

Jacobson J.W., Mulick J. A, Schwartz AA. A history of facilitated communication: science, pseudoscience, and antiscience. *Am Psychol.* 1995; 50 : 750-765

Jacobson R. (1986) Disorders of facial recognition, social behaviour and affect after combined bilateral amygdalotomy and subcordate tractotomy: a clinical and experimental study. *Psychological Medicine* 16: 439-50.

Johnston, J. M., & Pennypacker, H. S. (1986a). The nature and functions of experimental questions. In A. Poling & R. W. Fuqua (Eds.), *Research methods in applied behavior analysis: Issues and advances* (pp. 55-84). New York: Plenum.

_______________ & Pennypacker, H.S. (1986b). Pure versus quasi-behavioral research. In A. Poling & R. W. Fuqua (Eds.), *Research methods in applied behavior analysis: Issues and advances* (pp. 29-54). New York: Plenum.

Jordan, R. Jones, G. and Murray, D. (1998.) *Educational Interventions for children with Autism. A Literature Review of Recent and Current Research.* University of Birmingham: DFEE.

Jyonouchi (2001)."Innate and Adaptive Immune Responses in Children With Regression Autism: Evaluation of the Effects of Environmental Factors Including Vaccination". *Journal of Allergy and Clinical Immunology,* February 2001, Part 2, vol. 107, No. 2.

_______________ (2001). "Proinflammatory and Regulatory Cytokine Production Associated With Innate and Adaptive Immune Responses in Children With Autism Spectrum Disorders and Developmental Regression". *Journal of Neuroimmunology,* vol. 120, nos. 1-2, January 11, 2001, pp. 170-9.

Kanner, L. (1943). Autistic disturbances of affective contact. *The Nervous Child,* 2, 217-250.

_______________ (1946). Irrelevant and metaphorical language in early infantile autism. *American Journal of Psychiatry,* 103, 242-246.

______________ (1971). Follow-up study of eleven autistic children originally reported in 1943. *Journal of Autism and Childhood Schizophrenia,* 1(2), 119-145.

______________ Rodriguez, A., & Ashenden, B. (1972). How far can autistic children go in matters of social adaptation? *Journal of Autism and Childhood Schizophrenia,* 2(1), 9-33.

Karmiloff-Smith, A., Klima, E., Bellugi, U., Grant, J., Baron-Cohen, S. (1995). Is there a social module? Language, face processing and theory of mind in individuals with Williams Syndrome. *Journal of Cognitive Neuroscience,* 7, pp. 196–208.

Kawashima et al. (2000), *"Detection and Sequencing of Measles Virus from Peripheral [Blood] Mononuclear Cells from Patients with Inflammatory Bowel Disease and Autism". Digestive Diseases and Sciences,* vol. 45, no. 4, April 2000, pages 723-9.

Koegel, L., Koegel, R. & Dunlap, G. (1996). *Positive behavioral support.* Baltimore, MD:PaulBrookes.

Koegel, R.L., Russo, D.C., Rincover, A., & Schreibman, L. (1982) *Assessing and training teachers.* In R. L. Koegel, A. Rincover, & A. L. Egel (Eds.). *Educating and understanding autistic children* (pp. 178-202). San Diego: College-Hill Press.

Koomar, J.A. & Bundy, A.C. (1991). The art and science of creating direct intervention from theory. In A.G. Fisher, E.A. Murray, & A.C. Bundy (Eds.), *Sensory Integration Theory and Practice* (p.252). Philadelphia: F.A. Davis Company.

Kranowitz, Carol Stock. *The Out-of-Sync Child: Recognising and Coping with Sensory Integration Dysfunction.* 1998. New York: The Berkley Publishing Group.

Kundu (2000). Special education in India: Current status and future directions. *The Journal of International Special Needs Education, 3.*

LeDoux J.E., Wilson D.H., Gazzaniga M.S. (1977) Manipulo-spatial aspects of cerebral lateralisation: clues to the origin of lateralisation. *Neuropsychologia* 15: 743-50.

______________ , (1984). Cognition and emotion: Processing functions and brain systems. In M. S. Gazzaniga (Ed.), *Handbook of cognitive neuroscience.* NY: Plenum Press.

Leopold, D.A. and Logothetis N.K. (1996): Activity changes in early visual cortex reflect monkeys' percepts during binocular rivalry. *Nature.* 379 (6565): 549-53.

Lee K., Eskritt M., Symons L., and Muir D. (1998). Children's use of triadic eye gaze information for "mindreading". *Developmental Psychology,* 34(3) 525-539

Lohr, L. Sharon. (1999). *'Sampling: Design and Analysis'*, Duxbury Press.

Lovaas, O. I. (1993). Teaching developmentally disabled children: Theme book. Austin, TX: Pro-Ed.

Lord C. and Magill-Evans J. (1995). Peer interaction of autistic children and adolescents. *Development and Psychopathology*,17, 611-626.

Mahoney,W.J., Szatmari, P, Maclean, E., Bryson, S.E. Bartolucci G., Walter, S.D. Jones, M.B. and ZwaigenbaumL. (1997), Reliability and accuracy of differentiating Pervasive Developmental Disorders, *Journal of American Child & Adolescent Psychiatry*, 37 (3) 278-85.

Mason, S.A., & Iwata, B.A. (1990). Artifactual effects of sensory-integration therapy on self -injurious behavior. *Journal of Applied Behavioral Analysis*, 23, 361-370.

McDonough, L., Mandler, J.M., McKee, R. & Squire, L. (1994) The deferred imitation task as a nonverbal measure of declarative memory. *Proceedings of the National Academy of Sciences*, Vol. 92, 7580-7585.

McEachin, J. J., Smith, T., & Lovaas, O. I. (1993). Long term outcome for children with autism who received early intensive behavioral treatment. *American Journal on Mental Retardation*, 4, 359 - 372.

McEvoy R., Rogers S., and Pennington B. 1993 Executive function and social communication deficits in young autistic children. *Journal of Child Psychology and Psychiatry*, 34, 563-578.

McTear, M. & Conti-Ramsden, D. (1992). *Pragmatic Disbaility in Children*, London.

Mesibov, G.B. Adams, L.W and Klinger, L.G. (1997) *Autism Understanding the Disorder*. New York and London, USA: Plenum Press.

Miller, L. J., McIntosh, D. N., McGrath, J., Shyu, V., Lampe, M., Taylor, A. K., Tassone, Fl, Neitzel, K., Stackhouse, T., & Hagerman (1999). Electrodermal responses to sensory stimuli in individuals with fragile X syndrome: A preliminary report. *American Journal of Medical Genetics, 83*(4): p. 268-79.

Misra, A. (2000). Special education in India: Current status and future directions. *The Journal of International Special Needs Education, 3.*

Montinari, M., et al (1996). *Role of Immunogenetics in the Diagnosis of Postvaccinal CNS Pathology*, Department of Pediatric Surgery, University of Bari, Italy, presented May 9, 1996.

Mundy,P., Sigman, M., Ungerer,J.A., & Sherman, T. (1986) Defining Social deficits in autism: The contribution of nonverbal communication measures. *Journal of Child Psychology and Psychiatry*, 27, 657-669.

_______________, M., Kasari C. Joint attention, developmental level, and symptom presentation in young children with autism. *Dev Psychopathol* 1994:6:389–401.

Murray, E.A. and Mishkin, M. (1985). Amygdalectomy impairs crossmodal association in monkeys. *Science* 228: 604-6.

Murray, E.A., Anzalone, M. E. (1991). Integrating sensory integration theory and practice with other intervention approaches. In A.G. Fisher, E.A. Murray, & A.C. Bundy (Eds.), *Sensory Integration Theory and Practice* (p. 378). Philadelphia: F. A. Davis Company.

Nalini, Hema, V. (2002). 'A Special Friend', *Kovai Times,* Volume 1, Issue 9, December 8,2002.

_______________, V. (2003). 'A Special Friend', *The Hindu* – 'Young World- Quest', October, 11, 2003.

Nelson, C.A & deHaan, M. (1996). A Neurobiological approach to the recognition of facial expressions in infancy. In J.A. Russell (Ed) *The Psychology of Facial Expressions* (pp. 176-204). Cambridge: Cambridge University Press.

Nelson, D., Anderson, V. & Gonzales, A. (1984). Music activities as therapy for children with autism and other pervasive developmental disorders. *Journal of Music Therapy,* 21.(3),100-116.

Nelson, K. (1973). Structure and strategy in learning to talk.

_______________, Nelson, D., Anderson, V. & Gonzales, A. (1984). *Music activities as therapy for children with autism and other pervasive developmental disorders. Journal of Music Therapy,* 21.(3),100-116.

Ottenbacher, K. (1982). Sensory integration therapy: Affect or effect. *American Journal of Occupational Therapy.* 36. 571-578.

_______________, (1991). Research in sensory integration: empirical perceptions and progress. In A.G. Fisher, E.A. Murray, & A.C. Bundy (Eds.), *Sensory integration theory and practice* (pp 388-389). Philadelphia: F.A. Davis Company.

Peck, C.Z. (1998) (32). Program Evaluation of a Family Systems Model of Service Delivery for Parents of Children with Autism: Promoting Adaptation to Family Stress. *Special Services in the Schools* (6), Volume 14, Issue ½, pp 127-145.

Paul R. and Cohen D. (1984) Responses to contingent queries in adults with mental retardation and pervasive developmental disorders. *Applied Psycholinguistics* 5 349-357.

Piaget, J. (1972). *The psychology of the child.* New York: Basic Books.

_______________ (1990). *The child's conception of the world.* New York: Littlefield Adams.

_______________ Gruber, H. (Ed.), & Voneche, J. J. (Ed.). *The Essential Piaget* (100th anniversary Ed.). New York: Jason Aronson.

Pletnikov, M.V., Moran, T.H., & Carbone, K.M. (2002). "Borna Disease Virus Infection of the Neonatal Rat: Developmental Brain Injury Model of Autism Spectrum Disorders," *Frontiers in Bioscience,* March 1, 2002, vol. 7, pages D593-607.

Potter, C. and Whittaker, C. (2001) *Enabling Communication in Children with Autism.* London and Philadelphia, GB: Jessica Kingsley Publishers.

Price,S & Price,L. (1999) *Aromatherapy for Health Professionals* (Second edition) London: Churchill Livingstone.

Prior, M., and Cummins, R. (1992). Questions about facilitated communication and Autism. *J. Autism Dev Disord, 22,* 231-338.

_______________ , Fisenmajer, R., Leekam,S., Wing, L., Gould, I., Ong, B., Dowe, D. (1998). Are there subgroups within the Autistic Spectrum? A Cluster Analysis of a Group of Children with Autistic Spectrum Disorders, *Journal of Child Psychology and Psychiatry,* 39 (6) 893-902.

Ramaa, S. (1998). *Autism: A Complex Learning Disorder—A Multidisciplinary Perspective,* Regency Publications, New Delhi.

Rapin, I. & Allen, D. (1987). Developmental Dysphasia and Autism in PreSchool Children : Characterising & Shape in J. Martin & Fletcher. P Grunwell and D.Hall (eds.) *Proceeding of the First Inter-symposium of Specific Language Disorder in Children.* pp. 20-35, Land AFASIC.

_______________ , Ed. *Preschool Children with Inadequate Communication: Developmental Language Disorders, Autism, Low IQ.* London UK: Mac Keith Press. 1996. (Report of a large comparative study of historical, neurological, neuropsychological, language, behavior, sociability, and play in these three groups of preschoolers.)

Ray, T., King, L., & Grandin, T. (1988). The effectiveness of self-initiated vestibular stimulation in producing speech sounds in an autistic child. *The Occupational Therapy Journal Of Research,* 8 (3): 186-190.

Restall,G. & Magill-Evans, J. (2) (1994), Play and Preschool Children with Autism. The *American Journal of Occupational Therapy,* Volume 48, Issue 2, pp 113-120.

Rutter, M. (1985). Infantile autism and other pervasive developmental disorders. In M. Rutter & L. Hersov (Eds.), *Child and Adolescent Psychiatry: Modern approaches* (2nd ed., pp. 545-566). Oxford: Blackwell.

Saini, A. (2000). Literacy and empowerment: An Indian scenario. *Childhood Education Infancy through Adolescence, 76,* 381-389.

Schopler, E., & Mesibov, eds. (1988), *Diagnosis and Assessment in Autism.*

_______________ Reichler, R. J., & Renner, B. R. (1986). *The Childhood Disorders.*

Seigal, B (1996). *The world of the autistic child: understanding and treating autistic spectrum disorders,* Oxford: Oxford University Press.

Seitz, J. A. (1996a). Metaphor, symbolic play, and logical thought in early childhood. *General, Social, and Genetic Psychology Monographs.*

_______________ (1996b). The development of metaphoric understanding: Implications for a theory of creativity. *Creativity Research Journal.*

Shaw, W. (1998). Biological Treatments for Autism and PDD, 1998. *Autism and Clostridium Tetani: An Hypothesis" [Medical Hypotheses,* vol. 51, 1998, pp. 133-144.

Sidman, M. (1960). *Tactics of scientific research.* New York, NW: Basic Books.

Sigman, M. & Capps, L. (1997). *Children with Autism: A Developmental Perspective,* Harvard University Press: Cambridge, MA.

_______________ , & Capps, L. (1997). *Children With Autism: a Developmental Perspective* (Harvard University Press), pp 170-174.

_______________ , (1998). Change and continuity in the development of children with Autism. *Journal of Child Psychology and Psychiatry,* 39(6) 817-827.

_______________ , Mundy, P., Sherman, T., & Ungerer, J. (1986). Social interactions of autistic, mentally retarded and normal children and their caregivers. *Journal of Child Psychology and Psychiatry,* 27(5), 647-656.

_______________ , Ungerer, J. A., Mundy, P., & Sherman, T. (1987). Cognition in autistic children. In D. J. Cohen, A. M. Donnellan, & R. Paul (Eds.), *Handbook of autism and pervasive developmental disorders* (pp. 103-120). NY: Wiley.

Simpson, K. E. (1997). Effect of musical attunement on the behaviour of children with autism. Unpublished masterís thesis, University of Calgary.

Singh, V. (2002). Abnormal Measles Serology and Autoimmunity in Autistic Children," *Journal of Allergy and Clinical Immunology* (vol. 109, no. 1, S232, January 2002, abstract #702.

Singh, V.K. (2001). "Neuro-immunopathogenesis in Autism," Chapter 5, *Clinical Neuroimmune Biology* (vol. VI, New Foundation of Biology series, Elsevier Science, 2001).

Smith, T. (1996). Are other treatments effective? In Maurice, C., Green, G., & Luce, S., (Eds.), *Behavioral interventions for young children with autism: A manual for parents and professionals.* (pp 45-46). Austin, Texas: Pro-Ed.

_______________ , & Bryson, R. (1994). Autism. In T. R. Giles (Ed.). *Handbook of effective psychotherapy* (pp. 107 - 133.) New York: Plenum.

Smith, D. D. (2001). *Introduction to special education: Teaching in an age of opportunity* (4th ed.). Needham Heights, MA: Allyn & Bacon.*

Sperry, L.A., Whaley, K.T., Shaw, E., & Brame, K. (1999). 'Services for Young Children with Autism Spectrum Disorder: Voices of Parents and Providers'. *Infants and Young Children* (56), Volume 11, Issue 4, pp 17-33.

Stancliff, B.L. (55) (1998). Play with a purpose: Sensory Integration treatment and developmental disability, *OT Practice* (258), Volume 3, issue 9, pp 34-40.

Steege, M. & Northup, T. (1998). Brief functional analysis of problem behavior: A practical approach for school psychologists. *Proven Practice,* 1, (1), 4 - 11 and 37 - 38.

______________ , (in press). *Functional assessment: An odyssey.*

Stern, D. N., Barnett, R. K. & Spieker, S. (1983). Early transmission of affect: Some research issues. In J. D. Call, F. Galenson, & R. L. Tyson (Eds.), *Frontiers of infant Psychiatry.* NY: Basic Books.

Sulzer-Azaroff, B. & Mayer, R. (1991). *Behavior analysis for lasting change.* Fort Worth, TX: Holt, Reinhart & Winston, Inc.

Szatmari,P., Jones,M.B., Zwaigenbaum,L., & MaClean, J.E.. (1999). Genetics of Autism: Overview and New Directions. *Journal of Autism and Developmental Disorders* 55: 55-69.

Tager-Flusberg, H. (1981). On the nature of linguistic functioning in early infantile autism. *Journal of Autism and Developmental Disorders,* 11(1), 45-56.

______________ *What language reveals about the understanding of minds of children with autism.* In: Baron-Cohen S, Tager-Flusberg H, Cohen D. eds. *Understanding other minds: Perspectives from autism.* New York: Oxford Publications, 1993:138–157.

Tawney, H., & Gast, D. (1984). *Single subject research in special education.* Columbus, OH: Merill.

Teunisse, J.P., de Gelder, B. (1994). Do autistics have a generalised face processing deficit? Int. *J. Neurosci.* 77, 1–10.

______________ , de Gelder, B., (2001). Impaired categorical perception of facial expressions in high-functioning adolescents with autism. Neuropsychological Development & Cognition, Sect. C, *Child Neuropsychology.* 7, 1–14.

Tisserand, R.(1999) The Art of Aromatherapy (Nineteenth Edition) Saffron Walden: The C W Daniel Company Limited.

Trottier G., Srivastava L, Walker C.D. (1999). Etiology of infantile autism: a review of recent advances in genetic and neurobiological research. *J Psychiatry Neurosci.* 2:103-15.Trottier

______________ , et al. (1999). "Etiology of infantile autism: a review of recent advances in genetic and neurobiological research". *Journal of Psychiatry and Neuroscience,* vol. 24, no. 2, March 1999, pp. 103-15.

Turnbull, A.P. & Turnbull, H.R. (1999) "Parent Involvement in the Education of the Handicapped Children: A Critique". *Mental Retardation,* 20:3,119.

Vygotsky, L. S. (1978). *Mind in society: The development of higher psychological processes.* Cambridge, MA: Harvard University Press.

Wagner, A.E. & Lockwood, S.L (1994). Pervasive Developmental Disorders: Dilemmas in diagnosing very young children. *Infants and Young Children* (56), Volume 6, Issue 4, pp 21-32.

Walsh, W.J. & Usman, A. (2001). "Disordered Metal Metabolism in a Large Autism Population," 154th Annual Meeting, American Psychiatric Association, New Orleans, May 5-10, 2001

Waterhouse, S. (1995) 'Sensory overload'. *Special Children,* Jan (80) pp19-22.

Watling, R., Deitz, J. ,Kanny, E.M & McLaughlin, J.F. (1999). Current Practice of Occupational Therapy for Children with Autism. *The American Journal of Occupational Therapy.* (443), 1999 Sep/Oct (13), Volume 53, Issue 5, pp 498-505.

Wetherby, A. & Prutting, C. (1984). Profiles of communicative and cognitive-social abilities in autistic children. *Journal of Speech and Hearing Research.* Vol. 27, pp. 364-377.

Wetherby, A. (1986) Ontogeny of communicative functions in autism. Journal of Autism and Developmental Disorders Vol. 16, 295-316.

Whitaker P., Barratt P., Joy H., Potter M. and Thomas G. (1998). 'Children with Autism and peer group support, using "circles of friends"'. *British Journal of Special Education* 25(2) 60-64.

Wing, L., & Gould, J. (1979). 'Severe impairments of social interaction and associated abnormalities in children: Epidemiology and classification'. *Journal of Autism and Developmental Disorders,* 9(1), 11-29.

______________ , (1986). 'Clarification on Asperger's syndrome'. *Journal of Autism and Developmental Disorders,* 16(4), pp. 513-515.

Yirmiya, N., Sigman. M.D., Kasari and Mundy, P. (1992). Empathy and cognition in high-functioning children with autism. *Child Development* 63:150-160.

______________ , Shulman C. Seriation, conservation, and theory of mind abilities in individuals with autism, mental retardation and normally developing children. *Child Dev.* 1996; 67:2045–2059.

Zisserman, L. (1992). 'Case Report: The Effects of Deep Pressure on Self-stimulating Behaviors in a child with Autism and other Disabilities', *The American Journal of occupational Therapy,* 1992 June, Volume 46, Issue 6, pp 547-551.

Other references and websites

A Report to the Legislature: Changes in the Population of Persons With Autism and Pervasive Developmental Disorders in California's Developmental Services System: 1987 Through 1998 (Department of Developmental Services, California Health and Human Services Agency, Sacramento, CA: March 1, 1999), section IV, Rates of Occurrence, p. 5, http://www.dds.ca.gov/autismreport.cfm see also http://www.garynull.com/Documents/autism_99.htm

Post to the Autism electronic mail discussion list originating from St. John's University, New York [listserv@maelstrom.stjohns.edu], April 12, 1999, 19:09:49 -0700, subject lined "Is Autism a Public Health Problem?"

Barbara McDonald, Assessment, Evaluation and Support Unit, Special Education Division, California Department of Education (Bmcdonal@cde.ca.gov), to Raymond Gallup (truegrit@gti.net) via electronic mail, April 9, 1999, 10:10 a.m.

Statistics extracted from correspondence between Ray Gallup and the Illinois State Board of Education, posted to Vaccine Information and Awareness (VIA) discussion list [via@access1.net] April 28, 1999, 4:12 p.m.

The Autism Autoimmunity Project P.O. Box 293144, Davie, FL, 33329-3144 phone 954-506-5654; fax 954-587-6509 autism@CasiQuest.org; http://www.autismautoimmunityproject.org

The Centers for Disease Control, [1998], "Vaccines and Autism: Is There a Relationship?" (http://www.cdc.gov/nip/vacsafe/vac_autism.htm):

info@cureautismnow.org

Network Appliance, Inc.

info@cureautismnow.org

Accu-Find Internet Services

(http://www.rebcouncil.org/).

http://www.autism.org/si.html.

http://www.dinf.ne.jp/doc/prdl/othr/z00ap/002/z00ap00209.htm.

http://www.rebcouncil.org/).

(http://www.ncbi.nlm.nih.gov/entrez/query.fcgi?cmd=Retrieve&db=PubMed&list_uids=11553936&dopt=Abstract

http://lib.tcu.edu/www/staff/lruede/www.jorsm.com/~binstock

http://www.dds.ca.gov/autismreport.cfm

http://www.dinf.ne.jp/doc/prdl/othr/z00ap/ 002/z00ap00209.htm.

(http://www.nature.com/ni/special_focus/autoimmunity/home_welcome.html)

http://members.aol.com/nitrf/autism1.htm, accessed May 20, 1998.

http://www.pubmedcentral.nih.gov/articlerender.fcgi?tool=pubmed&pubmedid=10518583):

http://www.healthy.net/library/articles/coulter/biochem.htm).

http://www.hriptc.org/APA_abstract.htm).

http://www.dinf.ne.jp/doc/prdl/othr/z00ap/002/z00ap00209.htm.

http://www.cet.fsu.edu.NICHY.

Ministry of Social Justice and Empowerment. Rehabilitation Council of India.

Report to UNESCO of the International Commission on Education for the Twenty-first Century., 1996.

Autism Center http://www.patientcenters.com/autism/news/pdd47990601.htm

Autism Resources http://www.autism-resources.com/

OASIS(informationaboutAspergerSyndrome)http://www.udel.edu/bkirby/asperger/#education

TEACCHProgram(Treatment and Education of Autistic and Related Communication HandicappedChildren)University of North Carolina, Chapel Hill http://www.unc.edu/depts/teacch/

Autism Society of America7910 Woodmont Avenue, Suite 650 Bethesda, MD 20814-3015301.657.0881http://www.autism-society.org/

Autism Research Institute 4182 Adams Avenue San Diego, CA 92116619.281.7165 http://www.autism.com/ari

Cure Autism Now (CAN) 5225 Wilshire Blvd., Suite 503 Los Angeles, CA 90036 213) 549-0500 CAN@primenet.com

Index